New Parties in Government

Party literature is largely focused on the rise and success of new parties and their effects on party systems and older parties. This book, on the other hand, provides a valuable and original addition to such literature by analysing what happens to a party when it enters government for the first time.

Leading contributors assess how these parties, whether old or new, change when entering government by answering a set of questions:

- How and why has their role changed?
- What are the consequences of change?
- What explains the evolution from principled opposition to loyal opposition and eventually to participation in the executive?
- Which characteristics of the parties can be held responsible?
- Which characteristics of the parties' context should be brought into the picture?
- What have been the effects of the status change on party organization, party ideology and electoral results?

Covering a wide range of European parties such as the Finnish Greens, right-wing parties (FN, *Lega Nord* and *Alleanza Nazionale*) and new parties in Italy, the Netherlands and Sweden to name a few; this book will be of particular interest to scholars and students concerned with party systems, political parties and comparative politics.

Kris Deschouwer is Professor of politics at the Vrije Universiteit Brussel, Belgium.

Routledge/ECPR Studies in European Political Science

Edited by Thomas Poguntke

Ruhr University Bochum, Germany on behalf of the European Consortium for Political Research

The Routledge/ECPR Studies in European Political Science series is published in association with the European Consortium for Political Research – the leading organisation concerned with the growth and development of political science in Europe. The series presents high-quality edited volumes on topics at the leading edge of current interest in political science and related fields, with contributions from European scholars and others who have presented work at ECPR workshops or research groups.

Democratic Governance and New Technology
Technologically mediated innovations in political practice in Western Europe
Edited by Ivan Horrocks, Jens Hoff and Pieter Tops

Democracy without Borders
Transnationalisation and conditionality in new democracies
Edited by Jean Grugel

Cultural Theory as Political Science
Edited by Michael Thompson, Gunnar Grendstad and Per Selle

The Transformation of Governance in the European Union
Edited by Beate Kohler-Koch and Rainer Eising

Parliamentary Party Groups in European Democracies
Political parties behind closed doors
Edited by Knut Heidar and Ruud Koole

Survival of the European Welfare State
Edited by Stein Kuhnle

Private Organisations in Global Politics
Edited by Karsten Ronit and Volker Schneider

Federalism and Political Performance
Edited by Ute Wachendorfer-Schmidt

Democratic Innovation
Deliberation, representation and association
Edited by Michael Saward

Public Opinion and the International Use of Force
Edited by Philip Everts and Pierangelo Isernia

Religion and Mass Electoral Behaviour in Europe
Edited by David Broughton and Hans-Martien ten Napel

Estimating the Policy Position of Political Actors
Edited by Michael Laver

Democracy and Political Change in the 'Third World'
Edited by Jeff Haynes

Politicians, Bureaucrats and Administrative Reform
Edited by B Guy Peters and Jon Pierre

Civil Societies and Social Movements
Potentials and problems
Edited by Derrick Purdue

Resources, Governance and Civil Conflict
Edited by Magnus Öberg and Kaare Strøm

Transnational Private Governance and its Limits
Edited by Jean-Christophe Graz and Andreas Nölke

International Organizations and Implementation
Enforcers, managers, authorities?
Edited by Jutta Joachim, Bob Reinalda and Bertjan Verbeek

New Parties in Government
Edited by Kris Deschouwer

Also available from Routledge in association with the ECPR:

Sex Equality Policy in Western Europe
Edited by Frances Gardiner

Democracy and Green Poltical Thought
Edited by Brian Doherty and Marius de Geus

The New Politics of Unemployment
Edited by Hugh Compston

Citizenship, Democracy and Justice in the New Europe
Edited by Percy B. Lehning and Albert Weale

Private Groups and Public Life
Edited by Jan W. van Deth

The Political Context of Collective Action
Edited by Ricca Edmondson

Theories of Secession
Edited by Percy Lehning

Regionalism Across the North/South Divide
Edited by Jean Grugel and Wil Hout

New Parties in Government
In power for the first time

Edited by Kris Deschouwer

Routledge
Taylor & Francis Group

LONDON AND NEW YORK

First published 2008
by Routledge
2 Park Square Milton Park Abingdon Oxon OX14 4RN

Simultaneously published in the USA and Canada
by Routledge
270 Madison Avenue, New York, NY 10016

*Routledge is an imprint of the Taylor & Francis Group, an informa
business.*

First issued in paperback 2011

Typeset in Times New Roman by Prepress Projects Ltd, Perth, UK

British Library Cataloguing in Publication Data
A catalogue record for this book is available from the British Library

Library of Congress Cataloging-in-Publication Data
New Parties in Government: in power for the first time/edited by Kris
Deschouwer
        p.c.m – (Routledge/ECPR studies in European political science; 53)
        ISBN 978-0-415-40499-0 (hardback: alk. paper) – ISBN
        978-0-203-93859-1 (e-book: alk. paper) 1. Political parties–Europe–
        Case studies. 2. Power (Social sciences)–Europe. 3. Europe–Politics
        and government–1989– I. Deschouwer, Kris
        JN94.A979N47 2008
        324.2094–dc22
                        2007033768

ISBN 10 0–415–40499–1 (hbk)
ISBN 10 0–415–66369–5 (pbk)
ISBN 10 0–203–93859–3 (ebk)

ISBN 13 978–0–415–40499–0 (hbk)
ISBN 13 978–0–415–66369–4 (pbk)
ISBN 13 978–0–203–93859–1 (ebk)

Contents

xii   *Contents*

Tables

Figures

Contributors

Tim Bale joined the Department of Politics and Contemporary European Studies at Sussex in 2003 after five years at Victoria University of Wellington in New Zealand. He specializes in comparative politics and political parties. He is the co-editor of the European Journal of Political Research's annual Political Data Yearbook and his latest book is *European Politics: a Comparative Introduction*, published by Palgrave.

Nicole Bolleyer has recently completed her PhD thesis at the European University Institute in Florence, Italy. From September 2007 onwards she will work as a junior lecturer at Exeter University in the UK. Her dissertation accounts for the organizational patterns of intergovernmental relations in federal systems. Her research interests also include political parties and party systems in Western Europe, institutional theory and concept formation in comparative politics. Recent publications have appeared in *Publius: The Journal of Federalism*, *Regional and Federal Studies*, *the Swiss Political Science Review* and *West European Politics*.

Magnus Blomgren is a senior lecturer at the Department of Political Science at Umeå University, Sweden. He has mainly been interested in the impact of the European integration on political parties and national parliamentary institutions. He has published work on political representation in the European Parliament, national adaptation to the European political arena and post-war constitutional development in Western Europe.

Jo Buelens is a research assistant at the Vrije Universiteit Brussel. His research topics are new political parties, multilevel government and elections. He was involved in the development of the Belgian electoral database. His special interest is in the Democratic Republic of Congo, where he was invited as an expert to assist with the elaboration of the electoral law of DRCongo.

Pascal Delwit is Professor of Political Science at Université libre de Bruxelles (ULB) – Centre d'étude de la vie politique. He has published numerous contributions on Belgian and European political life and political actors. He is the author of *Social Democracy in Europe* (2005) and *Extreme Right Parties and power in Europe* (2007) which were published by Editions de l'Université de Bruxelles.

Kris Deschouwer is Professor of Politics at the Vrije Universiteit Brussel. He has published on political parties, elections, comparative regionalism and federalism and consociational democracy. He is the editor of the *European Journal of Political Research*.

Christian Pierre Ghillebaert is a PhD student in Political Science at the Centre d'Etudes Politiques sur l'Europe du Nord (from the Institut d'Etudes Politiques in Lille). His disseration deals with crossborder Dutch and Flemish nationalisms (Dietse gedachte). He is currently an English teacher and has taught sociology and the history of French institutions in several French universities.

Emilie van Haute is a PhD student in the Department of Political Science at Université libre de Bruxelles. Her thesis examines party membership at the Belgian level. Her research interests include political participation, party membership, intra-party democracy, parties and elections, and Belgian politics. She has published articles on these topics in national and international journals.

Airo Hino is Associate Professor of Political Science at Tokyo Metropolitan University, Japan. He received his PhD from the Department of Government at the University of Essex and has worked as Flemish Community Fellow at the Institute of Social and Political Opinion Research of Katholieke Universiteit Leuven, and as Post-doctoral Fellow at the Centre of Comparative Politics of Université Catholique de Louvain in Belgium. His research interests include political parties and party systems, voting behaviour, electoral systems, party finance, party manifestos, Green politics, extreme-right parties, new challenger parties, and comparative research methodology.

Jonathan Hopkin is a senior lecturer in the Department of Government at the London School of Economics, and an associate fellow of the Johns Hopkins University Bologna Center. He is the author of *Party Formation and Democratic Transition in Spain* (1999 Macmillan) and has published widely on party politics, decentralization and political corruption, with particular reference to Southern Europe.

Piero Ignazi is Professor of Comparative Politics at the University of Bologna. He is currently Chairman of the Committee for Political Sociology of the International Political Science Association. His research interests focus on party politics with a theoretical approach, a comparative approach (mainly European-wide) and a case study approach (on Italy). His most recent publications include *Extreme Right Parties in Western Europe* (OUP 2006, second expanded edition), *Political Parties and Political Systems* (co-edited with A. Roemmele and D. Farrell; Praeger 2005), *Il Parlamento Europeo* (with L. Bardi; il Mulino 2004), and *Il Potere dei Partiti: la Politica in Italia Dagli anni Sessanta ad Oggi* (Laterza 2002).

Elisabeth Ivarsflaten is currently a Postdoctoral Prize Research Fellow in Politics at Nuffield College, University of Oxford. From August 2007 she will be Associate Professor of comparative politics at the University of Bergen, Norway. She received her PhD from Oxford University in 2006 for a dissertation entitled 'Immigration Policy and Party Organization: Explaining the rise of the populist right in Western Europe'. Her work on European immigration politics and populist right parties has been published in journals such as *Comparative Political Studies* and the *European Journal of Political Research*.

Paul Lucardie received a PhD in Political Science at Queen's University (Kingston, Canada) in 1980. Since 1979 he has been Research Fellow at the Documentation Centre on Dutch Political Parties (DNPP) at the University of Groningen; since 1991 he has also been affiliated with the Canadian Studies Centre at the same university. His research interests focus on political ideologies and new parties in the Netherlands, Canada and Germany.

Jan Sundberg holds the Swedish Chair in Political Science at the University of Helsinki. His main research interests cover party organizations, local politics, and ethnic relations. He has contributed with several books on these topics written in Swedish and English. In addition, he is the former president of the Nordic Political Science Association, and the former vice chair and treasurer of ECPR.

Liam Weeks is a lecturer in the Department of Government, University College Cork. He has previously held an appointment in the Department of Political Science, Trinity College, Dublin. His main research interests include political parties, voting behaviour and electoral systems. He has published work in *Politics in the Republic of Ireland, How Ireland Voted 2002, Irish Political Studies*, and *Representation*. He is currently working on a study of Independent candidates and their voters, the dynamics of the single transferable vote, and election campaigns in Ireland.

Niklas Wilhelmsson (PhD candidate) works as a researcher at the Centre for Research on Ethnic Relations and Nationalism (CEREN) at the University of Helsinki. He has been involved in research projects dealing with the integration of immigrants, political participation and political parties.

Series editor's preface

Anybody who has followed the development of Green parties on their way from protest to governmental power cannot fail to agree with the former Green Foreign Secretary of Germany, Joschka Fischer, who remarked that the march through the institutions has tended to change the marchers far more than the institutions. Entering the game of established politics confronted them with a number of organizational and political challenges that left significant marks on their policies, their strategy and the way they organized. Coming from the opposite end of the political spectrum, right-wing populist parties faced comparable junctures: entering parliament meant that they also had to choose between continuing irresponsible, provocative behaviour or subscribing to the rules and norms of parliamentary work. Still, parliamentary representation allows protest parties to pursue a 'double strategy' in that they may attempt to exploit the parliamentary stage in order to promote their cause without renouncing their commitment to protest or to the demand for radical, fundamental change. Arguably, they approach an even more fundamental juncture when they decide to pursue governmental office. Being in government (or wanting to get into government) makes it impossible to continue sitting on the fence between protest and power and this is why this volumes takes a close look at the effects of entering into government for the first time.

However, this book is not just about parties that originated from new social movement protest or populist discontent with established politics. The editor has cast his net much wider and includes all new parties, many of which have not challenged the party system from 'outside' but are simply breakaways of existing parties. To be sure, they are, in a way, also protest parties because they were formed in protest against their former party's alleged failure to represent interests or constituencies which were considered important by those who decided to break away. Finally, there are parties which were considered to be unacceptable for government until this ban was finally lifted as a result of either ideological moderation or changed political circumstances (or both). The Italian Alleanza Nazionale is an example of this, and the German Left Party may become one in the future.

Whenever a party joins government for the first time it is confronted with a set of potential gains and losses which are similar irrespective of the party's origin or ideological orientation. First and foremost, it loses a set of powerful arguments.

There is no way back to pure protest or criticism: being part (or having been) of the executive means that certain arguments can no longer be used because the party itself has shared responsibility for the circumstances it wishes to criticize. Famously, when a German Green Minister for the Environment had to organize nuclear transports, his credibility with the anti-nuclear protest was damaged for ever. Similarly, when the Austrian Freedom Party joined the national government the credibility of its anti-establishment posture began to erode quickly. Second, ideological moderation is often an essential precondition of being admitted to government which, in turn, carries the risk of giving rise to another new party which claims to carry the can of ideological continuity. Third, governing requires organizational efficiency, because the number of required decisions tends to rise sharply while the permissible response time is likely to drop.

Not all parties rise to these challenges. Some are severely punished at the polls, some disappear altogether, like the List Pim Fortuyn which came from nowhere straight into government in the Netherlands in 2002 and officially dissolved itself five years later. Others bounce back, like the German Green Party, which lost for four consecutive years at each and every Land election following their admission to national government in 1998. And there are success stories like the Italian Forza Italia, which was created by its leader Silvio Berlusconi as a vehicle to attain prime ministerial office.

This short, and by no means complete, list indicates that newly governing parties have become a more widespread phenomenon in recent years, and while they differ widely as regards their ideological acceptability, their size, their age and their organizational power, they share similar problems of adaptation to a new and very important organizational environment, that is, the realm of executive power. To be sure, there are good reasons to disagree as regards the degree of adaptive success one would hope for in different cases but the very fact that coalition formation has become more inclusive is *also* a sign of the ability of modern democracy to integrate new (and old) outsiders. However, the price cannot be a compromise over democratic values, and there are sometimes good reasons for concerns. On the other hand, the fact that some challengers have also failed as a result of governmental participation may indicate that moderate forces are capable of dominating competitive party democracy in the long run.

Thomas Poguntke
Series Editor
Bochum
August 2007

1 Comparing newly governing parties

Kris Deschouwer

New and newly governing parties

One of the important indicators of party system change during the past few decades is the increasing promiscuity in national coalition formation (Bartolini 1998). Coalitions are indeed often formed (or supported) by new combinations of parties, including parties that are either new or that were before not considered to be governing parties. One of the explanations for this promiscuity and for these innovative combinations is the sheer presence of a large number of new parties able to attract a substantial number of voters. In the 1990s the average electoral result for parties created after 1960 in 15 West-European countries was a quite impressive 23.7 per cent (Mair 2002: 134).

Newly governing parties are the focus of this book, which intends to explore what happens when parties experience for the first time the pleasures and pressures of being in government. How does being in government affect their internal organization, their procedures of participation and decision-making, their relations with their voters and with their members? Does it affect the party ideology, the programme and the policy preferences?

Some of the parties that joined these innovative coalitions (Mair 1997: 211) are themselves indeed also new. They have seen the light as a consequence of the mobilization of new values and interests from the 1960s on. The literature has paid a great deal of attention to the explanation of their rise and success. Broadly comparative studies have looked at the interaction between the strategies of parties and the institutional context in which they try to break through (e.g. Harmel and Robertson 1985; Hug 2001; Tavits 2006). Different types of new parties have been identified on the basis of the role they want to play in the system, on the way in which they try to attract voters. Rochon (1985) classifies new parties into 'challengers' of existing parties and 'mobilizers' of new issues or cleavages. Lucardie (2000) labels the latter 'prophetic' parties and further divides the challengers into 'purifiers' of an old ideology and 'prolocutors' trying to revive neglected values and interests.

Most attention in the study of new parties went to their political sociology, to the societal changes that explain the realignment of voters and the emergence of more or less solid new alignments around new values (e.g. Dalton *et al.* 1984).

Prominently present in this literature are the Greens. The clear and evident link between their rise and success and the ingredients of the silent revolution (Inglehart 1977), their meaningful presence in a large number of party systems and undoubtedly also the mild sympathy they enjoyed from many academics has produced a stream of literature and insights that is probably only rivalled by the amount of studies of the social-democratic family. The new and challenging organizational forms displayed by the Green parties (Poguntke 1987) were another good reason for taking a closer look at them. More recently the family of right-wing populist parties has attracted more attention. And again the political sociology has been very prominent, trying to explain who the voters of these new parties are and why they vote for them (e.g. Von Beyme 1988; Ignazi 1992; Kitschelt 1996; Betz and Immerfall 1998; Lubbers *et al.* 2002). Rather than their special or experimental party organization their radical ideology and its compatibility with democratic values has been at the core of the research (Mudde 2000).

The dominance of Greens and right-wing populists in the recent party literature (on new parties) gives the wrong impression that they do indeed dominate the scene. Yet half of the electorate of new political parties in the 1990s voted for parties other than these (Mair 2002). Many new parties are indeed challengers rather than mobilizers. They are new in the party system but do not necessarily place themselves outside the existing competition. They are new but mobilize on old issues. This can be the economic left–right cleavage (with for instance leftist and anti-tax parties) or the religious cleavage (with for instance new Christian Democratic parties or radical religious parties).

This actually means that there are three different dimensions of 'newness' that can be identified. The first is the *age* of the party, or its 'organizational age' (Chapter 2). If a party is young, it is probably still building and institutionalizing its organizational structures. These are still a bit fluid. The party might have to go through its first major leadership change, always a crucial test for the institutionalization of an organizational structure. The second dimension is *ideology*. Mobilizing parties build their success on new issues and ideas. They compete on new conflict dimensions. They can do this in a very radical way, by deeply questioning the existing order or by fiercely blaming the existing political establishment. And a third dimension of newness is the *type of party organization*. A number of new parties – the Greens very obviously – are not just further evolutions or adaptations of the mass party model, but really new and alternative models. The 'business-firm party' (Hopkin and Paolucci 1999) is also typically a form for new and recently created political parties.

These three dimensions are very important for our purpose. One can indeed assume that each of these aspects of being 'new' affects the way in which a party can move from opposition towards executive power. This is not likely to be a move that is easy to digest. Yet not all parties that have recently joined a government are physically new parties. Some have been around for quite a long time, but remained outside the circle of governing parties. That is especially true for a number of (former) communist parties who have recently come 'in from the cold' (Bale and Dunphy 2007). The often renamed communist parties have since the end of the Cold War left their pariah status behind and have become part of and – in Italy for instance – even the leading party of coalition governments. For these parties the move from opposition to government after such a long time is also quite a change. Newly governing parties can thus be 'old' parties (age, ideology or organizational form) or 'new' parties.

A new phase in life

For both types of newly governing parties, the new parties and the older ones, the entering of a coalition marks a crucial *new phase in their lifespan*. Pedersen (1982) suggests the use of this metaphor to conceptualize the evolution of political parties. The basic idea is that a party goes through a number of stages, starting with being born and possibly ending with the death of the party. Parties can however remain in one of these stages for a very long time. Other authors have already used this model to look explicitly at new parties, and more in particular at new parties moving towards government (Buelens and Lucardie 1998; Rihoux 2001; Müller-Rommel 2002). Pedersen distinguishes between four stages, also assuming that a party can go back and possibly disappear again. The four stages are *declaration* (announcing the will to become a party), *authorization* (passing the necessary requirements to be recognized as a party), *representation* (winning seats) and *relevance*.

This lifespan model is a very useful heuristic tool. It allows us to identify crucial stages and crucial changes in the evolution of political parties. In order to assess the meaning and importance of participating in government, we add a new phase in the life of parties: *being in government*. That phase follows the phase of relevance. Relevance is indeed not the same as governing. According to Sartori (1976) there are two sources of relevance for a party: blackmail potential and governing potential. The latter means that a party has already been in government or that it is seen – both by itself and by the other parties – as a possible governing party. A party with blackmail potential is one that is not prepared to enter government or that is, for the others, not acceptable as a governing party.

The phase of relevance can therefore be broken down into these two different statuses. And by breaking up the phase of relevance and especially by adding the phase of governing (Figure 1.1) we claim that something important happens when a party moves from opposition to government. Governing is a new phase in life. It is a transition, the crossing of a new threshold. Still following Pedersen, we do not need to assume that a party will stay forever in that position. It can (and indeed most will) go back, just as it can lose its representation or simply die and

Figure 1.1 An amended model of the life span of political parties.

disappear. The move from opposition to government can also be for some parties a two-step process. Some parties start their life as political outsiders, as challengers not only of the other parties but also of crucial aspects of the political system itself. These parties can reach the status of relevance because of their blackmail potential. For these parties to become a potential or an actual governing party, they need to leave behind their outsider status in the first place. Both steps – from blackmail to governing potential and then to government – can be taken simultaneously or can involve a longer transition process.

Deciding to cross the threshold of government is a 'hard decision' (Müller and Strøm 1999). It means that a party has added the seeking of office to its mix of strategic goals (Harmel and Janda 1994). It is taking the risk of being blamed at the polls for what goes wrong, but hopes to take advantage of the visibility that comes with being in power. It is taking the risk of being challenged by its militants for having accepted compromises, but hopes that being in power is a more effective way to influence policy. It goes without saying that moving from opposition to government is not a minor event in the life of a party. That is the simple starting point of our analysis. A governing party is confronted with a different role to play. It has to select office-holders. It has to attract the necessary expertise to follow up not only its own portfolio's or its own chosen themes but the full action of the government. It is faced with new organizational challenges, like giving a place to the members of the cabinet in the decision-making procedures. Its internal life is likely to be affected much more by the agenda of the cabinet than by issues of its own choice. The party will be more visible in the media and will have to explain its positions and decisions more often than when it was in opposition.

There is another important element that makes the transition to power a major step in a large and still growing number of European countries. When a party joins the government at a lower tier of the system – like the substate in a federal country – that does not necessarily involve the entering of the central government. A party can decide to limit its governmental ambition to this lower tier only, as for instance some of the regional parties in the Spanish Autonomous Communities do. But entering the government at the level of the national state does automatically involve the entering of the higher-level European 'government'. Of course, the European Union is not a state with a normal (coalition) government, but exactly this peculiar nature of the EU means that whoever is in power at the national level becomes deeply involved in decision-making at the European level. The European decision-making processes entail a high degree of intergovernmentalism, of negotiations between national executives. It involves meetings of the Council of Ministers and possibly even the chairing of these meetings. In other words, the move from opposition to government at the national level means that it is impossible – or at least fairly difficult – to be in opposition to the European Union. Entering the national government means a twofold accession to the 'system', to the 'establishment'. It is one more element that makes the transition from opposition to government quite a difficult one. Especially for Eurosceptic parties, the switch from being against Europe to being active in Europe is not easy to manage.

Being in government is a new step in the life of parties, but some parties can of course get used to it. Once they have been in power and have experienced the consequences of it, they can decide to keep the office-seeking as one of their major goals. The second or the third time in government will not be the same as the very first time. Being in government will always be different from being in opposition – for the reasons given above – but the first time is special. And that is the second starting point of our analysis: *being new in government is more difficult*. There is only one first time,

There are indeed a number of good reasons to assume that crossing the threshold of power is more difficult when it happens for the first time. The first reason has already been spelled out above: it is the sheer newness of the role, the lack of experience, the absence of a storybook, the need to invent solutions for brand new problems. The lack of routine can be a problem for the internal organization of a newly governing party, but also for the way in which it organizes the relations with the other party or parties in the coalition. A newly governing party is likely to govern with more experienced partners, maybe even partners that have a history of being in government together. In that case the external relations, the relations between the party and the government also need to be invented and organized.

Although there are notable exceptions, like Forza Italia, a newly governing party will most often be a smaller partner in a coalition. Newly governing parties will not immediately receive extremely weighty or visible portfolios. Although their voting power or 'walk-away power' might be substantial – especially if the coalition is a minimal one – the use of that power supposes some experience about when and how and how often to use it. Being a smaller partner in a coalition can be quite a burden for a new party in government. This weaker position and possibly lower visibility can also affect the electoral results at the end of the governing period. Governing means that the chances to lose at the polls increase (Rose and Mackie 1983). The electoral risk that is being taken when joining a coalition can be higher for newly governing parties, especially if they are smaller. Not only are they then a less visible partner in the coalition, but the loss of votes can be much more painful. A larger party can more easily take the risk of losing some votes. A smaller party losing votes comes immediately close to the risk zone. It might simply end below the electoral threshold and lose all its MPs.

Newer parties – especially when the newness refers to the post-dealignment period – have yet another reason to fear the loss of votes. Parties that mobilize new values and interests are less likely to have an electorate that is deeply rooted in a clear societal subgroup whose relation to the party is obvious. They lack the 'diffuse support' (Easton 1965) by which they can get off the hook when or if the government policies are not fully and exactly those that had been promised.

Moving from opposition to government also involves an identity change. That is especially the case when a party moved towards government by a transition through the blackmail potential phase. If a party has built its place in the party system as a protest party, an anti-establishment party, a principled opposition party, then its joining the government is nothing less than a deep transformation. If a party has first been excluded by the others and then finally accepted as a governing or supporting partner, it becomes almost a new and different party.

Even if a party gradually moves away from an extreme position in the system by slowly being accepted or slowly making itself available for the game of coalition formation and compromising – for instance by playing the game at a lower tier of government – the final step will remain one that marks the end of the old status and identity. And once more this makes the first entry in government an important, visible, new and possibly painful step.

Exploring diversity

Being in government is a clearly different position and phase in a party's life, and entering that position is likely to have a clear impact on a party when it happens for the very first time. That is the working hypothesis of this book. So far the comparative analysis of newly governing parties has (again) focused very much on the Greens (Müller-Rommel 2002; Rihoux and Rüdig 2006). This is indeed a very peculiar and in this respect very interesting party family because its members did not only enter the party systems with a clearly new and radical ideology, but also with a party organization that was meant in the first place to offer generous possibilities for participation by the grass-roots (Poguntke 1987). These are characteristics that are at first sight not very compatible with being in government. Organizational adaptations before and after being in government, ideological adaptations, and electoral consequences of being in power have thus been among the topics covered by the research. As explained above, these dimensions are not only interesting for Green parties only. They are relevant for all parties in power for the first time (on right-wing populist parties in office, see Heinisch 2003; Minkenberg 2001; Luther 2003; De Lange 2007).

In this volume we describe and discuss a variety of parties in a variety of countries. Most chapters describe and compare a limited number of parties. Rather than aiming at sweeping generalizations, we try to take a look inside the parties to tell the story of the route towards power and the manner in which being in power was dealt with. We look at what happened afterwards. Was the party able to stay in government or to come back to government at a later stage? Did it win or lose votes after being in power?

The explored variety is, however, limited to parties in government in western European countries (and New Zealand). Many more newly governing parties could be analysed in East Central Europe, where most of the parties are new and where coalitions are likely to involve many parties governing for the first time. The context of newly governing parties in East Central Europe is, however, quite different. What is absent is the very specific contrast between traditionally governing parties and newly governing parties. It is exactly that contrast and the dynamics that it produces when a party enters government for the first time that justifies the limited scope of this book.

Three major topics are dealt with. The first is the party organization. How did the party cope with the new demands, with new tasks and new groups to integrate in the party structures? The second is the party ideology and identity. Did the newly governing party change its ideological profile? Did it soften its discourse?

Was it able to accept compromises? And the third topic is the party's relation with society. Was it able to keep its voters after governing? Did it attract more or different members? Did it keep or change its relations with civil society?

In Chapter 2, Nicole Bolleyer further develops the idea that for new parties the cost of public office is likely to be higher than for older parties. She conceptualizes new parties as being 'organizationally young' and discusses how moving from principled opposition to coalition potential, and then from coalition potential to being in power, creates a number of pressures. These are related to the need to co-ordinate between the central party organization and the party in public office, the need to select candidates for the executive functions and the need to acquire broader expertise outside the core themes of the party.

In Chapter 3, Jonathan Hopkin and Piero Ignazi deal with Italy, which is a very special and even extreme and exceptional case of new parties in government. After the collapse of the old party system in the early 1990s, coalitions were formed with unseen combinations of parties. One of the reasons for this was the creation and quite spectacular breakthrough of Forza Italia, a new party that would immediately obtain access to the highest office of prime minister. Hopkin and Ignazi look at three newly governing parties: Forza Italia, *Lega Nord* and DS. The last of these – the reformed PCI – is not a new party. Its organization can also not be labelled young or new. To the contrary: here is a party with a very old and solid organization. Entering and also leading the coalition made it fully feel the necessity to adapt, and so it did. The *Lega Nord* started as a typical principled opposition party, and brought down the first Berlusconi government in which it participated. It was invited to govern again, and quite surprisingly it was able to keep its old and very populist discourse. It managed to play a double role. Hopkin and Ignazi show that, actually, Forza Italia has been able to stick quite closely to its original populist discourse.

Chapter 4 also looks at several parties in the same country. Paul Lucardie and Christian Pierre Ghillebaert explain and show how, in the Netherlands, the very low electoral threshold allows new parties to gain representation fairly easily. A number of these new parties then move quite swiftly towards power. The chapter discusses D66, DS70, PPR and the List Pim Fortuyn. The fragmentation of the Dutch party system seems to facilitate the access to power for smaller partners. Being asked by the major parties is however the key that opens the door. Lucardie and Ghillebaert make very clear that entering a coalition is not an easy task. There is quite some evidence of strong pressures on the new parties to adapt and to change. Yet there is less evidence of real and substantial change. Newly governing parties are able to resist. The exception to this is the LPF, basically a political entrepreneur party with a barely existing party structure. Its immediate accession to the coalition in the absence of the then murdered party leader meant the beginning of the end.

In Chapter 5, Tim Bale and Magnus Blomgren look at two countries – New Zealand and Sweden – where minority governments are quite common. In such a context the very meaning of 'being in government' needs to be broadened. New parties supporting a government without actually holding office occupy a 'half-way house' (Bale and Bergman 2006), possibly combining the advantages and disadvantages of being in power and of being in opposition. Newly governing parties can thus also be nearly governing parties. The chapter looks at the fate of four New Zealand parties (United, New Zealand First, the Alliance and the Greens) and of four Swedish parties (New Democracy, the Christian Democrats, the Greens and the Left Party). Bale and Blomgren conclude that joining or supporting a government has not led to fundamental changes in the party organization, partly because some change and adaptation had preceded the move towards power. Major ideological changes are also absent, but the electoral losses suffered by newly or nearly governing parties are quite substantial.

Chapters 6 and 7 both tell the story of a Green Party moving into government and having to leave it again. Pascal Delwit and Emilie van Haute look at the Belgian Francophone Green party Ecolo. It joined a six-party coalition in 1999, but was never able to get fully used to being in power. Leadership teams were frequently replaced, and Ecolo kept on hesitating between a governing and an opposition role. Its ministers left the government two weeks before the next elections, at which they lost heavily. They did not return to government.

The story of the Finnish Greens is quite different. Jan Sundberg and Niklas Wilhelmsson describe the long process of party formation, related to the high thresholds of 'declaration' and 'authorization' in Finland. In 1995 the Finnish Greens join a multiparty 'rainbow coalition' and are well rewarded at the polls in 1999. And they join the next coalition, only to leave it in 2002 because they disagree with the policy on nuclear plants. Again, at the next elections in 2003 the party improved its score, without however returning to power immediately. Sundberg and Wilhelmsson show how the relative electoral stability of the Greens could be based on the existence of a well-defined social base in the Finnish electorate. Delwit and Van Haute focus more specifically on the evolution of the membership of Ecolo. Distinguishing between the pre- and post-1999 members, they are able to show that the members who joined the party after it entered the coalition do differ – but not dramatically – from those who had joined earlier.

The contrast between these two Green parties is quite striking. While the Belgian Greens found governing really hard and paid the price for it at the polls, the Finnish Greens were able to keep the tensions much lower. The consensual tradition of Finland possibly reduces the line between government and opposition and therefore softens the crossing of the border. Although Belgium is a typical consensus democracy, the coalition in which the Greens entered government was one that wanted to exclude the Christian Democrats and thus to mark the end of an era. It meant that the expectations were extremely high, and that the governing parties all had to prove that they were able to succeed. That has put much more pressure on the Belgian than on the Finnish Greens.

In Chapter 8, Liam Weeks looks at the role of independents or non-party candidates and MPs in the Irish system. He asserts that these independents are very similar to small parties, among others because many of them are actually not simply individuals but have been nominated by organizations. Independents have played a significant role in coalition formation, since they have often supported a government. Participation in government has generally had a positive effect – at the polls – in the cases where independents were able to bring home some tangible advantages for their constituencies. By looking at the way in which these independents play a role in government formation, Liam Weeks is able to illustrate how important it is for a new or minor player in that process to be asked by the larger parties. This was also very evident in the Dutch case.

Jo Buelens and Airo Hino explore in Chapter 9 a very important question: do newly governing parties lose at the polls? In the previous chapters we have seen that the evidence seems to be quite mixed. Some parties do lose, while others are able to survive or even to improve their score. Using a large comparative database Buelens and Hino do find some interesting patterns. Although generally all parties risk losing after having governed, the newly governing parties do lose a bit more often. The chances of losing are also higher for parties of the extreme left and of the extreme right (see also Heinisch 2003), while Greens show very mixed results. Winning or losing is also very much a matter of what happens to the coalition partners. Partners of an outgoing coalition seldom win together. If one party wins, one of the others is likely to pay the price. For newly governing parties this is not different. If they lose, their partners win. And when they are able to win, at least one of the partners loses.

In the final chapter Elisabeth Ivarsflaten takes us to a much wider effect of newly governing parties. One very special case was the inclusion of the Austrian populist right party FPÖ in the national coalition in 2000. This was widely contested with – among others – the argument that allowing such a party in the coalition would increase anti-immigrant sentiments among the population. Comparing Austria with Denmark (a right-wing populist party as support party) and Flanders (a right-wing populist party fully excluded from power) she shows how the impact of the new party in government has been limited. The very fact of being in government has limited the degree in which the FPÖ could further focus on anti-immigrant views. Especially the role of the major party in government – the ÖVP – that clearly communicated that this was not a coalition with a normal but with a potentially problematic party, has rather led to a decrease in anti-immigrant sentiments in public opinion. And indeed, the fate of the FPÖ in the Austrian government cannot be seen as a success story (see also Luther 2003).

Common patterns?

We have gathered a variety of stories and insights about parties entering or supporting government for the first time. These do not add up to one simple and straightforward pattern that would allow us to make strong and reliable predictions about what is likely to happen when a party joins a coalition. Yet there are some conclusions that can be taken on board for further research into the topic of newly governing parties but also of government and coalition formation in general.

In the first place, it goes without saying that the difference between being inside and outside government is crucial. We have slightly amended and expanded

Pedersen's lifespan model of parties to mark the presence in government as a very specific position. It involves the crossing of a threshold; it involves making a hard choice. We have been able to describe to what extent this status change affects a party crossing the line for the first time. In all cases the pressures to adapt to new demands and requirements have been quite visible. There is only one story of a fairly smooth move towards government, but that is a very special and peculiar one: Forza Italia. Its very special genesis and its creation as a party specifically intended to take over the governing power in Italy as soon as possible means that it was a party built to govern. Most parties start their life as challengers or mobilizers and concentrate on some electoral success in the first place. And from there they can start moving towards government.

For the parties that have entered government for the first time, we have been able to see that crossing that threshold does not pass unnoticed. That is actually no surprise. As we already said above, being in government is a different role and position than being in opposition. A governing party needs to defend policies rather than criticize them. A governing party needs to defend compromises rather than criticizing the concessions that were made to strike the agreement. Being in government creates a new relationship with the voters, with the different party organs and with the other parties.

The first and most obvious pressure to change is seen in the party organization. This is indeed a pressure that is almost impossible to avoid. Membership of a government introduces new roles in the party organization and these new roles are taken up by important people in the party. The dominance of the governmental agenda on the party life and the increased speed with which intra-party decisions have to be reached give quite some power to these new roles. That does not mean however that those newly governing parties suddenly change their organizational structure or organizational identity. The evidence shows rather that parties are trying to avoid changes, trying to find a way in between the necessities of government and the willingness to keep their organizational identity alive. That is especially the case for Green and radical parties for which avoiding oligarchic tendencies is a very central issue. The Belgian Green party Ecolo invented a word for this double and ambiguous position: '*participposition*'. During most of its time in the federal government (1999–2003) it was lead by a leadership trio opposed to government participation. The same ambiguous attitude and strategy is found in the Dutch D66. This party has been in and out of government several times, but remains – as Lucardie and Ghillbebaert conclude in Chapter 4 – a party led by amateurs.

For these new-politics parties, one can easily understand why shifting straight from a grass-roots-led party to an elite-driven party is quite difficult. But parties less concerned with internal democracy do feel the same pressure. The decision of the FPÖ leader Jörg Haider not to become a member of the Austrian government himself but to stay outside and thus to keep the real leadership of the party away from the members of government illustrates the same attempt to keep the old party organization – its power relations in particular – out of the hands of new party actors. In general the empirical evidence gathered by the contributions in this book shows very clearly that newly governing parties feel a strong pressure to change and to adapt to their new situation, but also reveal a strong resistance to change and creative attempts not to be too deeply transformed by the needs of being in government.

There is an interesting example, though, of a party that did consciously change its internal organization: the Italian (P)DS. Ignazi and Hopkin describe in detail how the former communist party that acceded to power in 1996 did reform its decision-making structures to make the transition from an opposition party to a (leading) governing party. With its old party organization, the DS does differ from most of the other newly governing parties. It is not a young and still fluid organization, but one that has a long history and that has institutionalized as an opposition party. In that sense the DS lacks the flexibility of newer and generally also much smaller new parties to cope with new challenges and tasks. Young age can be a problem for an organization (Chapter 2), but while old age might offer more chances for survival it also reduces the flexibility of an organization.

What Ecolo, D66 and DS have in common, though, is the fact that they paid a hefty electoral price for their participation in government. Looking at the electoral results of newly governing parties we do also find mixed results, but with some patterns emerging. Like traditionally governing parties, newly governing parties tend to lose after governing, but not all of them and not always. The more radical parties are more vulnerable, and of the radical parties the extreme right-wing parties are the most vulnerable. They are indeed the most recent example of parties that have put themselves and that are seen by the others as parties that are quite far away from the mainstream. They are (and for some of them have been) considered as pariah parties, as parties that might acquire blackmail potential but that can not be seen as potentially governing parties. The entry of the Austrian FPÖ into the federal government in 2000 has shown that most clearly. The fierce reaction of the then 14 other EU member states was meant to say that a line had been crossed. The rituals accompanying the installation of the ÖVP–FPÖ coalition, with special declarations about the protection of democratic values and with the president of the country only reluctantly accepting the new government did also make clear that this newly governing party was not just a new partner in government but a partner that did not fully belong there. Although other parties of the right-wing extremist family did enter or support national governments after 2000 (De Lange 2007), they are not yet all seen as governing parties. In France and in Belgium they remain pariah parties.

What makes the accession to power even more difficult for these parties is their clear and unambiguous Euroscepticism (Taggart 1998). Entering government is for these radical parties a very marked shift in identity, and the obligation to 'enter' the EU when in government makes it even stronger. These are certainly elements that explain why the more radical parties, and the right-wing radical parties in particular, are seldom able to win at the polls after having been in government. Italy is again offering the exception with the *Alleanza Nazionale*. But then the AN had clearly made its move towards a more mainstream and therefore potentially governing party *before* entering the governing coalition.

In general governing is thus a risky business. Opting for office does indeed mean that a number of voters are likely to punish the party at the next election. In a volatile environment, voters are more available, and they move more easily from one party to another. Even if these moves can be considered as intra-bloc moves (Bartolini and Mair 1990), they have important consequences for the parties who lose their voters. For newly governing parties that are also new parties, the danger of paying the price for governing is high. We distinguished above between three dimensions along which a party can be new: young age, new ideas and new type of organization. All three dimensions of newness can be a source of electoral instability. If a party has only a short history, if it was created recently, it will not have had the time to build a stable and loyal electorate. Only after a few elections – if the party can keep some kind of representation – can a loyal electorate possibly develop. Moving swiftly through the phases of the lifespan from declaration to government is almost asking for trouble. The many new (and small) Dutch parties entering coalitions are very good examples of this. Parties that have been able to build some history – as it is the case now for the Green parties – have more chances to keep (enough of) their voters after having governed.

The second dimension of newness – ideology – also adds to the electoral risks. Parties defending new ideas, especially if they are 'mobilizers' on new issues, have almost by definition an electorate that has been dealigned from old conflict lines and that still needs to develop – if they ever do – a habit of voting (almost) every time for the same new party. Again, the Greens seem to have secured a (small) niche in the party systems, allowing them to cope with electoral fluctuations. Sundberg and Wilhelmson claim that the presence of a well-defined Green electorate helps to explain why the Finnish Greens have been able to keep their voters, both when in opposition and when in government. The evidence is, however, still mixed in this respect. In the Italian DS we have a party that is not young at all and that does not mobilize on new values or issues. One could therefore expect that it has a stable and loyal electorate. Yet its participation in government caused the defection of one quarter of its voters. No party is shielded from electoral defeat.

Liam Weeks in his analysis of independents in Irish politics does find some recipe for success. To survive after supporting a government, it is important for them to be able to get some tangible rewards home to their constituency. But this is then a story that has no relation with party age or party ideology. Absence of ideology seems to be the key to success here. But it is a special and quite exceptional one. The Irish independents are indeed not fully fledged parties. Political parties normally come with some ideological identity, with policy proposals that go beyond pork barrel logic.

Ideology is – after organization and electoral fate – a third element for which we assumed that changes would occur in newly governing parties. We expect that governing parties adopt a different language, a different way to refer to their ideological identity. We expect a certain softening of the ideological profile. Yet like for organizational change, the evidence that we found does not point in the direction of strong or radical change. Again, resistance to change seems to be the rule.

There are two major reasons why there is so little change. The first is the very meaning of the ideological profile for a political party. It is not a peripheral attribute. It is an important reference point for party militants, members, voters and party elites. A sudden change of this core element of the party identity is not likely to happen overnight. But it does make life in government quite hard. Newer parties or parties coming from the opposition benches have been used to focusing much more prominently on their ideological profile. It cannot be easy to first defend in principle the independence of northern Italy and then enter a coalition that is – possibly – only prepared to start thinking about some further devolution. This is the point where the 'halfway house' between government and opposition can be a quite attractive solution. Staying outside, and supporting the government only on those items for which the party ideology and the policy proposals do not need to be stretched too far, allows a party to keep its ideological identity much 'cleaner' than when it has to share responsibility for all government decisions. But the conclusion is and remains that parties like the *Lega Nord* and actually many of the other newly governing parties have not been very eager to become a different party after having accepted to be in power.

The very nature of party ideology also explains why it will probably not change rapidly. Ideologies are broad and general views that do change over time, but at a rather slow pace. Entering government for the first time is certainly an event that contributes to the evolution of the way in which a party refers to its core ideas. But we should keep in mind that when a party crosses the threshold of power, this is not a sudden and surprising affair. Some parties do indeed jump the phases of the lifespan model and move almost directly from declaration into representation and government (see the List Pim Fortuyn or *Forza Italia*). But for most parties there is a – sometimes even very long – growing process. That can involve awareness that staying in the opposition and focusing on vote-seeking and policy-seeking without access to power might in the long run be a dead end (Dumont and Bäck 2006). The idea that entering or supporting a government is another possible way to position itself in the party system makes the party move and adapt in anticipation (Poguntke 2002). It has already changed when it crosses the threshold to power.

Coalition theory tells us that parties are more likely to form coalitions with partners that are not too far away in terms of ideology and policy proposals (e.g. De Swaan 1973). Parties at the margin of the party system are not potentially governing parties. But parties that have moved closer to at least one of the major and normally governing parties have more chance to be asked to join a government. Research on right-wing populist parties shows that proximity to the formateur party is an important predictor of the presence of these parties in a coalition (De Lange 2007). Moving first towards the core of the party system is not a guarantee but at least a major facilitator for getting in power.

Entering governing is not something that happens to a party. Although a newly governing party will need to be asked by others before it can enter government, it knows that in order to be asked it needs to have – in the eyes of the traditionally governing parties – enough coalition potential. Being in government is not a default position. It is the result of a deliberate choice. It is a choice that – with some exceptions – is made over a period of time. It is a learning process during which some adaptation and change occurs in anticipation.

While crossing the threshold of power does mark a new phase in the life of parties, it is not necessarily a step that leads to important *subsequent* changes in the party. The changes might and often have occurred earlier. And like all changes in and from political parties, this is a gradual process. Party change is hardly ever radical and total. Change is a piecemeal process. There might be a large amount of little alterations of rules and procedures and ways of communicating that lead only in the long run to a party that has been really transformed. In this long chain of little moves, the first time in government is an important event. Even if changes are adaptations in anticipation, and even if parties seem to resist to subsequent changes in the first place, the cases analysed in this book have shown that moving towards and entering government for the first time is a crucial phase in the life of a party.

Bibliography

Bale, T. and Bergman, T. (2006) 'A taste of honey is worse than none at all? Coping with the generic challenges of support party status in Sweden and New Zealand', *Party Politics*, 12(2): 189–202.

Bale, T. and Dunphy, R. (2007) 'In from the cold: left parties, policy, office and votes in advanced liberal democracies since 1989', paper presented at the 57th Political Studies Association Annual Conference, Bath, April 2007.

Bartolini, S. (1998) 'Coalition potential and governmental power', in P. Pennings and J.-E. Lane (eds) *Comparing Party System Change*, London: Routledge.

Bartolini, S. and Mair, P. (1990) *Identity, Competition, and Electoral Availability: The Stability of European Electorates, 1885–1985*, Cambridge: Cambridge University Press.

Betz, H.-G. and Immerfall, S. (1998) (eds) *The New Politics of the Right: Neo-Populist Parties and Movements in Established Democracies*, New York: St Martin's Press.

Buelens, J. and Lucardie, P. (1998) 'Ook nieuwe partijen worden oud: Een verkennend onderzoek naar de levensloop van nieuwe partijen in Nederland en België', in G. Voerman (ed.) *DNPP Jaarboek 1997*, Gronigen: University of Gronigen.

Dalton, R.J., Flanagan, S., Beck, P.A. and Alt, J.E. (1984) *Electoral Change in Advanced Industrial Democracies*, Princeton: Princeton University Press.

De Lange, S. (2007) 'The formation and reformation of radical right-wing populist government coalitions: a formal theoretical approach', paper presented at the 57th Political Studies Association Annual Conference, Bath, April 2007.

De Swaan, A. (1973) *Coalition Theories and Cabinet Formations: A Study of Formal Theories of Coaliton Formation Applied to Nine European Parliaments after 1918*, Amsterdam: Elsevier.

Dumont, P. and Bäck, H. (2006) 'Why so few, and why so late? Green parties and the question of governmental participation', *European Journal of Political Research*, 45: S35–68.

Easton, D. (1965) A *Systems Analysis of Political Life*. Chicago: Chicago University Press.

Harmel, R. and Janda, K. (1994) 'An integrated theory of party goals and party change', *Journal of Theoretical Politics*, 6(3): 259–87.

Harmel, R. and Robertson, J.D. (1985) 'Formation and success of new parties: a cross-national analysis', *International Political Science Review*, 6: 501–23.

Heinisch, R. (2003) 'Success in opposition – failure in government: explaining the performance of right-wing populist parties in public office', *West European Politics*, 26(3): 91–130.

Hopkin, J. and Paolucci, C. (1999) 'The business firm model of party organisation: cases from Spain and Italy', *European Journal of Political Research*, 35(3): 307–39.

Hug, S. (2001) *Altering Party Systems. Strategic Behavior and the Emergence of New Political Parties in Western Democracies*, Michigan: University of Michigan Press.

Ignazi, P. (1992) 'The silent counter-revolution: hypotheses on the emergence of extreme right-wing parties in Western Europe', *European Journal of Political Research*, 22(1): 3–34.

Inglehart, R. (1977) *The Silent Revolution: Changing Values and Political Styles Among Western Publics*, Princeton: Princeton University Press.

Kitschelt, H. (1997) *The Radical Right in Western Europe*, Ann Arbor: University of Michigan Press.

Lubbers, M., Gijsberts, M. and Scheepers, P. (2002) 'Extreme right-wing voting in Western Europe', *European Journal of Political Research*, 41(3): 345–78.

Lucardie, P. (2000) 'Prophets, purifiers and prolocutors: towards a theory on the emergence of new parties', *Party Politics*, 6(2): 175–85.

Luther, Kurt R. (2003) 'The self-destruction of a right-wing populist party? The Austrian parliamentary election of 2002', *West European Politics*, 26(2): 136–52.

Mair, P. (1997) *Party System Change: Approaches and Interpretations*, Oxford: Clarendon Press.

Mair, P. (2002) 'In the aggregate: mass electoral behaviour in Western Europe, 1950–2000', in H. Keman (ed.) *Comparative Democratic Politics: A Guide to Contemporary Theory and Research*, London: Sage.

Minkenberg, M. (2001) 'The radical right in public office: agenda-setting and policy effects', *West European Politics*, 24(4):1–21.

Mudde, C. (2000) *The Ideology of the Extreme Right*, Manchester: Manchester University Press.

Müller, W.C. and K. Strøm (eds) (1999) *Policy, Office, or Votes? How Political Parties in Western Europe make Hard Decisions*, Cambridge: Cambridge University Press.

Müller-Rommel, F. (2002) 'The lifespan and the political performance of Green parties', in Müller- Rommel F. and Poguntke T. (eds) *Green Parties in National Governments*, London: Frank Cass.

Pedersen, M. (1982) 'Towards a new typology of party lifespans and minor parties', *Scandinavian Political Studies*, 5: 1–16.

Poguntke, T. (1987) 'New politics and party systems: the emergence of a new type of party?', *West European Politics*, 10(1): 76–8.

Poguntke, T. (2002) 'Green parties in national government: from protest to acquiescence?' In F. Müller-Rommel and T. Poguntke (eds) *Green Parties in National Governments*, London: Frank Cass.

Rihoux, B. (2001) *Les Partis Politiques: Organisations et Changemen: Le Test des Ecologistes*, Paris: l'Harmattan.

Rihoux, B. and Rüdig, W. (2006) 'Analyzing Greens in power: setting the agenda', *European Journal of Political Research*, 45: S1–34.

Rochon, T.R. (1985) 'Mobilizers and challengers: towards a theory of new party success', *International Political Science Review*, 6(4): 419–39.

Rose, R. and Mackie, T.T. (1983) 'Incumbency in government: asset or liability?' In H. Daalder and P. Mair (eds) *Western European Party Systems, Continuity and Change*, London: Sage.

Sartori, G. (1976) *Parties and Party Systems: A Framework for Analysis*, Cambridge: Cambridge University Press.

Taggart, P. (1998) 'A touchstone of dissent: Euroscepticism in contemporary European party systems', *European Journal of Political Research,* 33: 363–88.

Tavits, M. (2006) 'Party system change: testing a model of new party entry', *Party Politics*, 12: 99–120.

Von Beyme, K. (1988) *Right-Wing Extremism in Western Europe*, London: Frank Cass.

2 The organizational costs of public office[1]

Nicole Bolleyer

New parties and the challenge of public office

In the course of declining party identification and growing electoral volatility, newly founded parties face increased opportunities to attract electoral support in a range of established Western democracies (Harmel and Robertson 1985; Hug 2001; Keman and Krouwel 2006; Mair 1999, 2002). This is reflected by the growing number of party foundations in the last decades and, even more importantly, by the frequent success of these new parties in gaining parliamentary representation on the regional and the national level. Such an empirical development has quite naturally motivated scholars to examine the reasons for the success or failure of new parties. Three questions are relevant here. They are logically connected but point to only partially overlapping if not different sets of explanatory factors (Hug 2000): first, under which circumstances are new parties founded? Second, when do they overcome electoral thresholds and, as a consequence, gain representation? And third, a question which, so far, has attracted lesser attention: under which conditions are new parties able to enter government and what are the consequences of doing so?

This chapter is devoted to the last question. Interestingly, if asked, the question of new parties' long-term success is often linked to assessing the nature of change new parties introduce in Western European party systems: do they represent genuinely new cleavages, or simply address neglected issues usually covered by traditional lines of conflict and survive only temporarily (Mair 1983: 411)? To ask for the *organizational challenges* following from the take-over of public office is much less prominent. As done with regard to party families in general, new parties tend to be analysed with an eye to their societal origin and their ideological profile (Mair and Mudde 1998) shaping the lens through which new parties are usually perceived.

This is surprising in face of the considerable theoretical and empirical work on party organization and its obvious relevance when approaching not only ideologically but also organizationally new political actors. As Kitschelt convincingly points out with regard to the group of left–libertarian parties, to understand the future, and thus the long-term impact of new parties on established Western party systems, one needs to assess their strategic capabilities to 'become effective political players both in terms of electoral appeal and of impact on public policy' (Kitschelt 1988: 233–4). Yet due to the dominant focus on new parties as vehicles to fill 'representational niches' (Lucardie 2000; Rohrschneider 1993) or, alternatively, as channels of protest reacting to traditional parties' 'representation failure' (Katz and Mair 1995; Mair 1997, 2005) the organizational costs of public office are rarely systematically specified. To become politically effective in public office in general and in government in particular creates *functional*[2] and *intra-organizational pressures* which parties need to respond to and which are often not made sufficiently explicit.

This chapter tries to make some first steps towards assessing these organizational challenges, looking at new parties as young organizations, and hence as organizations which have had only a limited time span to mature. Often starting out as principled opposition parties, later on new parties often try to access government institutions they have been shut out from so far (Heinisch 2003:102). This is when new parties try to develop coalition potential (Sartori 1976: 122–3; 300–1); when they try to become acceptable as potential coalition partners and are equally eager to exploit and willing to carry the costs of government participation. Although the challenges resulting from the coordination of votes, office and policy primarily concerns established parties, recent developments have shown that a considerable group of new parties is now ready to face or are currently facing this challenge.

This development has started to motivate scholars to study the organizational implications of incumbency (Burchell 2001a,b; Heinisch 2003; Minkenberg 2001; Müller-Rommel 2002; Poguntke 2002) which this chapter builds upon. However, instead of starting with a focus on an ideologically defined subgroup of new parties or following a case study approach, as is predominant in the literature, this chapter takes a broader focus and concentrates on new parties as such. It discusses the costs of taking over public office in the legislature and in government from the following viewpoint: due to new parties' often fluid, open organizational character, the costs of public office tend to be higher for them than for older and, hence, organizationally mature parties.

The chapter proceeds as follows: The first section identifies the analytical lens through which new parties have been analysed. It points at those caveats which tend to generate a neglect of the organizational pressures new parties face when entering parliament and, later onwards, participating in government. To address this gap, in a second step, 'new' parties are conceptualized as a particular type of actor distinct from 'established' or 'traditional' parties. It is hypothesized that the two core consequences resulting from new parties' youth are a pronounced *electoral* and *organizational vulnerability*. A third part discusses the gains of office which provide the motivation for new parties to aspire government entry in the first place. In the fourth and major part, the consequences of moving into public office will be discussed. This is done in three steps. First, the move from principled opposition status to the development of 'government potential' will be specified as a precondition for government entry. Second, the challenges of acquiring 'governmental relevance' will be analysed from an actor-centred perspective. Third, I will theoretically assess the intra-organizational and functional pressures that parties are confronted with when taking over legislative and executive office. The conclusion elaborates on the implications of the issues discussed for the debate on party change in Western democracies.

New parties as representatives and organizations: analytical lenses and conceptual caveats

It is already a commonplace in the party literature that the reorientation towards the balanced co-ordination of votes, policy and office – in contrast to a clear prioritization of one goal only – creates strategic dilemmas. Strategies to maximize votes can reduce the chances to enter government and vice versa. Yet while approaches are well-established that compare the context-specific payoffs of government participation (Strøm 1990; Strøm and Müller 1999), it has been widely ignored that costs and benefits also vary with the type of actor. When estimating a party's capacity of goal co-ordination, scholars need to consider a party's properties, since these directly affect its strategic choices. Evidently, properties such as 'newness' or 'smallness' directly affect an actor's cost–benefit calculations (Bolleyer 2007). For this reason, the next section will take an actor-centred perspective on new parties.

Further, when using the triad of votes, office and policy to study new parties, one needs to be aware of two problematic caveats, one related to the conceptualization of new parties, the other related to the conceptualization of public office.

First its implications for the conceptualization of new parties: Since Rose's and Mackie's widely cited article on government as a liability, the 'currency' through which the costs of governing have been measured are votes (Rose and Mackie 1983; for more recent analyses, see Mattila and Raunio 2004; Narud and Valen 2005). Albeit electoral costs are crucial when analysing parties' strategic choices, the corresponding focus on the trade-offs between votes, office and policy systematically blinds out those intra-organizational and functional costs generated by entering public office unrelated to supporters' policy goals or to vote-losses. For instance, the organizational costs resulting from the recruitment of competent aspirants to office, or the need to co-ordinate the 'party in public office' internally, receive too little attention.

In general, the literature on new parties has strongly concentrated on new parties' electoral fates, which is doubtless legitimate: the proliferation of new parties was considered striking since it questioned the heavily influential 'freezing hypothesis' put forward by Lipset and Rokkan. This hypothesis asserted the long-term stability of Western European party systems from the 1920s onwards (Lipset and Rokkan 1967; for a discussion, see Mair 2001). Since new parties proved to be more than a short-term phenomenon in a wide range of Western European party systems, the interest shifted to the parties' success, understood as repeated parliamentary entry. Yet, despite the move from accounts of the emergence of new parties to accounts of their success, the perspective on new parties remained surprisingly unchanged: new parties still tend to be perceived as vehicles for voicing and representing interests and attitudes neglected by traditional parties.

This viewpoint gains additional weight from the increasingly prominent position in the party literature on traditional parties' decline that I will return to in the conclusion of this chapter. Following this line of argument, it is claimed that traditional parties have begun to strongly emphasize their governing function by establishing tight linkages to the state, while functioning less and less as voluntary associations for citizen representation. New parties are perceived as a counter-reaction to this development. As a consequence, the emphasis on the new parties' representative function is reinforced (Katz and Mair 1995; Mair 1997; for a critical discussion, see Kitschelt 2000).

Unfortunately, such an analytical lens makes us easily forget that, as traditional parties do, new parties might want to govern at some point as well. Particularly after more and more new parties started to move from the 'representation stage' to the 'government stage' (Pedersen 1982), this lens became increasingly problematic: when assessing 'incumbency effects' in terms of vote gains and losses and, simultaneously, understanding new parties as representative channels and not as organizations which have to recruit policy entrepreneurs to occupy public office, the organizational costs public office imposes on new parties are easily overlooked.

Indeed, scholarly work has clearly emphasized that new parties are new not only in terms of issues but also in terms of organizational styles (Mair 2002: 133). A comparison with the traditional parties usually associated with the mass party model led to descriptions of new parties either as a less hierarchical organizational alternative, allowing for more direct individual influence from the ground often identified with the new left (Burchell 2001a: 113), or as a per se anti-organizational, anti-bureaucratic counter-model, usually associated with the new populist right (Van der Brug and Fennema 2005: 2). Only recently an organizational perspective has gained more prominence in comparative studies either focusing on the new left (see Burchell 2001a,b; Kitschelt 1989; Müller-Rommel 2002; Poguntke 2002) or the new right (see Heinisch 2003; Minkenberg 2001).[3] Facing these 'organizational counter-images' to traditional models of party, it is a valuable exercise to move up the ladder of abstraction a couple of steps in order to specify the pressures of public office on new parties as organizationally young actors irrespective of their ideological profile.

The second problematic implication of the triad of votes, office and policy refers to the specification of public office. When applying the distinction between 'vote-seeking' and 'office-seeking', one easily overlooks that, as soon as parties enter the parliamentary stage, an increase of votes directly leads to an increase of public offices. The party occupies more and more legislative seats which create resources available to the party to further invest in vote-maximizing strategies (e.g. through state funding). Simultaneously, this process causes intra-organizational costs which should not be overlooked. To give only one example, as soon as it enters parliament, a party needs to cope with the need to bridge the divide between the parliamentary party, the party central office and the party on the ground (if this last exists). Government entry represents a further qualitative step by complicating the challenge of further intra-organizational co-ordination and by creating additional functional pressures.

Therefore the conceptual equation of 'office' and 'incumbency' usually flowing from the triad of votes, office and policy, needs to be avoided. Simply speaking, when new parties – after having repeatedly gained parliamentary representation – try to enter government, they do not shift from mere vote-seeking to office-seeking, but 'expand' within the public realm from solely occupying legislative office towards the occupation of executive office.

Based on these lines of reasoning, this chapter puts forward the following argument: in order to understand the challenges new parties face when gaining parliamentary representation and, later on, aspiring government entry, one needs to specify the intra-organizational and functional demands towards party as an organization in each of the two phases. This is done so from an actor-oriented viewpoint focusing on the organizational and electoral vulnerability likely to affect new parties.

New parties as organizational actors: newness and two dimensions of vulnerability

To ask for the problems new parties as a distinct group of actors face when entering public office leads to obvious conceptual problems. As soon as new parties enter the group of parties with government potential, one might argue that what we associate with 'newness' vanishes to a considerable degree; when defining new parties as organizations which represent genuinely new issues, one might point out that, by then, new parties are no longer a symptom of party system change but instead an indication of its transformation, implying that what has once been a 'new demand' is today a 'normal', 'established' or 'accepted' claim. Facing this problem, what is the feature that nevertheless makes them genuinely new and justifies examining them as a group of parties opposed to the 'not-new' or 'already established' ones?[4] One solution pointed to above is defining new parties as 'organizationally young'.

Among the few systematic studies of the success of new parties as such, one can indeed find the application of 'ageist' criteria in the general sense without focusing on the issues put forward by new parties. Yet this is not very common-place: Mair, for instance, defines as new any party which has not contested elections before 1965 and, by doing so, characterizes the time period after 1965 as one in which new parties have started to proliferate due to electoral re-alignment in Western European democracies. In this sense, the criterion chosen characterizes the period after 1965 as 'an age of new parties', but does not refer to the concrete implications of the 'age of a new party' taking the single party as unit of analysis. More crucially, he does not conceptualize new parties as organizational actors (Mair 1999: 209–10; for a similar conceptualization, see Hug 2001: 80–1).

In order to understand the impact of public office on new parties, such a conceptualization is, however, necessary. Work on party systems in Eastern and

Southern Europe supports this viewpoint. There, party systems are mostly composed of newly created parties which are particularly vulnerable to intra-party conflicts easily generated between the different party units inside and outside public office (van Biezen 2000: 410–11). When referring to the organizational repercussions of age and, simultaneously, focusing on new parties as strategic actors, two properties seem to be crucial for new parties' capacity to coordinate votes, office and policy: their *electoral* as well as *organizational vulnerability*, two sources of weakness which are easily accelerated when moving into public office as laid out in detail later.

Although the organizational vulnerability of new compared to old parties is in principle unrelated to their actual moment of birth and refers to the time span needed for organization-building, the period since the mid-1960s, when new parties increasingly emerged, naturally affects the phenomenon of the 'new party' itself and thereby its strategic capabilities, in particular new parties' electoral vulnerability as one core dimension. Traditional parties also suffer from the growing electoral volatility which has been intensifying over the last few decades, but they can usually rely on a security net of reliable core voters still closely affiliated to their party. Those voters need to be mobilized, but not convinced to change their orientation; evidently, this is an easier task than to establish a new pool of reliable voters in the first place, which constitutes the core of new parties' electoral vulnerability.

Their usually small size reinforces this weakness.[5] While for established parties, especially those of medium or large size, vote-seeking tends to circle around the question 'how much?' while taking entry for granted, new and small parties are easily threatened by entry barriers. In sum, 'newness' – especially when related to small size – tends to make vote-seeking more pressing as a goal, since elections become easily a game not only of relative success or failure but also of survival (Bolleyer 2007).

All in all, in order to discuss the costs of public office, I understand new parties as a group of actors that can be characterized by the following set of structural properties, being a function of their young age: new parties tend to be disadvantaged by (1) the absence of a 'security net' of reliable core voters which is reinforced by (2) their small size. Finally, they are (3) organizationally less developed than established parties.

The operational implications of this conception for empirical analyses are obvious: most fundamentally, only new parties actually entering parliament are considered. 'Promoter parties', whose major objective is to bring attention to a particular issue but which do not succeed electorally (Harmel and Robertson 1985: 517), are excluded. Moreover, since electoral and organizational vulnerability are considered as the two main implications of newness, 'newly born' parties are the core group of analysis because they are most likely to be characterized by both dimensions although also new parties often draw elements of their leadership from established parties (Mair 1999: 216). Mergers – if established parties are involved – should be excluded since it is unlikely that their electoral vulnerability is very pronounced. Although it creates costs to unite two or even more separate organizations, a process which can generate conflicts, the resulting organizational strains should be less problematic than when setting up a new organizational structure from scratch.[6] New parties resulting from splits from established parties, by contrast, should be included. Although they might draw voters from their mother party, they need to build up a new organizational structure able to stabilize party–supporter relations and need to present themselves as independent actors in the political arena. If the deviating faction does not succeed in doing so, voters are easily tempted to return to their original party (Rochon 1985).[7]

The gains of government

Before assessing the costs of public office in general, a few words are necessary about the system-specific incentives to enter government, assuming that parties do not per se prioritize one goal – votes, office or policy – over the other (for an alternative approach, see Harmel and Janda 1994). Further, if new parties faced no clear incentives to enter government, the discussion of the costs of the latter would forfeit a lot of its relevance. There are three types of incentives which affect parties' cost-benefit analysis concerning government entry. Most prominently, Strøm (1990) argued that strong negative incumbency effects in votes[8] and strong opposition influence on policy making through parliamentary committees devalue government entry and thereby favour the formation of minority cabinets. Hence, besides assessing whether government parties are systematically more punished in a system than opposition parties, a crucial factor to look at is the degree to which the executive monopolizes policy-making structurally. Irrespective of these factors, it is also important to indicate whether the presence of minority cabinets allow for policy influence of opposition parties which have not acquired government potential.[9] In such a context, new parties can function as support parties in single issue areas without formally taking over government responsibility.[10]

Although it is important to assess these cross-national differences, in the end, one needs to recognize that no matter how favourable the impact of opposition parties on policy formulation, in parliamentary systems legislative initiative is dominated by the executive (Döring 1995; Döring and Hallerberg 2004). The policy influence of opposition parties remains necessarily limited compared with the influence of government parties, not to speak of their power over policy implementation. Supporting this point, Strøm's (1990) account of minority governments has indicated that committee power provides a weaker incentive for parties to remain in opposition than the threat of losing votes. Accordingly, if a new party enters parliament repeatedly, its followers – especially the active members – are likely to demand the realization of core policy goals (presupposing of course that the party's message transcends mere protest). At that point, active efforts to enter government become a matter of maintaining political credibility.

When talking about the resources linked to public office, in most systems parties have access to state funding as soon as they gain parliamentary representation. Other resources, such as appointments in the bureaucracy, however, tend to be accessible only by executive office-holders. These resources to pay off supporters are particularly useful for those new parties which are not rooted in social movements and may therefore lack a back-up of intrinsically motivated followers whose support need not be maintained through selective incentives primarily. At the same time, parties without an external organizational back-up are likely to be particularly vulnerable to vote losses possibly related to government participation. Paradoxically, the weaker a new party is organizationally, and the more useful government resources would be as a pool of selective incentives to maintain supporters' loyalty, the more the possible electoral costs of government might be perceived as problematic. External roots in movements, in contrast, can reduce the manoeuvrability of party leaders once they have entered office. Simultaneously, they can function as an organizational safety net, able to stabilize the party when confronted with organizational strains resulting from public office.

In sum, although government is often conceptualized as liability, in view of the power, the resources and the prestige related to government, electorally successful new parties will, more likely than not, aspire to government participation at a certain point. This makes the conceptualization of the costs of public office even more necessary than if anticipation of these costs prevented new parties from entering right away.

The costs of public office

In order to assess the implications of new parties' office-aspirations, two steps are necessary. First, the move from principled opposition status to the development of coalition potential will be specified. On this basis, the jump into coalition government will be discussed from an actor-centred perspective considering new parties' strategic capacities during formation bargaining. Second, the intra-organizational and functional pressures parties face as soon as they hold legislative and executive office will be discussed.

From representing to governing: how to acquire government potential and governmental relevance

Given the rather large group of new parties starting out with an 'anti-system' or at least 'anti-establishment' profile, it is necessarily a challenge for new parties to develop coalition potential as a precondition for government entry. This potential – understanding 'potential' in the sense of the word – needs to be kept separate from success, since looking at Western European party systems, one faces a range of, in particular, small parties which regularly fail to enter government but are nevertheless potential government parties. The need for this distinction seems as self-evident as crucial when dealing with new parties. They usually pass through a transitory phase before actually entering government, during which they slowly give up their principled opposition status.

In order to capture this transitory phase conceptually and empirically, it is useful to return to Sartori's seminal book on parties and party systems (Sartori

1976). Following Sartori, coalition potential – in conceptual terms – captures the relevance of a party in a party system resulting from this party's decisiveness for the formation of possible government majorities (Sartori 1976: 122–3).[11] When it comes to the operationalization of the concept of 'coalition potential', however, Sartori deliberately collapses the two components of coalition potential – government potential and actual governmental relevance – while conceding that, in principle, two measures would be necessary to capture coalition potential fully (Sartori 1976: 300). Yet since the 'potential' relevance of a party cannot be captured by a systemic measure, he uses a party's participation in government, or, alternatively, the decisiveness of its support in a confidence vote for a government's survival, as indicators to construct a numerical measure of governmental relevance applicable to different party systems (Sartori 1976: 301–2; for an operationalization closer to the theoretical conception, see Abedi 2002: 555). Evidently, by demanding a party's decisive role for the particular outcome of formation processes, the phenomenon measured is far more narrow than the theoretical core of coalition potential defined as being decisive for a *possible*, thus not necessarily successful, government majority (Sartori 1976: 122).

Here we have arrived at the core difference between *government potential* and *governmental relevance* which makes the concept of *coalition potential* so complicated and yet so fruitful for the study of the development of new parties as soon as one shifts from a systemic to an actor-oriented perspective: government potential is *assigned by others*, making the new party a 'part' in the real sense of the word whose status is judged upon and defined by the core parties constitutive for the party system under analysis.[12] This passive role becomes empirically evident in that the formateur initiating formation bargaining tends to belong to the biggest, often formerly governing party (Warwick 1996: 474), a situation which prevents a new party from playing a proactive role.[13]

Governmental relevance, in contrast, directly flows from a party's properties such as its relative size or programmatic profile immediately effective during formation bargaining. As Sartori expresses it, in order to be relevant a party needs to be 'needed' by other parties in the system to form a particular government (Sartori 1976: 122). It is not a matter of *general acceptance* as political force, it is a matter of *bargaining power*, a power which only becomes relevant as soon as a party's status is evaluated based on the same criteria as any other established party in the system, which clearly presupposes government potential.

In sum, acquiring government potential means acquiring access to a bargaining arena regulated by the core of established parties in a party system; acquiring governmental relevance (entering government or playing the role of a support party) means exploiting strategic resources, of which Sartori mentions two – a party's relative size and its programmatic compatibility (Sartori 1976: 122) – and to which one needs to add a third one when it comes to the analysis of new parties: their organizational reliability.

New parties' government potential: anticipatory substantial or organizational adaptation?

The concept of government potential brings up the question on which dimensions there is a need for adaptation when new parties aspire to acceptability as potential coalition partners by established parties. Obviously, parties attracting votes based on an anti-establishment image are unlikely to be warmly welcomed from the outset. Whether established parties consider a new party as, in principle, acceptable as a government party is likely to depend on two different features related to a party's *substantial* profile. First, a new party's proclaimed attitude towards the established elites; the way the new party publicly positions itself towards mainstream parties in general and current executive office-holders in particular. Second, its programmatic orientation on the major axis of competition, the left–right continuum, is likely to be important. These two features are often inter-related, yet this need not be the case. Before the party becomes acceptable, the moderation of anti-establishment rhetorics is likely to be necessary irrespective of whether the party is programmatically located on one extreme end of the spectrum or not. This might not imply that the party will stop to attack minority groups in society as scapegoats, for instance. Yet the maintenance of a strong general opposition to the political class per se, and to governing itself, is hardly compatible with efforts to become an accepted player in the political arena, hence, to become a de facto part of the political class oneself.

Programmatic moderation is another step again, and is likely to involve the downplaying of those positions which cannot be reconciled with core positions of the mainstream parties.[14] This means nothing other than to increase policy compatibility ex ante, which is completely rational, since a new party's ideological position and its relative size are more crucial determinants for government participation than are vote gains (Mattila and Raunio 2004). To the same extent, it is evident that the more compatible a party's core preferences are with those of the established parties the more moderate it is per se, and the more manageable its demands are, the more likely the party will be accepted early, since a potentially non-credible programmatic reorientation will not be necessary.[15]

Anticipatory *organizational* adaptation towards a centralized leadership in order to acquire governmental potential is clearly more demanding than a *programmatic* or *rhetorical* reorientation. Research on Green parties in Western Europe identified cases of organizational restructuring in favour of centralized decision-making before these parties entered national government. Examples are the Italian Greens in 1993, the Flemish AGALEV in 1991 and the German Greens in 1990 (Poguntke 2002: 136). However, throwing a short glance at two of the cases, parties responded to a specific shock unrelated to the aim to acquire government potential: The German Greens engaged in reform after having lost representation in the national legislature in 1990, hence, attempted to regain legislative, not executive office. The Flemish AGALEV strengthened its leadership after their experience during government negotiations in 1991, hence, already possessed government potential at the time of reform and tried to increase the likelihood of successful government access.

While reform attempts have served a range of different purposes, research on both Green and new populist parties indicates that the transformation into a parliamentary party itself, hence, taking over legislative office, creates organizational strains in new parties which push them towards professionalization (Burchell 2001a,b; Minkenberg 2001). This allows us to conclude that the willingness of new parties' MPs to develop expertise and to engage in legislative projects with others, as well as the capacity of the parliamentary faction to act in a co-ordinated manner, are likely to contribute to the acceptance of new parties as established political players. Thus, a party's successful response to the demands of legislative office is likely to increase the chance to achieve government potential.[16] Moreover, it points to the need to assess the pressures resulting from legislative and executive office separately as done in a later section.

To conclude this section with a final word on operationalization: due to the multiple causes driving different adaptation processes, and the fact that government potential is assigned to new parties by the major established parties, it is useful to choose an indicator for government potential unrelated to the new parties' adaptation strategies themselves. One possibility is to refer to a new party's invitation to formation bargaining as an indicator for government potential irrespective of whether the new party finally enters government or under which conditions it might do so. Even if a new party is invited to negotiations only after several rounds of bargaining among established parties have failed, it still indicates the willingness of those established parties dominating the negotiation process to consider the party as a potential government partner. On the basis of this criterion, it is possible to systematically assess whether new parties which successfully gained access to government negotiations ex ante changed their rhetoric, their programmatic profile or basic organizational features. In particular, organizational reforms might not have been directed towards acquiring government potential but instead represent a reaction to the demands of legislative office. Nonetheless, they might be a favourable condition for becoming accepted in the political arena.

New parties' governmental relevance: strategic and organizational capacities in government formation

As pointed out before, when we discuss new parties' governmental relevance, we already presuppose that they possess governmental potential and they are not excluded from the outset. Starting from here, the two major questions are, first, which kind of strategic position new parties tend to occupy during formation bargaining within their party systems and, as a consequence, how much concessions can they demand from potential partners? Second, which are the tensions the individual party has to deal with when participating in a coalition government as a collective decision-making body? Within a coalition, the character of interaction is highly ambivalent. Who is the interest-maximizing actor – the coalition or the single participant? Even if the government receives maximal benefits, it does not automatically follow that each participant maximizes its individual benefit as well. That is, each single party is forced to balance out efficient internal co-opera-tion (regarding the government as one collective actor) and efforts to sufficiently discriminate between the single participants, who have to compete against each other at the following elections. Too many internal quarrels weaken the govern-ment's capacity to formulate and implement policies, or even worse, may lead to its dissolution. However, if parties adapt too much to their partners' positions, their electorates have fewer reasons to vote for them in upcoming elections.[17] As a consequence, intra-coalitional interaction cannot be unambiguously qualified as co-operative or competitive.

For this reason, when choosing coalition partners, two sets of factors are likely to be paramount which easily conflict with each other. The first refers to the power distribution among the partners of the coalition. Naturally each participant wants to maximize its individual share and prefers a coalition in which it has more rather than less weight. The second one refers to the workability of the coalition as a col-lective decision-making body which assures the survival of the government. Even if a party is very strong in a coalition, if it expects the coalition to break down after a short while, it is unlikely to enter it. The two factors which primarily determine a new party's strategic position in the party system are its relative size and its ideological position (Mattila and Raunio 2004). A factor of prior importance for the workability of a coalition – and especially critical in the case of new parties – is a party's organizational reliability.

Starting with the first question of new parties' strategic capacity during coali-tion negotiations, new parties tend to be in a rather weak bargaining position. Since they tend to be quite small, they are necessarily concerned about the possibility of being dominated within a coalition, a situation which a big actor normally does not need to fear. Their internal positions heavily affect their chances of realizing their own policies, especially when there is intra-coalitional disagreement over crucial issues. Although formation and coalition weight of a party are analyti-cally clearly distinct, their empirical linkage is obvious. Parties begin to strive for the future maximization of coalition weight already during formation bargaining. More concretely, the single actor tries to achieve as much control as possible with regard to the future coalition by demanding mechanisms to protect its status within the coalition, such as portfolios, formally fixed policy concessions, specific control mechanisms or decision-making rules for conflict resolution (Blondel and Müller-Rommel 1993). This is crucial since entering an agreement including many vague compromises easily provokes conflict later on (Timmermans 2006: 154) in which junior partners in particular are disadvantaged and which feeds back to the workability of the coalition in general. Given that new parties' sup-porters are less acquainted with the constraints of government, they might be also less tolerant towards resulting compromises necessary to maintain a coalition than supporters of traditional parties with considerable government experience. Therefore, the intra-coalitional performance new parties anticipate is likely to be a major concern for them.

But why are new parties usually in an unfavourable bargaining position? The two concepts frequently used to capture parties' strategic potential in parliamentary party systems are *centrality* and *pivotality*. During formation bargaining, centrality[18] generates two strategic advantages. First, due to its ideological position in between the leftist and rightist bloc, a small central party has more than one government option, and second, is therefore more likely to secure government entry. Yet, as pointed out before, most new parties which successfully enter parliament are not located in the centre space. Although new parties often try to avoid being located on the left–right continuum, due to the dominant patterns of competition in established party systems, they tend to be clearly associated with one side of the ideological continuum. Quite evidently, a distinct profile is easier to acquire at the fringes of a party system than in the centre space. In formation bargaining, a non-central status implies that a new party has only limited options to join a government. It tends to be dependent on a particular party or group of parties as potential government partners which weakens its strategic weight (Bolleyer 2007).

A new (usually small) party is pivotal, hence, can effectively demand high concessions when it numerically completes a majority by joining a big partner or a clearly coherent, distinct bloc, while there is no numerically and ideologically equivalent actor in the system. Then, a large party inviting a new party to enter negotiations cannot switch to an equally valuable alternative in the system and, in Sartori's terms, the new party is 'needed' (Sartori 1976: 122) and has considerable formation weight.[19] As with centrality, a new parties' pivotal status is unlikely. Pivotality of small actors tends to occur in concentrated party systems in which new parties are less numerous. A comparison of small parties' strategic positions in nine Western European party systems has shown that, in six of the nine party systems, small parties could occupy a pivotal status at certain points in time – with or without being central on the left–right dimension (Bolleyer 2007). With the exception of two small Portuguese parties, one of which no longer exists, all of them belonged to the group of organizationally mature parties.[20]

Overall, due to their (usually) non-central and non-pivotal status new parties tend to be in a weak bargaining position and their capacity to affect the final negotiation outcome can be assumed to decrease with the increasing complexity of the party system. Consequently, the weight of these parties within coalitions is likely to be limited. Since they often gain little during in formation phase, they possess only few resources in terms of portfolios and policy concessions within government. In sum, new parties' capacity to defend and realize core policy commitments during coalition formation and in government coalitions should be limited.

The discussion of new parties' strategic position can, in principle, be applied to any small party firmly established in the party system since it does not refer to the organizational features of new parties compared with established ones. When we now discuss the anticipated workability of a coalition, these differences become crucial. Luebbert (1986) has argued that it is often easier for party elites to agree on compromises across party lines than for party leaders to convince their respective followers of the final result. The perceived reliability of a party depends not only on the professionality of the respective leaders directly engaged in negotiations[21] but also on their position within their own party. They need to be able to ensure that compromises are accepted by the party on the ground and by party MPs, not only until entry is safe but, even more important, during the coalition's life-time. The capacity to make credible commitments is not only a question of the personal authority of the respective leader, often labelled as charisma, but also one of organizational procedures. On the one hand, a leader might need the agreement of the party congress to formally enter a coalition agreement. On the other hand, a leader (most likely a future government member if negotiations are successful) needs to be capable of implementing the coalition agreement and, if necessary, disciplining his parliamentary MPs and avoiding protest within the external arm of his party later on. This capacity is often a matter of access to sanctions and incentives, for example through controlling candidate selection (Sieberer 2006).

As with government potential, this capacity is likely to be stronger in new parties with a few terms of parliamentary experience during which MPs are likely to be one core pool from which executive office-holders are chosen and whose members can socialize professionally and demonstrate the capacity to adapt to the demands of office. As Burchell puts it with regard to the European Green parties, although comparatively young, 'many have now developed significant political experience. In these cases an activist base is emerging with invaluable experience of parliamentary negotiation and action' (2001b: 252). Such a development naturally affects new parties' capacity to perform well in government also.

Dimensions of vulnerability: electoral and organizational costs of public office

The previous section has already touched upon the impact of public office on new parties as organizational actors. Although new parties might seek to challenge the established system in terms of issues as well as organizationally, they simultaneously become entangled in systemic processes (Burchell 2001b: 251–2). Therefore it is useful to look at the demands resulting from public office from a functional viewpoint and to draw conclusions on the way these demands are likely to affect new parties in their strategic and organizational choices.

The costs of public office are assessed in two parts, each corresponding to one dimension of vulnerability considered as typical for new parties. The first part focuses on the widely studied phenomenon of the 'electoral costs' of public office. Since vote-maximization strategies automatically lead to a maximization of legislative seats, this part focuses directly on the electoral costs of incumbency. The second part looks at the often neglected organizational costs of public office. Here legislative and executive office need to be kept separate in order to adequately specify the functional and the intra-organizational pressures generated by each type of public office.

New parties and the electoral costs of incumbency

Whereas the organizational costs of government entry have not found considerable attention in scholarly work, the electoral cost of government participation is a widely studied phenomenon (e.g. Rose and Mackie 1983; Mattila and Raunio

2004; Müller and Strøm 2003). Government participation leads frequently to vote losses and these losses have – as a function of growing electoral volatility – constantly increased over the last few decades, a context which creates disincentives towards government entry. Thinking of new parties' core features, especially the lack of a reliable core of voters, new parties can be expected to be more vulnerable to vote losses than established parties. A considerable proportion of traditional parties' voters need to be mobilized, but not convinced to change their basic orientation; evidently, this is a much easier task than to establish a new pool of reliable voters in the first place, especially under conditions of growing individualization and political disaffection among the younger, in principle more open, parts of the electorate. Yet the fluidity of their vote support is not the only aspect which can induce new parties to prioritize vote-seeking over office-seeking. Their size in itself is relevant, since the overall number of new parties gaining representation tends to be small. Accordingly, the threat of entry barriers is likely to affect their calculation of government costs and benefits more negatively than for larger actors (Bolleyer 2004). The high number of new parties never entering parliament in the first place and the 'deaths' of new parties underlines this point (Keman and Krouwel 2006; Lucardie 2000; Mair 1999).

Also because of the profiles of new parties, the trade-off between votes and office is also likely to be more severe than for established parties – especially when joining a coalition for the first time. It is a frequently mentioned problem that new parties, usually starting out with an anti-establishment image, risk the alienation of core supporters when entering the realm of 'normal politics' and co-operating with the 'establishment' (Heinisch 2003). This is particularly risky for anti-establishment parties with an otherwise fuzzy ideological profile, as is often the case for the new populist right. However, conflicts between 'ideologues' and 'pragmatists' have been also observed in parties of the new left (Kitschelt 1989) and are considered as a general phenomenon of party organizational development (Panebianco 1988; Wilson 1973). Hence these conflicts tend to be a general problem for new parties when entering government, which creates the pressure to adopt a more pragmatic perspective on politics.[22]

In sum, one can expect that new parties react more sensitively to potential vote losses related to government entry than established parties, since their vote support is less reliable and their voter base tends to be small. This makes them particularly vulnerable to entry barriers. Moreover, inasmuch as they started their career with an anti-establishment image, the negative feedback of government entry is likely to be more substantial for them than for established parties (whose supporters might also be disappointed) since supporters might interpret the mere act of office participation as a fundamental betrayal. This is naturally reinforced if parties are simply unable to realize core policies against the will of their coalition partners, as mentioned before.

New parties and the organizational costs of public office

This section conceptualizes the organizational costs of public office. Two distinctions are crucial here: the one between legislative and executive office and the one between intra-organizational and functional pressures generated when entering public office. The first distinction helps to characterize the shift of electorally successful new parties in parliament to new parties in government, and points to the demands already present when entering parliament, which are easily overlooked. Intra-organizational and functional pressures need to be distinguished because the actors which the two types of pressures impact upon differ: whereas intra-organizational pressures refer to processes in the party organization inside and outside the public realm as the unit of analysis and point to a process of internal organizational differentiation following the take-over of public office, functional pressures most immediately impact upon party members in public office. Of course, functional pressures have intra-organizational repercussions by creating the demand for the party to provide the personnel able to cope with institutionally generated expectations. Nevertheless, to understand the link between these two types of demands which constitute the organizational costs of public office, it is analytically useful to keep them separate.

The organizational costs generated by public office can be subsumed under three types of demands. They involve the *coordination* between different arms of the party inside and outside public office, the *selection* of legislative or executive candidates or the *need for expertise* either on the level of individual office-holders or on the level of party. Primarily, the distinction between these types of demands helps to break down the regularly used label of 'professionalization' into interrelated yet separate components. It helps to better distinguish between organizational strains new parties are likely to face when being pushed towards professionalization. Another distinction which becomes important when discussing new parties' development is the one between the party in central office as the national leadership, the party in public office and the party on the ground (Katz and Mair 1993: 594).

Despite the obvious organizational differences across new parties flourishing at different ends of the ideological continuum, they tend to share the desire to distinguish themselves from the established parties organizationally as well. It has been pointed out already that both new parties on the left and the right regularly take an 'anti-party position' with regard to conventional party organization. Hence, their organizational foundation can be expected to be less stable than that of established parties for two reasons: on the one hand, because their major organizational structures still need to be built up; on the other, because many new parties – on principle – refuse to professionalize and to institutionalize their structures.

Although established parties tend to invest less and less in maintaining a broad membership basis, they are still dependent on a group of active members who are essential to maintain the external arm of the party (Panebianco 1988: 26). Despite a reorientation towards a smaller group of more qualified core members, the existence of a reliable basis of supporters is essential to a party's survival and recovery in bad electoral times (Seyd and Whitley 2004: 360). Given the pronounced electoral vulnerability of new parties, a stabilizing organizational core is likely to be essential for any new party which tries to be successful in the long run. How far the external organization of a new party approaches a closed form similar to that of traditional mass parties remains to be seen. In any case, studies on new parties in public office clearly identify adaptation processes that partially give up principled opposition to a more institutionalized type of party organization in order to assure greater efficiency and increase manoeuvrability (Burchell 2001a,b; Poguntke 2002). Drawing on these findings, this section argues that public office creates pressures to which a more institutionalized form of party organization is likely to provide an answer.

Generally speaking, institutionalization becomes visible in a process of internal organizational development, in particular a process of functional differentiation directed towards a more complex distribution of tasks to different offices or even sub-units and towards a more complex set of procedures (Judge 2003; Panebianco 1988). This process of functional differentiation accelerates when a new party enters public office. The move from legislative to executive office in part creates new demands, in part intensifies those already present when holding legislative office.

As Table 2.1 shows, legislative office creates different types of demands towards the party outside and inside of public office. It generates a need for expertise regarding office-holders in particular but not regarding the party organization in general. Conversely, it creates selection and co-ordination demands in the party as organization but not in the public realm. In contrast, executive office creates all three types of demands within the party and between different groups of office-holders in the public sphere. Consequently, it is justified to speak of a qualitatively new phase in a party's life cycle as soon as a new party enters government (Pedersen 1982).

Looking first at the *organizational costs* of *legislative office*, the most evident demand is the one of *candidate selection* which becomes critical as soon as the pool of potential candidates is bigger than the number of positions available. Although a party has to nominate candidates already when contesting elections, candidate nomination (including the ranking of candidates) becomes naturally more crucial when there is a realistic chance of winning seats or seats have been won already. Indeed, it could be observed that new parties faced shortages of active members willing to take over posts on the local level, especially when the party required a rotation of offices (Burchell 2001a), a problem established parties also face more and more often (Sundberg 2003). A shortage of volunteers, however, is unlikely when it comes to the distribution of the much fewer and more attractive offices in regional or national institutions. As soon as a party has access to them, the party needs selection procedures, which, due to their distributive implications, can easily generate intra-organizational conflict.[23]

Candidate selection and the smooth replacement of office-holders demand the recruitment of a pool of office aspirants in the first place. Controlling recruitment not only is in the interest of party leaders who want to maintain their privileged position in the party, but also adds to the outside credibility of parties able to deliver programs, policies and personnel in the long run. This becomes particularly crucial when parties transform from channels for representation or protest outside public institutions to active participants in the process of policy formulation

Table 2.1 Intra-organizational and functional pressures generated by public office

Pressure	Legislative office	Executive office
Intra-organizational pressure (party as unit of analysis)	Co-ordination: co-ordination between parliamentary party and party on the ground internal coordination of party MPs	Co-ordination: co-ordination between parliamentary party and executive members co-ordination between party on the ground and executive members co-ordination of executive members
	Selection: recruitment/replacement of legislative candidates	Selection: recruitment/replacement of executive members political appointments in the administration
		Expertise: development of a broader programmatic profile
Functional pressure towards office-holders (types of office-holders as units of analysis)		Co-ordination: co-ordination/compromise/ conflict resolution between coalition partners Co-ordination between executive and bureaucracy
		Selection: political appointments in the administration
	Expertise: MPs' need for expertise MPs' professional use of predefined channels for political/policy influence (e.g. issue legislative initiatives)	Expertise: executive members' need for expertise (e.g. regarding implementation)

inside public institutions. Such a transformation does not presuppose incumbency. Party members can already try to exert substantial influence in the legislature through committee work and demonstrate their endeavour to influence policy in the parliamentary arena. To do so, they have to acquire expertise regarding the issues dealt with but also regarding the procedures through which influence can be exerted.

Evidently, the challenge of establishing efficient and accepted intra-organizational selection procedures is closely tied to the functionally generated need for *qualified office-holders*. While party activists on the ground are usually political amateurs, holding office on the regional and national level is more often than not a full-time job. With the professionalization of politics, the expectations towards candidates in terms of skills as well as the burden of political life are increasing.

A rather closed party organization can provide an answer to a growing need for expertise of potential office aspirants. In developed party organizations, the latter tend to rise slowly through the ranks of the party to acquire professional experience (King 1981: 277) which functions as a mechanism of ex ante screening of candidates used by party leaders (Müller 2000). Again, the advantage of such intra-organizational career paths is control. Potential candidates have to move up the internal hierarchy before having access to public office, while current elites profit from aspirants' long-term engagement and gather information about their qualification.

The third type of demand is the one of *co-ordination*. Evidently, parliamentary entry creates the intra-organizational divide between the party on the ground and the party members in public office (van Biezen 2000: 411). Co-ordination between them is all the more important since MPs attract considerable media attention, and hence shape the public face of the party. Moreover, to maximize their influence in parliament and present the party as a serious political player, co-ordinated action is also necessary among party MPs. The structural incentives are evident: in most parliamentary systems individual member influence is severely restricted not only de facto but also in procedural terms (Döring 1995; Döring and Hallerberg 2004).

These co-ordination demands grow with the size of the parliamentary faction. Ironically, small size is a notorious problem in the electoral arena when it comes to the problem of jumping parliamentary entry barriers. Simultaneously, immediate and considerable electoral success can create considerable problems in the parliamentary arena. Coping with a medium-sized legislative faction can cause considerable organizational strains within a party represented by inexperienced candidates lacking professional expertise which have not been socialized within a firmly established party organization. Given that the organizational structure of the party in central office is also weakly developed, the party might be, on top of this, unable to impose discipline from outside.

In sum, demands for selection mechanisms, expertise and co-ordination easily create organizational costs, especially when a party is in an early stage of development. To cope with these pressures, a strengthening of the central party office is a likely answer.

When a new party takes over *executive office*, selection and co-ordination demands as well as the need for expertise already present when gaining legislative seats intensify. Furthermore, new demands are generated flowing from the specific nature of executive functions. Table 2.1 indicates that in contrast to legislative office, executive office creates all three types of demands in the intra-party and in the public sphere. Accordingly, the organizational costs of public office increase considerably when entering the governmental sphere.

Since executive positions are more prestigious and less numerous than legislative positions, the *challenge of selection* becomes more intense. Simply due to the relevance of the positions, intra-organizational quarrels over ministerial appointments are more likely than over the placement of legislative candidates. A party needs the organizational capacity to settle these conflicts. Also, the functional need for *qualified personnel* is obviously more crucial regarding executive office-holders, since the tasks ministers are confronted with are much more complex. Much more than MPs, ministers act in the centre of media attention and their performance will be exposed to public criticism.[24] While ministerial office-holders might have been good campaigners in the electoral arena, now they need to become policy managers, two roles which demand separate skills and are often difficult to reconcile: as good political tactics do not always produce good policies, the abilities that make a good candidate are not necessarily those who make a good MP or minister (Brittan 1975: 136). Further, in face of increasingly technical, complex and depoliticized policy-making processes accompanied by more personalized and less programmatically oriented electoral competition this tension between electoral campaigner and policy expert is likely to widen (Mair 2005: 23). On top of that, the pressure to generate expertise due to executive office does not only concern the public realm. Government responsibility for a wide range of policies implies that very specialized government parties need to develop standpoints and knowledge on a wider range of issues. This need sets incentives for developing policy expertise more broadly within the external party organization.

With regard to *co-ordination demands* generated by government entry, executive actors need to cooperate with their MPs, a divide within the party in public office itself. Further, as party MPs, ministers need to co-ordinate among themselves in order to strengthen the party within the cabinet. However, since the new party is unlikely to have many ministers, this is a minor challenge compared to the need to find compromises across party lines. The conflict between individual interests of a coalition partner and the collective interest of the government as a whole in a working coalition government has already been discussed. Further, this functionally generated co-ordination demand within the cabinet easily conflicts with the interests of party members in the legislature as well as in the party outside. Thus, effective coordination within government resulting in policy compromises easily complicates party co-ordination in public office as well as between the three faces of party – the party in public, in central office and the party on the ground. Correspondingly, parties in new democracies have strengthened the party central office to assure party cohesion within and across different party units (van Biezen 2000: 411), an argument directly applicable to organizationally new parties in established party systems.

The co-ordination demands mentioned so far refer to the stage of policy formulation. Government entry also brings in the task of policy implementation, again an area in which the minister needs to have, and to develop, expertise. The necessity of finding the personnel capable of fulfilling the policy management tasks related to executive office is reinforced by the need to monitor policy experts in the bureaucracy which are heavily involved in the drafting of legislative proposals later decided upon within cabinet. In fact, new demands are mutually reinforcing as well as inter-related: logically, the selection of competent candidates becomes more important if those selected are involved in selection processes themselves. Furthermore, the authority to select a new group of actors in the public realm generates new co-ordination demands. Depending on the system under analysis, political appointments in the administration can be the responsibility of single ministers or the cabinet, hence they fall into the category of functional pressure, or can be controlled by the party in central office. If political appointments in the bureaucracy are a privilege of the single ministers, the selection of loyal and competent ministers is all the more important. But also, if the party leadership controls these appointments, the latter are a desired good whose distribution can cause intra-organizational quarrels, especially if a party is programmatically weak and depends on these rewards to maintain followers' support. Again, the need to develop accepted procedures to handle internal demands is crucial.

Note that selection and co-ordination demands might be easy to handle as long as a strong leader is in place, able to make choices widely accepted within his party due to his or her personal authority only. For a while, an organizational back-up might be of little importance. However, in the long run two problems are likely to occur in particular when a party aspires to government. On the one hand, the need for neutral procedures will emerge as soon as a weaker leader has taken over. Hence, leadership succession will sooner or later become a crucial problem for any party heavily relying on the personal appeal of a particular person. On the other hand, personal authority can generate acceptance, but it is debatable whether, based on a 'patronage logic', the most qualified candidates will be chosen. If this is not the case, which is likely, the pressure to generate expertise will make it fairly difficult for parties to constantly refrain from organization-building. Accordingly, the most successful and prominent extreme right parties – which tend to unite strong leadership with anti-organizational tendencies – have in the end built up their organization (Hainsworth 2000: 14).

New parties in old party systems and the organizational costs of public office

Institutionally generated pressures on parties as organizations affect old and new parties alike. The assessment of these pressures provides a fruitful lens to compare parties' strategies to address these challenges in an environment of social transformation, changing electoral competition and growing expectations towards government. Organizationally, due to new parties' particular electoral and organizational vulnerability, they are likely to suffer more considerably from the costs of public office than older established parties. As van Biezen points out in her analysis of new parties in the new democracies of southern and Eastern Europe:

> When parties acquire governmental status at an early stage of organizational development – which is generally the case for parties in new democracies – they are particularly vulnerable to the destabilizing consequences that the intricate relationship between the party central office, the party in government and the parliamentary party may produce.
>
> (van Biezen 2000: 411)

Surprisingly, this perspective has hardly been applied to parties in established party systems. Due to the dominant perspective on new parties in Western Europe as channels for the representation of 'new' issues in established party systems representing 'old' lines of conflict, 'newness' is rarely conceptualized in terms of organizational age. Therefore the organizational costs of public office imposed on new parties, the major topic of this chapter, have not received much attention.

Understanding 'newness' in terms of organizational youth, the evolution of new parties in established party systems can be conceptualized depending on the type of public office – legislative or executive – they take over at a particular point of their development. In this sense, this chapter asked for the demands towards new parties as organizational actors and these demands' intra-organizational implications. Pedersen (1982) pointed to the need to treat parties as 'mortal organizations'. If organizations are perceived as mortal, their survival becomes a puzzle. This is most evident if parties are organizationally 'new' or 'young'. In contrast to old parties, new parties' long-term survival can be less easily taken for granted. In order to survive, they need to adapt. However, in a context of changing Western societies, this is equally true for traditional parties. One symptom of such an adaptation has already been mentioned above: traditional parties' stronger focus on their governing functions at the cost of their representative function (Mair 1997; Mair 2005). Taking an actor-centred instead of a structuralist perspective, new parties mirror this process when developing from channels for protest and neglected citizen demands to law-makers and policy-managers.

Accordingly, this chapter has tried to specify the organizational costs of public office which point towards a greater institutionalization and professionalization of parties in the long run. In particular, new parties' orientation towards governing pushes them to establish a new functional equilibrium which necessarily has organizational repercussions. With the stronger focus on governing in the case of traditional parties, new parties' first experiences in governing need to be seen as potential triggers for programmatic, strategic and organizational change. Substantially, the discussion indicates the need for new parties to develop a less fluid organizational basis which is capable of responding to these demands. Functionally speaking, one can hypothesize that traditional and new parties are likely to converge towards a model of party organization which neither corresponds with the mass party model nor frees itself completely from 'party as organization' in favour of 'party as a network'.[25] The 'party on the ground' might weaken in traditional parties and never play an 'institutionalized' role in new parties as it did in the traditional mass party. Still, public office generates the need to strengthen the party in central office as a means to control candidate recruitment in the face of increasing demands towards office aspirants and as a means to co-ordinate an increasingly functionally differentiated party in public office.

Put differently, if a party's public face becomes increasingly complex due to a growing functional differentiation as a response to the demands of public office, the party in central office as the organizational core of a party's external arm is likely to take up the role of a linchpin handling upcoming pressures (van Biezen 2000: 410–11). Although the parties in public and central office tend to overlap and the former could continuously increase its power (Katz and Mair 1995; Mair 1997), only the party in central office is able to assure organizational stability irrespective of a party's electoral success since it is less dependent on such success than the party in public office. Evidently, this is all the more the case for parties in an early stage of organizational development without a security net of reliable core supporters struggling with an increasing electoral volatility.

Notes

1 I am very grateful to Zsolt Enyedi, Peter Mair and Joost van Spanje for their help and comments on this chapter.
2 'Functional' denotes demands generated by public offices or posts which are directed towards particular purposes. The term 'functional' as used in this chapter is not associated with functionalist theory in the narrow sense.
3 This should not imply that there are no centrally located new parties. The Dutch D66 would be one example. However, as reflected in the dominant strands of the literature, new parties are not evenly distributed along the left–right continuum, which justifies a focus on these two major sub-groups as the two most important new party families in Western Europe (Mair 2002: 135).
4 In this context, it is important to distinguish 'new' parties and 'newly governing' parties. New parties might enter government immediately, while newly governing parties might actually be old. To belong to the group of established parties constitutive for the traditional party system does not presuppose any experience in government. Instead of starting from the feature of 'lacking government experience' in general and exploring the motivation to enter or not to enter and the consequences of doing so, the starting point here is new parties and the challenges they face when moving into office, challenges resulting from their status as comparatively young organizations.
5 For details on new parties' seat strength and vote strength in Western Europe, see Keman and Krouwel (2006) and Mair (1999).
6 Evidently, it also makes a difference whether parties can draw on established subcultures when building up an organization.
7 In Mair's comparison between different subgroups of new parties – 'new' new parties, mergers and splits – the group of mergers shows a higher survival rate (measured based on renewed electoral contestation) than splits. In 1965–1998, 52.6 per cent of the mergers (10 out of 19) and 33.3 per cent of splits (13 out of 39) survive, while the survival rate of 'new' new parties was 47.5 per cent (56 of 118). At the same time, both splits and mergers do much better than 'new' new parties in terms of average electoral support (Mair 1999: 217). This result is, however, not surprising, since factions within a party will only risk a split if they are strong enough to realistically expect sufficient electoral support to survive as a party. 'New' new parties, in contrast, might be mere promoter parties only intending to highlight a certain issue without ever even coming close to parliamentary representation, and might vanish after the issue has been picked up by established parties (Harmel and Robertson 1985: 517). Looking at the survival of these three groups of new parties in Western European parliaments in 1975–2003, 19 per cent of 'new' new parties died (4 of 21) after having gained parliamentary representation, as did 12.5 per cent of the splits (1 of 8), while all mergers (4 of 4) and all of the rebirths – indicating ideologically transformed old parties – (9 of 9) survived (Keman and Krouwel: 6–7). Evidently, due to the different sizes of the three groups, the comparison of percentages needs to be treated with a certain caution.
8 Measured by the vote losses of government parties compared to the vote losses of opposition parties.

 9 High opposition influence and the formation of minority cabinets are not necessarily related as indicated by, for instance, the Irish case where minority cabinets form in a context of a structurally weak opposition (Bolleyer and Weeks forthcoming).

10 In some cases, this might be a good solution for both sides: the established parties need not share government power formally and new parties might find themselves less in conflict with the anti-establishment image they push in the electoral arena. Alternatively, support status might be the only option new parties have to influence policy if established parties are not willing to take them in as a formal government member, as could be observed with the Swedish Greens (Bale and Bergman 2006).

11 Blackmail potential, as the second source of relevance Sartori introduces, is not discussed since it applies to large parties permanently excluded from government (Sartori 1976: 122).

12 This conceptualization points to the importance of studying established parties' reactions to the entry of new parties, which can range from immediate acceptance to outright exclusion. See, for instance, Van Spanje and Van der Brug (2007).

13 Exceptions are new parties which immediately win the biggest vote share which, however, in stable party systems rarely occurs.

14 The reverse strategy would be to take on board more extreme positions in order to increase vote-gains as chosen by the ideologically 'new' Austrian FPÖ.

15 To give one example, one new party might insist in better measures of environmental protection as a core preference; another might oppose European integration and the consequences of the internationalization of the national economy. When it comes to the adoption of measures to realize these preferences, not only is the first preference more concrete and therefore more manageable, its scope is also more limited. Hence, the implications for other policy fields are more restricted, which facilitates its realization within coalition governments where coalition partners have to reconcile measures to implement their different policy goals.

16 Correspondingly, Müller-Rommel uses the duration of pre-parliamentary and parliamentary experience of Green parties before government entry as one indicator for the likelihood of professional behavior in coalition negotiation and cabinet decision-making (Müller-Rommel 2002: 4).

17 Parties do not only strive for electoral success but also for support of their members, who contribute to them financially and are eager to see party policy realized.

18 There are two prominent possibilities to conceptualise this property (Daalder 1983) – either as a space (Hazan 1997; Keman 1994) or alternatively as a point, more concretely the inclusion of the median MP on the left–right continuum (Roozendaal 1992). Looking at concrete party systems, several parties frequently possess this freedom, not just the one positioned at the median (Hazan 1997; Keman 1994). Therefore a spatial conception seems to be more useful when analysing party system dynamics.

19 It is assumed here that large parties tend to prefer coalitions with small parties over coalitions with stronger parties.

20 Using a rather broad criterion for newness, parties having run elections for the first time only after 1965 are classified as new. While this is a useful cut-off point to identify the group of new parties in Western European party systems, it is less so regarding the southern European countries. Portugal had its first free elections only in 1975. Accordingly, the small Party of the Democratic Social Center was found in 1974 and, after 20 years in opposition, entered the government in 2002 after having gained a pivotal status. The Portuguese Renewal Party was found later in 1985, hence, represents also within the young Portuguese party system a new party. It immediately occupied a central-pivotal position and entered government. However, after two years it left the coalition preliminarily and afterwards, together with other opposition parties, brought the government to an end. In the following election, it lost 38 of its 45 seats and in 1991 all parliamentary representation.

21 It is therefore important to notice which social strata new parties' leaders belong to and whether, depending on their roots, they can be expected to adapt to the rules for professional behavior established in the political sphere.

22 The occupation of a concrete niche of neglected policy issues certainly facilitates the maintenance of vote support and the assurance of survival. Moreover, the focus of followers on substantial goals instead of mere protest increases the likelihood that supporters are more tolerant towards compromises for the sake of seeing policies implemented (Poguntke 2002).

23 This problem also exists with regard to internal party positions, although leadership replacement is not a problem related to public office directly but necessary to assure a party's long-term survival inside or outside public institutions.

24 New parties are unlikely to occupy the office of the prime minister.

25 For different conceptions of party formation and change, see van Biezen (2005).

Bibliography

Abedi, A. (2002) 'Challenges to established parties: the effects of party system features on the electoral fortunes of anti-political-establishment parties', *European Journal of Political Research*, 41: 551–83.

van Biezen, I. (2000) 'On the internal balance of party power', *Party Politics*, 6(4): 395–417.

van Biezen, I. (2005) 'On the theory and practice of party formation and adaptation in new democracies', *European Journal of Political Research*, 44(1): 147–74.

Bale, T. and Bergman, T. (2006) 'A taste of honey is worse than none at all? Coping with the generic challenges of support party status in Sweden and New Zealand', *Party Politics*, 12(2): 189–209.

Blondel, J. and Müller-Rommel, F. (eds) (1993) *Governing Together: The Extent and Limits of Joint Decision-Making in Western Europe Cabinets*, London: Macmillan.

Bolleyer, N. (2004) 'Kleine Parteien zwischen Stimmenmaximierung, Politikgestaltung und Regierungsübernahme am Beispiel Irlands und Dänemarks', *Zeitschrift für Parlamentsfragen*, 1: 132–48.

Bolleyer, N. (2007) 'Small parties – from party pledge to government policy', *West European Politics*, 30(1): 121–47.

Bolleyer, N. and Weeks, L. (forthcoming) *The Puzzle of Non-Party Actors in Party Democracy: Independents in Ireland*, San Domenico: EUI Working Paper Series.

Brittan, S. (1975) 'The economic contradictions of democracy', *British Journal of Political Science*, 5(2): 129–59.

Burchell, J. (2001a) 'Evolving or conforming? Assessing organisational reform within European Green parties', *West European Politics*, 24 (3): 113–34.

Burchell, J. (2001b) ' "Small steps" or "great leaps": how the Swedish Greens are learning the lessons of government participation', *Scandinavian Political Studies*, 24(3): 239–54.

Daalder, (1983) 'In the search of the centre of European party systems', *American Political Science Review*, 78: 92–109.

Döring, H. (ed) (1995) *Parliaments and Majority Rule in Western Europe*, Frankfurt: Campus.

Döring, H. and Hallerberg, M. (eds) (2004) *Patterns of Parliamentary Behaviour: Passage of Legislation Across Western Europe*, Aldershot: Ashgate.

Hainsworth, P. (2000) 'Introduction: the extreme right', in P. Hainsworth (ed.) *Politics of the Extreme Right, From the Margins to the Mainstream*, New York: Pinter.

Harmel, R. and Janda, K. (1994) 'An integrated theory of party goals and party change', *Journal of Theoretical Politics*, 6(3): 259–87.

Harmel, R. and Robertson, J.D. (1985) 'Formation and success of new parties: a cross-national analysis', *International Political Science Review*, 6: 501–23.

Hazan, R.Y. (1997) *Centre Parties: Polarization and Competition in European Parliamentary Democracies*, London: Pinter.

Heinisch, R. (2003) 'Success in opposition – failure in government: explaining the performance of right-wing populist parties in public office', *West European Politics*, 26(3): 91–130.

Hug, S. (2000) 'Studying the electoral success of new political parties: a methodological note', *Party Politics*, 6(2): 187–97.

Hug, S. (2001) *Altering Party Systems: Strategic Behavior and the Emergence of New Political Parties in Western Democracies*, Michigan: University of Michigan Press.

Judge, D. (2003) 'Legislative institutionalization: a bent analytical arrow?' *Government and Opposition*, 38(3): 497–514.

Katz, R.S. and Mair, P. (1993) 'The evolution of party organization in Europe: three faces of party organization', *American Review of Politics, Special Issue: Political Parties in a Changing Age*, 14: 593–617.

Katz, R.S. and Mair, P. (1995) 'Changing models of party organization and party democracy: the emergence of the cartel party', *Party Politics*, 1(1): 5–28.

Keman, H. (1994) 'The search for the centre: pivot parties in West European party systems', *West European Politics*, 17(4): 124–48.

Keman, H. and Krouwel, A. (2006) 'The rise of a new political class? Emerging new parties and the populist challenge in Western Europe', *Working Papers Political Science Vrije Universiteit Amsterdam*, 2006: 02.

King, A. (1981) 'The rise of career politicians in Britain – and its consequences', *British Journal of Political Science*, 11(3): 249–85.

Kitschelt, H. (1988) 'Left-libertarian parties: explaining innovation in competitive systems', *World Politics*, 40(2): 194–234.

Kitschelt, H. (1989) *The Logic of Party Formation: Ecological Politics in Belgium and West Germany*, London: Cornell University Press.

Kitschelt, H. (2000) 'Citizens, politicians, and party cartellization: political representation and state failure in post-industrial democracies', *European Journal of Political Research*, 37: 149–79.

Lipset, S. and Rokkan, S. (eds) (1967) *Party Systems and Voter Alignments: Cross-national Perspectives*, New York: Free Press.

Lucardie, P. (2000) 'Prophets, purifiers and prolocutors: towards a theory on the emergence of new parties', *Party Politics*, 6(2): 175–85.

Luebbert, G.M. (1986) *Comparative Democracies: Policy-Making and Governing Coalitions in Europe and Israel*, New York: Columbia University Press.

Mair, P. (1983) 'Adaptation and control: towards an understanding of party and party system change', in H.M. Daalder and P. Mair (eds) *Western European Party Systems, Continuity and Change*, London: Sage.

Mair, P. (1997) *Party System Change: Approaches and Interpretations*, Oxford: Clarendon Press.

Mair, P. (1999) 'New political parties in long-established party systems: how successful are they?', in E. Beukel, K.K. Klausen, M.N. Pedersen and P.E. Mouritzen (eds) *Elites, Parties and Democracy: Festschrift for Professor Mogens N. Pedersen*, Odense: Odense University Press.

Mair, P. (2001) 'The freezing hypothesis: an evaluation', in L.K. Karvonen and S. Kuhle (eds) *Party Systems and Voter Alignment Revisited*, London: Routledge.

Mair, P. (2002) 'In the aggregate: mass electoral behaviour in Western Europe, 1950–2000', in H. Keman (ed.) *Comparative Democratic Politics: A Guide to Contemporary Theory and Research*, London: Sage.

Mair, P. (2005) 'Democracy beyond parties', *Center for the Study of Democracy*, paper 05–06.

Mair, P. and Mudde, C. (1998) 'The party family and its study', *Annual Review of Political Science*, 1: 211–29.

Mattila, M. and Raunio, T. (2004) 'Does winning pay? Electoral success and government formation in 15 West European countries', *European Journal of Political Research*, 43: 263–85.

Minkenberg, M. (2001) 'The radical right in public office: agenda-setting and policy effects', *West European Politics*, 24(4): 1–21.

Müller, W.C. (2000) 'Political parties in parliamentary democracies: making delegation and accountability work', *European Journal of Political Research*, 37: 309–33.

Müller, W.C. and Strøm, L. (eds) (2003) *Coalition Governments in Western Europe*, Oxford: Oxford University Press.

Müller-Rommel, F. (2002) 'The lifespan and the political performance of Green parties in Western Europe', in F. Müller-Rommel and T. Poguntke (eds) *Environmental Politics, Green Parties in National Government*, London: Frank Cass.

Narud, H.M. and Valen, H. (2005) 'Coalition membership and electoral performance in Western Europe', paper read at the NOPSA Meeting, Reykjavik, 11–13August 2005.

Panebianco, A. (1988) *Political Parties: Organisation and Power*, Cambridge: Cambridge University Press.

Pedersen, M. (1982) 'Towards a new typology of party lifespans and minor parties', *Scandinavian Political Studies*, 5: 1–16.

Poguntke, T. (2002) 'Green parties in national government: from protest to aquiescence?', in F. Müller-Rommel and T. Poguntke (eds) *Green Parties in National Governments*, London: Frank Cass.

Rochon, T.R. (1985) 'Mobilizers and challengers: towards a theory of new party success', *International Political Science Review*, 6(4): 419–39.

Rohrschneider, R. (1993) 'New parties versus old left realignment: environmental attitudes, party politics, and partisan affiliation in four West European countries', *The Journal of Politics*, 55(3): 682–702.

van Roozendaal, P. (1992) *Cabinets in Multi-party Democracies: The Effect of Dominant and Central Parties on Cabinet Composition and Durability*, Amsterdam: Thesis Publisher.

Rose, R. and Mackie, T.T. (1983) 'Incumbency in government: asset or liability?', in H. Daalder and P. Mair (eds) *Western European Party Systems, Continuity and Change*, London: Sage.

Sartori, G. (1976) *Parties and Party Systems: A Framework for Analysis*, Cambridge: Cambridge University Press.

Seyd, P. and Whiteley, P. (2004) 'British party members, an overview', *Party Politics*, 10(4): 355–66.

Sieberer, U. (2006) 'Party unity in parliamentary democracies', *The Journal of Legislative Studies*, 12(2): 150–78.

Strøm, K. (1990) *Minority Government and Majority Rule*, Cambridge: Cambridge University Press.

Strøm, K. and Müller, W.C. (1999) 'Political parties and hard choices', in W.C. Müller and K. Strøm (eds) *Policy, Office or Votes? How Political Parties Make Hard Decisions*, Cambridge: Cambridge University Press.

Sundberg, J. (2003) *Parties as Organized Actors: The Transformation of the Scandinavian Three-Front Parties*, Helsinki: The Finnish Society of Sciences and Letters.

Timmermans, A. (2006) 'Standing apart and sitting together: enforcing coalition agreements in multiparty systems', *European Journal of Political Research*, 45: 263–83.

Van der Brug, W. and Fennema, M. (2005) 'Explaining support for "new" right wing populists with "old" models: the case of Pim Fortuyn', paper read at the ECPR Joint Session, Nicosia, 25–30 April 2005.

Van Spanje, J. and Van der Brug, W. (2007) 'The party as pariah: the exclusion of anti-immigrant parties and its effect on their ideological positions', *West European Politics*, 30: 1022–40.

Wilson, J.Q. (1973) *Political Organizations*, New York: Basic Books.

Warwick, P.V. (1996) 'Coalition government membership in Western European parliamentary democracies', *British Journal of Political Science*, 26: 471–99.

3 Newly governing parties in Italy

Comparing the PDS/DS, Lega Nord and Forza Italia

Jonathan Hopkin and Piero Ignazi[1]

Introduction

After a long period of relative stability in Western European party systems (Bartolini and Mair 1990), the 1990s saw a dramatic increase in the presence of new political parties in national governments. Party system cartels (Katz and Mair 1995) have come under severe pressure, as new parties have forced their way into government coalitions (Mair 2002). This chapter examines this problem through the prism of an extreme case of new party penetration into the government structures: Italy since the early 1990s. The Italian case differs from all the other Western European cases in at least two respects. First, the emergence of new parties was in part a response to the spectacular collapse of the existing party system in 1992–93. Whereas in other West European countries new parties had to push hard to open a door which the established parties sought to keep locked, in Italy the door was left wide open and unattended, and the new parties found themselves in the unique position of having to govern themselves with little help from the previous governing elites. The second important difference is that, unlike in many other Western European cases where new parties were 'prophets' (to use Lucardie's (2000) terminology)[2] articulating new political demands unmet by the existing party system, in Italy the new parties had, at least in part, to represent a large constituency of voters who had little interest in 'new' issues and hankered after a degree of stability and continuity.

These differences may cause some problems in generalizing from the Italian experience, and it is not our intention here to present a grand theory of new parties in government. However, it may also be the case that the performance of new parties in government in rather exceptional circumstances brings out with particular clarity some of the dynamics which are present in other cases. This chapter will seek to illustrate the key features of the Italian case in terms which facilitate broader comparative enquiry.

Changes in the Italian party system: crisis and collapse 1992–94

In the early 1990s Italy experienced the total breakdown of a party system which had lasted in a relatively stable form since the immediate post-war period, leading to a complete redefinition of Italy's electoral dynamics between the 1992 and 1994 elections. Electoral volatility reached the unprecedented level of 36.8 per cent, and the most voted-for party in the 1994 general election was one founded just a few months before. The turnover of parliamentary personnel in the Italian lower chamber (the Chamber of Deputies) was an astonishing 71 per cent (Bardi and Ignazi 1998, Ignazi 2002, Bardi 2002).

This is not the place for an extensive analysis of this remarkable transformation of the Italian party system (the curious reader can consult, amongst others, Bardi and Morlino 1994, Morlino 1996, Gundle and Parker 1996, Bufacchi and Burgess 2001). For our present purposes, it is sufficient to note that a range of pressures became irresistible for the Christian Democratic (DC)-dominated centrist coalition which, in a variety of forms, had governed Italy since 1948. These pressures included: the end of the Cold War, which undermined the Christian Democrats' role as a bulwark against communism; the financial and currency crisis caused by years of loose fiscal policies and brought to a head by the Maastricht treaty and the crisis of the exchange rate mechanism (ERM); the emergence of the Northern League as a challenger to the DC in its northern heartlands; and in the shorter term, the judicial campaign against corruption launched in Milan on the one hand, and the successful campaign for a majoritarian electoral reform on the other. Between the 1992 and 1994 elections, dozens of Christian Democrat and Socialist parliamentarians were placed under judicial investigation for a range of misdemeanours relating to corruption and illicit party funding, whilst the reform of the electoral system left a discredited governing class uniquely exposed to the wrath of a dissatisfied electorate. A Mafia bombing campaign added to the political turbulence.

With the magnitude of the earthquake suffered by the Italian party system in the early 1990s, many new parties were created and most of the oldest ones disappeared. Just to give an idea of the change, no party in the 1994 general election had contested in the 1987 election: some were totally new; others had new names or symbols as a result of, often traumatic, transformations. As a consequence, the governments after 1994 were mostly made by newcomers.

Therefore, the Italian case provides abundant material for the analysis of 'new parties in government'. In this chapter we adopt a parsimonious strategy and reduce the cases under consideration to three parties only: *Partito Democratico della Sinistra/Democratici di Sinistra* (PDS/DS), *Lega Nord* (the Northern League) and *Forza Italia* (FI). The PDS/DS is the direct heir of the former Italian Communist Party (PCI) and therefore it has a long political–ideological and organizational tradition. The other two are newly formed parties: *Forza Italia* is organizationally lightweight, weak and flexible, whilst the *Lega* is somewhat more institutionalized, but still far less articulated than the PDS/DS.

Given the differences among the parties, it would be somewhat difficult and even inconclusive to analyse them on the same ground, in the same aspects. Therefore the analysis which follows adopts a slightly different focus in each case in accordance with data availability and the peculiarities of the individual parties.

The formation of new parties in contemporary Italy

The swift collapse of the dominant political parties after the 1992 elections made a change in governing coalitions appear inevitable, since the parties most threatened by the upheavals of 1992–3 had been the mainstays of governing coalitions for the previous decade and a half. This prospect of substantial turnover in the governing elites – a complete novelty in post-war Italy, where high levels of government instability masked a high degree of continuity in government personnel – accelerated the development of new political parties.

The main reason government turnover appeared traumatic was the presence of a dominant party of the left – the PDS – which represented a visible link with the PCI, for decades the most powerful communist party in Western Europe. The PDS/DS was the offspring of the PCI: it was founded in January 1991 after a long process of renewal initiated immediately after the fall of the Berlin Wall. While the PDS/DS has distanced itself from the PCI's ideological legacy, its organizational roots come from the former Communist party. The new party was founded with the clear intention to overcome the effective veto on the PCI's presence in Italy's national government in the post-war period. In 1993 the party was able to take a first step in this direction, by offering parliamentary support to Carlo Azeglio Ciampi's 'caretaker' government (Cotta and Verzichelli 1996). The Ciampi government's precarious parliamentary position made an early election a near certainty. The governing credentials of the new PDS/DS, added to the collapse of the Christian Democrat and Socialist parties in the face of economic crisis and corruption allegations, made the election of a left-dominated government a clear possibility for the first time in over 40 years.

This scenario played a major role in the development of a completely new party, *Forza Italia*, which formed an electoral alliance with other parties of the centre-right, including another newcomer: the *Lega Nord*. Media magnate Silvio Berlusconi used his financial clout and the organizational resources and nationwide presence of his own business empire (*Fininvest*) to build the new party, which recruited largely political novices to stand, under Berlusconi's leadership, as candidates in constituencies throughout Italy. *Forza Italia* became the pivot of a broad right electoral coalition which included both the Northern League and the post-Fascist party National Alliance (*Alleanza Nazionale*; AN). This hastily formed coalition, called the 'Pole of Liberty and Good Government' (*Polo delle Libertà e del Buongoverno*),[3] which had the clear purpose of averting a left-dominated government, won the elections of March 1994. The fractious parliamentary majority it produced collapsed after only nine months, and after a further period of caretaker governments, the 1996 elections were won by a centre-left coalition – the Olive Tree (*Ulivo*) – dominated by the PDS/DS. The centre-left governed during 1996–2001 before the centre-right, reconstituted as the House of Liberties (*Casa delle Libertà*), won power and governed throughout the 2001–06 legislature. These governing experiences for the PDS/DS, *Forza Italia* and the *Lega* provide the empirical sample for this chapter.

Newly governing parties in Italy: the centre-left

The 1996 general elections offered the opportunity for the PDS/DS to enter the governing arena directly for the first time. The centre-left coalition (the Olive Tree) led by Romano Prodi won a parliamentary majority which allowed the PDS/DS to remain in government for a full five-year legislature (1996–2001). As well as the PDS/DS, the largest party, the Olive Tree coalition also included the *Partito Popolare Italiano* (PPI – heir of the once powerful Christian Democrat party), the Green Party and the centrist–moderate *Rinnovamento Italiano* (Italian Renewal, led by Lamberto Dini), plus some minor fringe parties. This section focuses solely on the PDS/DS's first experience at the heart of government, paying particular attention to how this experience affected the party's electoral performance, the party organization, and the party's ideological/programmatic profile.

The electoral impact

In terms of the PDS/DS's electoral position, there is some evidence that government experience had the effect of depressing electoral mobilization. This is one possible expected consequence of new parties taking on government roles, since opposition parties of all kinds face the difficulty of adapting their ambitious promises and commitments to the constraints of government. The 'inexperience' of the political personnel in ministerial positions and the difficulty in managing the government coalition could also have contributed to poor electoral performance. In the 2001 general elections, after five years in office, the DS suffered one of the worst defeats ever suffered by either the new party or its predecessor the PCI, winning just 16.6 per cent, 4.5 per cent less than in 1996.

This electoral failure was not caused by any change in the geographical spread of the party's vote. The PDS/DS maintained its traditional strongholds in the 'red belt' in central Italy (Galli 1972; Diamanti 2003), collecting 27.2 per cent of the vote compared to the 16.6 per cent collected nationally. This result allowed the party to still dominate that area, notwithstanding significant losses there too: a drop of 7.2 per cent since 1996, higher than the national average (Diamanti 2003: 88). In sum, the geographical map of the DS was basically unaffected by the party's governmental participation, suggesting that the DS did not implement policies aimed at privileging their traditional strongholds.

The same cannot be said of the party's relationship to its social constituency, which did change in this period. This question is inevitably intertwined with the changes in the party programme over the 1980s and 1990s which modified the party's identification with a specific social class (the working class). The PDS/DS underwent significant changes in its identification with the welfare state, in its attitude toward state intervention and the market economy, liberalization and globalization, and in its relationship with the trade unions. Its predecessor, the PCI, overwhelmingly represented the blue-collar electorate (Galli 1966; Accornero *et al.* 1983). However, the birth of two competing parties in the early 1990s – the PDS's splinter party *Rifondazione Comunista* and the 'populist' *Lega Nord* – undermined the PDS/DS's privileged relationship with this social group.

In 1996, at the eve of its entry into government, the working class was slightly over-represented in its electorate (Bellucci *et al* 2000: 29). The PDS-DS was going to lose its social stronghold. The effects are even stronger regarding trade union support. Whereas in 1985 the members of the communist-led trade union the General Italian Confederation of Labour (CGIL) voted overwhelmingly for the PCI, in 2001 their loyalty towards the DS was limited: only 41 per cent of CGIL members voted for the DS (Bellucci and Segatti 2002: 912). The remainder largely voted for the minor parties of the left (above all *Rifondazione Comunista*) but also for the *Lega* which collected also, and especially, many non-unionized working-class voters.

Socialist parties' declining support amongst the working class is a well known phenomenon all over Europe. The PDS/DS has followed the general trend. However, the PDS/DS acquired governmental responsibilities much later than comparable parties, which may have slowed the process of dealignment. Once it was in power, this process accelerated. The policies highlighted by its 1996 programme and the ones enforced during the legislature diverged quite substantially. In 1996 the PDS presented a manifesto which followed the final document developed in the 1995 'thematic' national conference (Gilbert 1996). That document diverged from the traditional pro-interventionist standings because it accepted the privatisation of the public companies and recognized the need for a reform of the welfare state. The low profile accorded to this document helped the party maintain its core support in the 1996 elections. However, during the 1996–2001 legislature, the PDS (which took the name of DS in February 1998) moved along an unequivocal acceptance of the logics and constraints of the market economy, abandoning any reference to 'socialist' goals, and advocating a reform of the welfare state. The 1997 party conference represented the apogee of the leadership's attempt to redefine the party's profile as a more pragmatic, 'third way' party (Ignazi 1997, Vignati 1998) Opposition to this approach came, not by chance, from the CGIL leader (Sergio Cofferati) who invoked more attention to the traditional constituency. Cofferati's criticism was consistent with the progressive detachment of workers (especially in the northern regions) from the party and union. According to the Italian national elections survey, the DS won the votes of 24.2 per cent of the workers and clerks in the public sector against 25.3 per cent collected by *Forza Italia*, and a mere 16.6 per cent against 30.6 per cent collected by *Forza Italia* in the private sector (ITANES 2001: 95).

In sum, access to power 'forced' the PDS/DS to de-emphasise some traditional pro-state intervention and pro-welfare positions, but this shift caused discontent among the working-class constituency, a discontent which was voiced quite blatantly by the CGIL leader, in contrast with the party leadership. The result of this conflict appeared quite clearly at the polls.

The organizational impact

In organizational terms, we would expect the 'cartelization' or professionalization of parties to be reinforced by the access to power, because control of the resources which the parties acquire on entering government would be concentrated in the hands of the leadership. Newly governing parties would strengthen the centralization and professionalization – two basic traits of the professional new cadre/cartel/party.

In this case, the process of organizational change was already under way in the mid-1980s, and rapidly accelerated in connection with the transformation from PCI into PDS. An important turning point is represented by the national conference of March 1989, when 'democratic centralism' was formally ended, even if the prohibition of creating internal factions remained (Ignazi 1992). Only when the PDS was founded (January 1991) did the party finally acquire the organizational features of a 'standard' European social democratic party (Baccetti 1997). However, the earthquake of the party system in 1993–94 and the emergence of novel and successful political formations such as *Forza Italia* led to further redefinitions of its internal structure. The process reached its end only at the 2001 congress, after which the debate over internal changes ended.

Notwithstanding this long process of change, the PDS/DS entry into government produced some effects. First, it deepened the gap between party leadership and rank-and-file; second, it created a gap between the party leader and the national collective bodies (in particular the party executive); and third, it produced a new division between government personnel on the one hand and the parliamentary group and the party executive on the other. In general terms, in the first year of government participation the party accelerated the tendency towards centralization and personalization, although this tendency was halted by new rules introduced by the first DS congress held in January 2000.

The new process of leadership selection adopted by the congress involved more direct participation by the membership: the candidates present their candidature at the time of the local congresses (at the branch level) and accompany their candidature with a political–programmatic document. In this way, candidates are tied to their own programme, enhancing accountability, at least in principle. The 'candidate cum programme' is voted by the members at local level; thus the secretary is no longer elected by the delegates at the national congresses but by the members who participated in the selection processes in the local conferences. The national conference only ratifies the number of votes collected. This direct legitimation strengthens the secretary but its power is now counterbalanced by a more powerful national executive. The personalization is enforced, but the centralization into the secretary's hands is tempered by a greater emphasis on the national collective bodies and by the federalization of the party organization.

The other relevant innovation concerned the transformation of the organizational structure into a network model. The party became a federation of territorial units (centred around the regional level), of extra-party associations able to affiliate with the party, and of the elected officials (MPs, regional and local councillors). Finally the party opened up to the participation of non party members in its 'thematic associations', and allowed the formation of internal tendencies, which are allotted structures and funds and can be supported also by non party members. In fact, many of these innovations remained on paper, with only the leadership selection process enforced at the 2001 congress (after the electoral defeat). The other organizational reforms along the 'network model' went unfulfilled but for a growing centrality of the regional structures, which had increased their weight within the organization (even if this could be interpreted as the end-point of a long process initiated in 1991).

In conclusion, access to power affected the PDS/DS organization: the parliamentary party (including the governing figures) acquired a greater role and tended to distance itself from, and free itself from, the extra-parliamentary party; the personalization of the leadership increased, especially when the party leader became prime minister, but it was countered both by the attempt at stimulating membership involvement in the internal decision-making and leadership selection processes, and by the greater emphasis on the accountability and responsiveness of the leadership *vis-à-vis* the membership; the relationship with the traditional flanking organizations, such as, above all, the trade union CGIL, was relaxed in favour of a broader appeal to different social categories.

A final point to be discussed here concerns the level of recruitment and internal participation. Apparently the party did not suffer from its entry into government, nor was it benefited: recruitment remained more or less at the same level, over 600,000 members, with some uneven fluctuation (Bellucci *et al.* 2000: 35). On the other hand, internal participation followed a more precise pattern: it was quite low in 1997 (around 12 per cent of the members participated in the local congresses) during a period of stability for the party (one year after its victory at the polls and its entry into government), but much higher in 2000 (around 25 per cent participated in the local congresses) when the party was in an even better situation, 'crowned' by the party's premiership, and still higher in 2001 when, on the contrary, the party was defeated at the polls and out of government. The crucial variables to explain these different levels of participation are linked to the different degree of internal factionalism: non-existent in 1997, lively in 2000 and explosive in 2001. The declining percentage of members voting for the party secretary is just a partial example of the different settings: 98.7 per cent for D'Alema in 1997, 79.1 per cent, for Veltroni in 2000, and 61.8 per cent for Fassino in 2001. Moreover, a comparison of the middle-level elites' perception of the intensity of the pre-congress debates in 1997 and 2000 is illuminating; while in 1997 12.7 per cent declared that there were highly conflicting opinions in their local congress, 29.9 per cent declared so in 2000; and conversely, while 21.1 per cent estimated that there was practically no debate in 1997, only 12.9 per cent gave the same judgement in 2000 (Bellucci *et al.* 2000: 107).

Factionalization increased with the amount of time spent in government. Whether a causal link exists or not is a matter of speculation. Our answer is no: there is not a direct link. Participation in government might have been a facilitating factor of a longer process. In fact, participation in government enabled the PDS/DS to 'normalize' its internal life, finally purging itself of the residue of the communist traditions of unanimity, deference to the leadership and democratic centralism. Already in 1994 the defenestration of Occhetto by the young turks D'Alema and Veltroni represented a *first attempt* at introducing some element of democratic rituals in the leadership selection; but many undemocratic barriers were still present at that time (see Gilbert 1996, Ignazi 2002). Only with the contested and confrontational congresses of 2000 and 2001 did a more transparent and open decision-making process emerge. In sum, PDS-DS participation in government did not depress internal democracy: internal participation increased and competition between internal factions emerged, whilst leadership accountability was also enforced, thanks to the 2001 party's internal rules.

Party de-radicalization and ideological change

In terms of the effects of government participation on the party's ideological location, empirical data on the party's location demonstrate the abandonment of the more leftist leaning by the party middle-level elites. Compared to 1990, when more than 70 per cent located themselves on the two leftmost cases of the one-to-ten left–right continuum, only 24.6 per cent did so in 1997, and 19.9 per cent in 2000. The abandonment of the more leftist positioning is compensated by the dramatic increase of the centre-left location which goes from a mere 25 per cent at the time of the PCI (1990), to 68.1 per cent and 73.6 per cent respectively in 1997 and 2000 (Ignazi 1992, Bellucci *et al.* 2000: 116–18). The party's move toward the centre-left alliance in government has been metabolized by its middle-level elites. The party delegates attribute to their own party an even stronger identification with the centre-left (compared to their own) since 74.3 per cent of the them rated the PDS in 1997, and 76.9 per cent rated the DS in 2000, in the centre-left. A further indicator of de-radicalization is provided by the feeling of closeness or distance *vis-à-vis* the other parties. Here the PDS/DS middle-level elites signal a higher closeness to the centre-located partner of the coalition such as the PPI rather than to the more leftist fringes (PCDI and Rifondazione Comunista) (Bellucci *et al.* 2000: 126–7).

The PDS/DS entered government with a program which still contained many aspects of the traditional socialist identity absorbed in the passage from PCI to PDS, with some novelties inspired by 'third-wayism' and by the liberal–democratic tradition. However, the party did not dedicate as much intellectual energy to crafting a modern social democratic identity as it had devoted to rationalizing its detachment from communism. One could argue that abandonment of the communist heritage had exhausted the party, leaving little energy left to build a new, well-knit identity. It redefined itself as a socialist party, part of the social democratic family, and abandoned the Communist group in the European Parliament in 1990, joining the socialist Euro-group, the PSE; and the Socialist International, to which it was admitted in 1992. But the chaotic events in Italian politics since 1992 did not provide an appropriate environment for theoretical speculations, and the PDS entered government with a patchwork-like ideological identity.

The 'thematic' congress of 1995 and the II PDS Congress of 1997 did not enable the party to deepen and enlarge the debate which was instead sterilized into contingent problems. The so called 'liberal revolution' that the party leadership intended to promote at the time was no more than a slogan, implying only the acceleration of the privatization of the gigantic state economy sector. Proposals to reform welfare were inadequately articulated. The party was still dwindling between traditional and new references, with the further handicap of an insufficient theoretical elaboration by the renovators. Evidence of this imbalance comes from the evaluation of the democracy by the party's middle-level elites interviewed at the national congresses. The four items of the question concerning democracy are related to two different interpretations (Held 1994): the 'procedural' or liberal one (freedom, rules and constitutional guarantees), and the 'substantial' one (social justice and social rights). In the decade which goes from the last PCI congress (1990) to the last DS one (2001) an amazing stability in the middle-level elites' preferences emerges. More than half of the middle-level elites since 1990 (!) inclined to a liberal vision of democracy, and a sizeable minority indicated the substantial one, but the ratio between the two did not change much in ten years. Once liberal–democratic principles had been accepted, the party did not move along further.

A correlate of the PDS/DS' full acceptance of liberal democracy concerns adhesion to the market economy. While in 1990 the party documents still stigmatized the market and the private enterprise, the 1997 and 2000 party documents were quite unambiguous in their full acceptance. The 1997 party document stated, in fact:

> to free the capacity of individual entrepreneurality, to favour the creativity of the entrepreneurs, to develop a social market for health-care and welfare . . . are the bases of a reform of the welfare state and of a new relationship between citizens and the State.
>
> Documenti per il I congresso del PDS, Rome, 1997

Growth and development will be assured 'by the passage from a welfare of guarantees to welfare of opportunities'. The 2000 document was even more explicit and emphatic in exalting the virtues of free market. The same goes for the final document at the 2001 congress.

As for the party's middle-level elites, the reactions to this new profile are variegated. Again, since 1990, the market has been valued positively; but only after the 2001 electoral defeat did the middle-level elites abandon almost completely any diffidence toward the market, so that 85.6 per cent of those interviewed valued it in positive terms. But this 'pro-market' shift is only part of the story. The traditional Marxist interpretation of capitalism (exploitation of man by man), despite a sharp decline, is still shared by 59.6 per cent of the middle-level elites. This can be seen as a reaction to harsher and tenser labour relationships, just as the growing concern about unemployment (the highest since 1990) suggests a reaction to particularly difficult conditions in the job market and workers conditions. However this discontent with the market economy has not led to the revival of the ideal of workers' participation in the firm's management: only 43.1 per cent of the middle-level elites, less than half the level in 1990, still insist upon this goal. If we aggregate these items in two coherent sets of attitudes – pro-market and anti-market – the former gets almost half of the respondents while the latter around a quarter of them; the others represent mixed options (Bellucci *et al.* 2000: 145) However, analysing the change of the attitudes over time, in the two time points when the PDS/DS was in government (1997 and 2000), it appears that the middle-level elites have de-emphasized their pro-market convictions by eight percentage points, whereas the anti-market group have increased by four points. This shift highlights a certain difficulty in promoting inside the party the ever closer pro-market standing of the leadership stated in the official manifestos.

A more coherent picture emerges from another set of questions concerning, broadly speaking, civil rights issues. The question of citizens' rights represented a cornerstone in the ideological evolution from the PCI to the PDS (Ignazi 1992). The emphasis attributed to individual rights constituted a radical break with the communist tradition of social rights and class strife. That novelty was welcomed immediately by the party at the time: the 1990 survey confirmed this quite surprising support from middle-level elites (Ignazi 1991, 1992). In the years of PDS/DS participation in government, this set of attitudes has found a certain internal consistency. Two groups seem to emerge. The larger one could be defined 'liberal–secular' since it defends the secular profile of the state and advocates the full acknowledgement of civil rights, especially in the sexual and gender spheres. The other, smaller, group has a less definite profile: it combines more concern for 'traditional' issues concerning family values, censorship of pornography, and stricter rules for abortion, with post-materialist and pacifist attitudes. Comparing the 1997 and the 2000 surveys the trend displays a – rather limited – depression of the secular and liberal standings. It might be therefore argued that the participation in government has stimulated a more moderate set of attitudes within the party or even favoured the involvement of more 'traditional' constituencies. Even if it is difficult to find official statements in this direction, the centripetal drive implied by the party in government might have favoured this shift.

In conclusion, at the end of this journey around the PDS/DS in government, we can state that:

- The party was not rewarded by the polls as it lost votes in the 2001 general elections especially in its traditional strongholds (the 'red belt'); however its territorial distribution was not altered.
- The party lost its hold on the working class and also on the unionized working class; this decline was already in motion but it increased during the 1996–2001 legislature.
- The party reformed its internal organization along a network model which implied a federalization of its structure, the opening to non-party-members, the leader selection process via the local congresses, the return of the national executive countervailing the secretary's power which had increased in the previous years. Basically, the party attempted to introduce new mechanisms to improve internal participation and leaders' accountability; these mechanisms proved effective at the 2001 congress. The ongoing tendency toward professionalization and centralization was accelerated in the first part

of the legislature, especially with the premiership of Massimo D'Alema, but then it was soft-pedalled after D'Alema's resignation. In conclusion, the PDS-DS participation in government had a mixed impact on the internal organization.

- The party deradicalized its image since it redefined its location in the political spectrum as a centre-left party rather than a leftist party *tout court*.
- The party promoted some modifications in the party's ideological constellation especially concerning market economy and welfare; but this programmatic innovation promoted by the leadership and stated in the party manifestos was not completely absorbed by the party middle-level elites. They maintained the new set of values that the party had acquired during its transformation from PCI to PDS in 1990. After that radical change the party remained quite immune from further revisions. The experience in government did not further modify the party identity: on the contrary it constituted a dam against the recurring waves of change.

Newly governing parties of the centre-right

The League and *Forza Italia* (FI) are not as closely tied to previously existing organizations as in the case of the PDS/DS. Their leaderships (with a few exceptions in FI), and in good part their memberships, had not been formally affiliated with any of the established parties, although with their electoral successes they have subsequently acquired some of the personnel of those parties. Furthermore, they are both quite distinct from the parties they replaced in terms of ideology, discourse and organization, although they have both clearly inherited a substantial part of the electorate of the Christian Democrat-dominated governing coalitions. These two parties between them held just short of 35 per cent of the seats in the Lower House, and the majority of ministerial posts, in the 2001–6 legislature. Though both on the right of the political spectrum, and coalition partners in governments for almost six years, these two parties have very different origins, and their presence in government has had very different effects. This section focuses on the impact on these two parties of their period in office in 1994, and then in 2001–6. As in the previous case, we assess the consequences of office for electoral performance, party organization, and ideological/programmatic profile.

The electoral impact

The *Lega Nord* had been formally founded in 1991 through the federation of the various regional (northern) leagues that had flourished between the end of the 1980s and the beginning of the 1990s (Diamanti 1995, Biorcio 1997, Cento Bull 2002). The party won access to parliament with a resounding 8.6 per cent of the votes in 1992 (although the party's focus on the northern regions meant it won 17.3 per cent of the vote in the north and almost zero in the central south). After 1994, Berlusconi and his coalition allies spent a period of over six years in opposition. Berlusconi I was replaced by a caretaker administration supported by the centre-left, and in the 1996 elections, the *Lega* stood alone, causing the defeat of the Polo delle Libertà. The *Lega* did extraordinarily well in these elections, winning 10.1 per cent of the national vote (20.5 per cent in the north), and the remaining centre-right parties also did well, but their divisions were heavily penalized by the electoral system and the election was lost. The two parties therefore struck a deal for the regional elections of 2000, and in 2001 the *Lega* once again allied with Forza Italia and AN in the Casa delle Libertà.

The 2001 elections demonstrated the potential costs for the *Lega* of a strategy of government participation. Whereas in 1996 the party had approached the election with fiery rhetoric and a series of stunts designed to whip up support for the separation of the north from the Italian state, in 2001 the *Lega* had to adapt its message to fit in with the objective of the centre-right coalition to win a parliamentary majority and govern for a full legislature. In these circumstances the *Lega* clearly lost out to Forza Italia, winning just 3.9 per cent of the vote, whilst Berlusconi's party increased its share significantly. It could be argued that the *Lega* paid the price of its office-seeking strategy in votes lost to FI; however, the 2006 elections, held under a new electoral system based on proportional representation, gave the *Lega* a better performance, with 4.6 per cent. On the whole though, the party's best electoral performances – in 1992 and 1996 – have come when it has presented itself as a protest party outside and against the existing political system. Involvement with government has had a substantial electoral cost, almost certainly related to the difficulties for the *Lega* of implementing its formal programmatic goals with a centre-right coalition committed to the unity of the Italian state.

Forza Italia has also seen fluctuations in its electoral support consistent with the hypothesis of government experience proving particularly costly for new parties. Entering the political stage with a spectacular 21 per cent of the vote in the earthquake elections of 1994, FI polled a disappointing 20.8 per cent two years later, after a chaotic and short-lived experience at the heart of government in 1994. Correspondingly, the party's best performance to date came in 2001, after over six years in opposition, when its 29.4 per cent made it Italy's biggest party by some distance. After five years in government with the party leader as prime minister, this has fallen to just 23.7 per cent. These results can be interpreted in terms of voter disappointment as the mismatch between the party's eloquent promises during election campaigns and the more prosaic reality of its achievements in government. However, *Forza Italia* remains, unlike the *Lega*, a party with a clear governing vocation, which would lead us to expect the electoral costs of government incumbency to be lower.

The organizational impact

The nature of the two party organizations assessed here could hardly be more different. Whereas the *Lega* built a relatively strong and dynamic organization based on highly committed voluntary activists (Cento Bull and Gilbert 2001: 12–13), FI had no mass base at all to speak of when it won the 1994 elections. Instead,

FI was articulated by the territorial offices of Berlusconi's business empire, in particular, his TV advertising company Publitalia 80 (Farrell 1995). Regional Publitalia bosses screened and chose the party candidates and coordinated their election campaigns. Although a move was made to develop a kind of mass organization – in the form of the *Forza Italia* 'clubs' – this organization was kept formally separate from the party itself, and hastily abandoned after the 1994 elections. Although the party's disastrous showing in its first local elections convinced Berlusconi that some kind of mass organization was needed (Paolucci 1999), the mass membership has no formal capacity to influence central party policy, which remains in the hands of an unelected clique of Berlusconi's closest allies (for an account of the party statutes, see Poli 2001: ch. 6). The party's political campaigning rests very heavily on the use of Fininvest resources, most importantly its TV stations, but also its marketing and advertising arms.

These characteristics have led to descriptions of FI as a 'partito-azienda' or 'business firm party' (Diamanti 1995, Hopkin and Paolucci 1999). In its initial phase, there was not a clear dividing line between *Forza Italia* the party and Fininvest the corporation. Regional managers of Publitalia become regional organizers of FI (some of them remaining in position for several years); Fininvest TV channels faithfully broadcast the party's electoral propaganda even in the most unlikely formats (game shows etc.); and of course, the head of Fininvest was the undisputed leader of the party. Realization that some kind of more solid territorial presence was necessary has led to an attenuation of these characteristics over the decade of the party's existence. To a considerable extent, this has involved the 'recycling' of local elite groups previously to be found within the DC and PSI (Diamanti 2003); this is the case for areas such as Sicily (where a clientelistically mobilized 'captive' vote allowed the right alliance to win all 61 constituency seats in the 2001 elections) or Liguria. However in other areas where FI has a weaker electoral base (such as Emilia-Romagna) the party organization is almost non-existent. Given the weakness of the party apparatus, government power represents an opportunity to strengthen the party organization by attracting new members through patronage. Unlike the *Lega*, which has the option of reverting to anti-government protest from its Alpine heartlands, *Forza Italia* makes little sense as a protest party alone. This territorial presence has often drawn on the 'traditional' clientelistic practices of electoral mobilization, most obviously in Sicily. This suggests that the party could institutionalize along the lines of a modernized clientelist party model, distributing 'club goods' to identifiable electoral clienteles. A lengthy spell of government office is crucial to this kind of organizational strategy, suggesting that FI has benefited in these terms from its long period in government.

In the case of the *Lega*, the consequences of government participation are far less clear. Although there is relatively little secondary literature available on which to base the analysis, the *Lega* seems to come much closer than the other new parties to a traditional 'mass party' model, with an activist base capable of acting as a transmission belt between the party and its electorate, at least in those areas where the *Lega* is well entrenched. Mass participation events (although on a smaller scale than the classic mass party), such as the annual festival at Pontida, and mock referenda for the independence of Padania organized by party members, give the *Lega* a stronger link with its core electorate than for many other Italian parties. However, the demagogic and extremist tone of many party activities also entrench the *Lega*'s image as a protest party, an image which creates immediate problems when the party enters the government. Ultimately, the tensions between participation in a coalition government and maintaining a party activist base committed to radical and probably unrealistic goals has tended to be resolved in favour of the latter.

Party de-radicalization and ideological change

A reasonable expectation, apparently confirmed by the PDS/DS case, is that government participation is likely to curb ideological radicalism and instill a more pragmatic approach in new parties. The case of new parties on the Italian centre-right, however, does not lend strong support to this argument. Neither the *Lega* nor FI have taken clear steps towards more moderate policy proposals and discourses, although they accepted the need to compromise on policy while governing in coalition in the 2001–6 legislature.

The *Lega*, the most radical of the two, has its origin in several independent movements which expressed sentiments of cultural, linguistic and ethnoregional identity (see Diamanti 1993: ch. 3). Most prominent of these was the *Liga Veneta*, which built on a long tradition of Venetian historical and linguistic identity. As the movements grew, it was recognized that such particularist claims would be a brake on electoral growth, and under the leadership of Umberto Bossi of the Lombardy League, a process of unification took place leading to the formation of the Northern League. This unification diluted the ethnic and linguistic identity of the Leagues, and replaced it with a much broader identification with the 'north'[4] (later christened Padania) which made little sense in terms of any ethnic identity. As a result, the League cannot be considered a genuine 'peripheral nationalist' movement along the lines of the Basque or Catalan parties in Spain. However the lack of a coherent national identity has not prevented the party from regularly proposing the break-up of the Italian state and rejecting symbols of Italian unity, such as the tricolour flag.

In practice, this anti-Italian rhetoric has co-existed with the party's choice to participate in the state institutions in Rome and take part in government coalitions with parties based largely in the south (AN) and which identify themselves with the legacy of the DC (CCD-UDC, and indeed to an extent *Forza Italia*). There is also a degree of pragmatism in the way in which northern grievances have been addressed by the party, with regular changes of position from a 'tripartite' federalism, to outright secession, through to 'devolution'. The party's commitment to a greater fiscal decentralization through the devolution of powers over the education and healthcare systems to the Italian regions can be seen as a pragmatic strategy to maximize the advantage to its electoral heartlands within a coalition largely opposed to any fundamental territorial reform of the Italian state. This project emerged from an agreement with Berlusconi that the centre-right government would introduce decentralizing reforms to strengthen the north's fiscal autonomy (Loiero 2003: ch. 3). This agreement proved robust, with the League and *Forza Italia* establishing a very stable pattern of cooperation in 2001–6. The *Lega*'s public attitude to government participation – sharing power with the 'Fascists' of AN and the corrupt, pro-south UDC – was that it is a necessary evil, the only way to achieve a federal reform which will give the north the power to govern itself (see Vandelli 2002: ch. 2).

The *Lega* is rather more consistent about the social groups it aims to represent, and the broad political and economic grievances it expresses. The slogan '*Roma ladrona*' (thieving Rome) captures the essence of the League's message at its simplest. Rome, the capital city and seat of the national government, steals and wastes the money of ordinary hard-working citizens. The social groups the League seeks to represent are those most intolerant of the burden of taxation placed on productive activity in Italy: the owners and employees of small and medium-sized businesses (which are disproportionately numerous in the north-east), and the self-employed. The League articulates the frustration felt by these sectors at what they perceived to be an onerous burden of taxation, and at the waste of public money, which had undeniably in part been used by political leaders – either through patronage and clientelism, or through outright corruption – to buy electoral support and sustain expensive electoral machines. The *Lega* has therefore emphasized lower taxes, a position shared by Berlusconi and *Forza Italia*, and indeed many mainstream centre-right parties. Where the party parts company with mainstream conservatism is its demagogic approach to the international economy: whilst in the early 1990s the League mobilized support around the need to reform economic policy in order to help Italy meet the Maastricht criteria, once the Euro was actually adopted the League began to adopt a clearly Eurosceptic discourse, and more recently it has begun to advocate protectionist measures to safeguard Italian business against Chinese competition. So even though the League has an identifiable social base with reasonably coherent economic interests, this has not prevented frequent recourse to an essentially oppositional and demagogical political message, in part anti-statist in its appeal for lower taxes and less regulation, in part statist in its demands for protectionism.

The case of *Forza Italia* differs in that Berlusconi's party is not wedded to any clear ideological or programmatic goal, and certainly nothing so implausible as the dismantling of the Italian state. FI is a very different party from the League in a number of ways, although it shares with the League a strong populistic, even demagogical, tendency in its political discourse. Its origins and organization are very different and the governing experience presents FI with as many opportunities as constraints.

Whereas the League was the product of the growing dissatisfaction and anger with the existing political system amongst well defined social groups in northern Italy, FI was only founded after the collapse of the DC-dominated party system. The formation of FI can be seen as an emergency response to the collapse of the DC-PSI governing arrangement. The prospect in 1992–93 of a left-wing government, which alarmed many on the centre and right in Italy, and the effective disappearance of the DC and PSI, left the conservative electorate without a strong anti-left alternative for which to vote. The prospect alarmed Silvio Berlusconi even more. His business interests were heavily dependent on the political backing of the DC and PSI elites, and their disappearance left him exposed at a particularly difficult juncture for his Fininvest corporation. Without the protection of these political sponsors, Berlusconi ran the risk that his political adversaries would pass an anti-trust law which would result in expropriation of some of his TV interests, which would have serious ramifications for Fininvest as a whole.

FI is therefore neither a 'mobilizer' nor a 'challenger' (Rochon 1985); instead it is in many respects a 'substitute' party for the DC and PSI, and access to government protection and patronage is a key part of the rationale for FI's creation. FI is therefore very much a party that seeks to govern, and does not suffer the temptation to retreat to the opposition that can affect a movement such as the *Lega*. However, being in government also poses difficulties. FI's political message to mobilize the vote has been dominated by a negative message – anti-communism – which is of little use in guiding government policy. To the extent that FI has had a positive message, it is a set of unrealistic promises on valence issues: a 'new Italian miracle' of economic progress. Such a message is much easier to sell in opposition than in government.

From the point of view of its ostensible political programme, *Forza Italia*'s performance in government is in large part typical of the difficulties faced by all populist parties once they reach government. Its clear failure to deliver an economic 'miracle' – Italy's growth rate during the second Berlusconi government was even lower than under the centre-left – bears a close resemblance to the difficulties faced by populists such as Haider or the followers of Fortuyn when they won power: like them, FI promised a quick solution to a much broader, and therefore all the more intractable, problem.

There are two reasons why FI's programme was bound to disappoint. First, in order to ensure electoral success, it was hyperbolic in its promises. Instead of promising specific economic reforms which might help Italy to grow, Berlusconi committed himself explicitly to swingeing tax cuts which in the current European economic context could not possibly be sustainable, and also (even more imprecisely) promised a transformation of Italy's economic performance analogous with the country's remarkable development in the immediate post-war period. In short, whilst in opposition, FI garnered support by blaming all of Italy's many and well-entrenched problems on the ineptness of its political opponents and assuring voters that Berlusconi's managerial talent would succeed where others had failed. Once in government, Berlusconi's inability to live up to these high expectations undermined his credibility. FI's response to these difficulties in part revolved around a well-honed redistributive strategy aimed at shoring up support amongst the traditional support base of the Italian centre-right. One example of this is the second Berlusconi government's generous distribution of informal and ad hoc tax breaks to groups such as the self-employed, small business and small retailers (De Cecco 1994), a group which is much larger as a proportion of the working population in Italy than in other Western countries. Although this kind of strategy is increasingly difficult in an age of 'permanent austerity' (Pierson 1998) and external budgetary constraints, in combination with Berlusconi's media resources it offers FI a fallback position when the flamboyant rhetoric of election campaigns encounters the reality of Italy's deep-seated economic and social problems. Although this suggests that FI is adapting pragmatically to the opportunities and constraints of government, there is relatively little evidence of any toning down of the oppositional rhetoric typical of new parties. After the centre-right's narrow defeat in the 2006 election, Berlusconi failed to acknowledge the official election results and set out to undermine the legitimacy of the new centre-left government, suggesting an attachment to aggressive and demagogical campaigning characteristic of new oppositional and protest parties.

Conclusion

In very different ways, the *Lega* and *Forza Italia* provide clear indications of the difficulties facing new parties in government. These difficulties, for the most part, stem from the essentially oppositional, and usually populist, strategies for electoral mobilization that new parties adopt. Such messages play well in opposition, but are quickly exposed as unrealistic and impracticable once these parties are called to take up government responsibilities. As a result, 'success in opposition, failure in government' (Heinisch 2003) is a common pattern. The case of the PDS/DS suggests opposite conclusions: a party moulded from a more radical predecessor adapted itself to government by removing the most contentious elements of its ideological and programmatic identity and firmly establishing itself in the mainstream. All of these parties seem to have suffered electoral costs as a result of their government experience, suggesting that a return to 'outsider' politics could be a fruitful strategy. However the *Lega* is in a rather different situation to FI and PDS/DS, unwilling to abandon its 'protest party' status. Both FI and PDS/DS have taken on the role of articulating potential governing coalitions around them, with consequences for their electoral base – which has come under pressure after governing experiences – and their ideological identity, which has become more mainstream and pragmatic after periods in office (rather more in the case of the PDS/DS than in that of FI). As a tentative conclusion, it can be argued that involvement in government does not produce a predictable response, but it does force new parties to make a choice about whether to enter the mainstream of party politics, or whether to remain outside, shouting from the sidelines.

Notes

1 This chapter is jointly authored. The authors' names appear in alphabetical order.
2 Or, alternatively, most new parties in Western Europe have been 'mobilizers' rather than 'challengers' (Rochon 1985).
3 To be more precise, FI and the League stood together in the north as the *Polo delle Libertà*, whilst FI and AN stood together in the centre and south as the *Polo del Buongoverno*. The coalition also included other smaller parties, most notably a group of conservative Christian Democrats, the CCD.

4 The 'north' includes all the regions from the Po valley upwards: the original north-eastern regions, plus the north-west (Val d'Aosta, Lombardy, Piedmont and Liguria), and the central northern region of Emilia-Romagna (where the League's support is minimal). At some points in its development the League also won a little support in Tuscany. However, the League's inability to penetrate Emilia-Romagna and Tuscany implies that the 'north' stops more or less at the river Po itself. This vagueness over boundaries confirms that the League lacks a clear idea of the confines of its ethnic and territorial identity.

Bibliography

Accornero, A., Mannheimer, R., Sebastiani, C. and CESPE (1983) *L'identità Comunista*, Milan: Feltrinelli.

Baccetti, C. (1997) *Il Pds*, Bologna: Il Mulino.

Barbacetto, G., Gomez, P. and Travaglio, M. (2002) *Mani Pulite: La Vera Storia*, Rome: Editori Riuniti.

Bardi, L. (2002) 'Italian parties: change and functionality', in P. Webb, D. Farrell and I. Holliday (eds) *Political Parties in Advanced Industrial Democracies*, Oxford: Oxford University Press.

Bardi, L. and Morlino, L. (1994) 'Italy: tracing the roots of the great transformation', in R.S. Katz and P. Mair (eds) *How Parties Organize: Change and Adaptation in Party Organizations in Western Democracies*, London: Sage, pp. 242–77.

Bardi, L. and Ignazi, P. (1998) 'The Italian party system: the effective magnitude of an earthquake', in P. Ignazi and C. Ysmal (eds) *The Organization of Political Parties in Southern Europe*, Westport: Praeger, pp. 91–109.

Bartolini, S. and Mair, P. (1990) *Identity, Competition and Electoral Availability: The Stabilization of European Electorates 1885–1985*, Cambridge: Cambridge University Press.

Bellucci, P. and Segatti, P. (2002) 'Le risorse di un leader della sinistra: il caso Cofferati', *Il Mulino*, 403: 911–15.

Bellucci, P., Maraffi, M. and Segatti, P. (2000) *PCI, PDS, DS*, Milano: Donzelli.

Betz, H.-G. (1993) 'The new politics of resentment: radical right-wing populist parties in Western Europe', *Comparative Politics*, 25: 413–27.

Betz, H.-G. (1994) *Radical Right-Wing Populism in Western Europe*, Basingstoke: Macmillan.

Biorcio, R. (1997) *La Padania Promessa*, Milan: Il Saggiatore.

Biorcio, R. (2002) '*Forza Italia* and the parties of the centre-right', in J. Newell (ed.) *The Italian General Election of 2001*, Manchester: Manchester University Press, pp. 88–104.

Bufacchi, V. and Burgess, S. (2001) *Italy Since 1989: Events and Interpretations*, 2nd edn, Basingstoke: Macmillan.

Burnett, S. and Mantovani, L. (1998) *The Italian Guillotine: Operation Clean Hands and the Overthrow of Italy's First Republic*, Lanham, MA: Rowman and Littlefield.

Cento Bull, A. and Gilbert, M. (2001) *The Lega Nord and the Northern Question in Italian Politics*, London: Palgrave.

Cento Bull, A. (2002) 'Towards a federal state? Competing proposals for a revision of the constitution and the institutional referendum of 7 October 2001', in P. Bellucci and M. Bull (eds) *Politics in Italy*, Oxford: Berghahn Books.

Cotta, M. and Verzichelli, L. (1996) 'La chasse politica italiana: cronaca di una morte annunciata?', in M. Cotta and P. Isernia (eds), *Il gigante dai piedi di argilla: Le ragioni della crisi della prima republica*, Bologna: Il Mulino.

De Cecco, M. (1994) 'L'economia italiana e la tempesta perfetta', *La Repubblica Affari e Finanza* 22 March 2004, p. 7.

Diamanti, I. (1993) *La Lega: Geografia, Storia e Sociologia di un Nuovo Soggetto Politico*, Rome: Donzelli.

Diamanti, I. (1995) 'Partiti e modelli', *Almanacco di Politica ed Economia* January: 71–81.

Diamanti, I. (2003) *Bianco, Rosso, Verde . . . e Azzurro: Mappe e Colori dell'Italia Politica*, Bologna: Il Mulino (2003).

Farrell, J. (1995) 'Berlusconi and *Forza Italia*: new force for old?', *Modern Italy*, 1: 40–52.

Galli, G. (1966) *Il bipartitismo imperfetto: comunisti e democristiani in Italia*, Bologna: Il Mulino.

Galli, G. (1972) *Il difficile governo*, Bologna: Il Mulino.

Gilbert, M. (1996) 'L'Ulivo e la quercia', in M. Caciagli and D.I. Kertzer (eds) *Politica in Italia 96*, Bologna: Il Mulino, pp. 121–38.

Gold, T. (2003) *The Lega Nord and Contemporary Politics in Italy*, New York: Palgrave.

Gundle, S. and Parker, S. (eds) (1996) *The New Italian Republic: From the Fall of the Berlin Wall to Berlusconi*, London: Routledge.

Heinisch, R. (2003) 'Success in opposition, failure in government: explaining the performance of right-wing populist parties in public office', *West European Politics*, 26: 91–130.

Held, D. (1994) *Modelli di Democrazia*, Bologna: Il Mulino.

Hopkin, J. (2003) 'Political entrepreneurship or predatory rule? Party formation and the case of *Forza Italia*', paper presented at the annual meeting of the Società Italiana di Scienza Politica, University of Trento, 14–16 September.

Hopkin, J. and Paolucci, C. (1999) 'New parties and the business firm model of party organization: cases from Spain and Italy', *European Journal of Political Research*, 35: 307–39.

Ignagi, P. (1991) 'Attori e valori nella trasformazione del PCI', *Revista Italiana di Scienza Politica*, 21: 523–49

Ignazi, P. (1992) *Dal PCI al PDS*, Bologna: Il Mulino.

Ignazi, P. (1997) 'Il PDS, l'Ulivo e il governo', *Il Mulino*, 370: pp. 252–60.

Ignazi, P. (2002) *Il Potere dei Partiti: la Politica in Italia dagli Anni Sessanta ad Oggi*, Roma-Bari: Laterza.

ITANES (2001) *Perché ha Vinto il Centro-Destra*, Bologna: Il Mulino. Available at: http://sda.berkeley.edu.7502/cattaneo.html

Katz, R.and Mair, P. (1995) 'Changing models of party organisation and party democracy: the emergence of the cartel party', *Party Politics*, 1: 5–28.

Kitschelt, H. (1988) 'Left-libertarian parties: explaining innovation in competitive systems', *World Politics*, 15: 194–234.

Kitschelt, H. (1989) *The Logics of Party Formation*, Ithaca, NY: Cornell University Press.

Loiero, A. (2003) *Il patto di ferro*, Rome: Donzelli.

Lucardie, P. (2000) 'Prophets, purifiers and prolocutors: towards a theory on the emergence of new parties', *Party Politics*, 6: 175–85.

Mair, P. (2002) 'In the aggregate: mass electoral behaviour in Western Europe, 1950–2000', in Hans Keman (ed) *Comparative Democratic Politics*, London: Sage, pp. 122–40.

Morlino, L. (1996) 'Crisis of parties and change of the party system in Italy', *Party Politics* 2: 5–30.

Newell, J. (2000) *Parties and Democracy in Italy*, Aldershot: Ashgate.

Paolucci, C. (1999) '*Forza Italia* a livello locale: un marchio in franchising?', *Rivista Italiana di Scienza Politica*, 29(3): 481–516.

Pierson, P. (1998) 'Irresistible forces, immovable objects: post-industrial welfare states confront permanent austerity', *Journal of European Public Policy*, 5: 539–60.

Poli, E. (2001) *Forza Italia*, Bologna: Il Mulino.

Rochon, T. (1985) 'Mobilizers and challengers: towards a theory of new party success', *International Political Science Review*, 6: 419–39.

Sivini, G. (1971) *Sociologia dei Partiti Politici*, Bologna: Il Mulino.

Vandelli, L. (2002) *Devolution e Altre Storie: Paradossi, Ambiguità e Rischi di un Progetto Politico*, Bologna: Il Mulino.

Vespa, B. (2001) *Scontro Finale: Ultimo Atto*, Milan: Mondadori.

Vignati, R. (1998) 'Il leader e il partito: Il PDS dopo il II congresso', in L. Bardi and M. Rhodes (eds) *Politica in Italia 98*, Bologna: Il Mulino, pp. 87–108.

Willey, J. (1998) 'Institutional arrangements and the success of new parties in old democracies', in R. Hofferbert (ed.) *Parties and Democracy*, Oxford: Blackwell, pp. 229–46.

4 The short road to power – and the long way back

Newly governing parties in the Netherlands

Paul Lucardie and Christian Pierre Ghillebaert

Introduction

The Dutch political system has been relatively kind to new parties. Even if we use a rather strict definition – a new party has to start from scratch, building an organisation, developing a (more or less ideological) project and conquering a niche in the party system – then we find eighteen new parties gaining seats in Dutch parliament from 1946 to 2006. Mergers of established parties or transformations of old parties do not meet these requirements, but a breakaway or split from an established party does qualify, as other political scientists agree (Hug 2000; Ignazi 1996). Ten of the new parties broke away from an established party; eight were founded without any direct connection with existing parties. Two of each category joined a government coalition.

The relative success of new parties can be attributed to the electoral system as well as to the complicated cleavage structure of the Dutch party system. The electoral system in the Netherlands is a pure example of proportional representation: seats in the lower house of parliament (*Tweede Kamer*) are distributed to parties according to the votes they won in the whole country. The country is divided into 19 electoral districts for administrative purposes only. As the lower house contains 150 seats, a party needs only 0.67 per cent of the popular vote (at present about 60,000 votes) to obtain a seat. There is no legal threshold (as exists in, for example, Germany, Denmark and Austria).

Even before the introduction of proportional representation in 1918, the Dutch party system was rather fragmented. Almost every religious denomination and every social class produced, as it were, its own political party. Catholics supported the Catholic party (since 1946 named the Catholic People's Party: *Katholieke Volkspartij*, KVP), while Calvinists founded the Anti-Revolutionary Party (ARP, *Anti-Revolutionaire Partij*) and later the Christian Historical Union (CHU, *Christelijk-Historische Unie*). Secular workers would vote for the Social Democrats (since 1946 the Labour Party: *Partij van de Arbeid*, PvdA) or the Communists, while the secular middle classes tended to support one of the competing liberal parties. In recent years competition has tended to be fairly open and centripetal most of the time. Ideological distances between the main parties are limited – at least on the dominant socio-economic dimension; to a lesser extent on the cultural–religious dimension (Andeweg and Irwin 2005: 57–62, 100–5). In spite of secularisation, the party system could still be considered tripolar. One pole comprises the Christian Democratic party (CDA, *Christen Democratisch Appèl*) – resulting from a merger between ARP, CHU and KVP – and the smaller Protestant parties. The other two poles are the Dutch Labour party PvdA – followed by the Green Left and the more radical Socialist Party – and the Liberal Party VVD (*Volkspartij voor Vrijheid en Democratie*). True to Dutch consociationalism, all three major parties, CDA, PvdA and VVD, are willing to join coalitions – though 'purple coalitions' between PvdA and VVD governed only between 1994 and 2002.

In this chapter we will focus on the four parties that participated in a government: Democrats 66 (D66, *Democraten 66*), the Radical Party (PPR, *Politieke Partij Radikalen*), Democratic Socialists '70 (DS'70, *Democratisch Socialisten '70*) and the List Pim Fortuyn (LPF, *Lijst Pim Fortuyn*).

What distinguished these four parties from the other fourteen that never left the opposition benches? Probably four features. In the first place, parties that took part in government adhered to a mainstream ideology, even if they advocated a more extreme variety than established parties. In the second place, they aggregated a broad range of interests instead of concentrating on one particular group such as farmers or senior citizens. Thirdly, they were not too small: with less than six seats (out of 150), a new party will probably never be asked to nominate a minister, no matter what its political project. A fourth factor might be summed up as the political opportunity structure, the configuration of power or political contingencies; do established parties need the newcomer to form a majority, and under what conditions? In 1989 D66 won twelve seats yet remained in the opposition; in 2003 it obtained only six seats but joined the government – mainly because the Christian Democrats and Liberals needed a partner close to the political centre.

Government participation and ideological change

Do new parties adapt their ideology once they take part in government (in a more pragmatic, 'realistic' direction)? Ideology is here used in a rather broad sense: a more or less coherent set of beliefs about state and society. Some parties refer explicitly to a comprehensive ideology, as in the case of a party that calls itself Liberal or Communist. Other parties combine elements from different ideologies while proclaiming to be 'pragmatic' or 'realistic'.

In this sense, the ideologies of D66, PPR, DS'70 and LPF will be analysed briefly here, before and after they participated in government.

D66: Liberals coming out of the closet

Democrats 66 (D66) was founded in 1966 by young intellectuals from different political backgrounds, united only by a common political project (Gruijters 1967; Godschalk 1970; Van der Land 2003: 19–34). This project entailed reforming the elitist and consociational Dutch political system in a radical democratic direction.

Surprisingly, it won seven seats in the parliamentary elections of 1967, less than a year after it had been founded. Its sudden success could be attributed to several factors: the charisma of its political leader, the journalist Hans van Mierlo; the favourable publicity, partly arranged by Van Mierlo and his colleagues; but also to its political project. In 1967 all three factors may have reinforced each other; seven years later they had lost much of their vigour and D66 almost disbanded; yet it recovered with a new leader and (partly) new issues, such as the environment. In the 1980s it repeated this cycle: success in 1981, followed by defeat, crisis, and rebirth under a new leader – in fact Van Mierlo again. In 1994 it broke all records, winning 24 seats and a central position in the new government – until the next crisis occurred with Van Mierlo's retirement and substantial electoral losses in 1998 and 2002 (Table 4.1). Even so, the party continued to take part in government until 2002 and again from 2003 to 2006.

The founders of D66 wanted to be modern and 'pragmatic'. They regarded ideologies as outdated obstacles on the road to progress. Unlike other Dutch parties, D66 did not adopt a declaration of principles. Yet it did cherish principles (called *actiebeginselen* or *uitgangspunten*), which were articulated in election platforms and more elaborate 'policy programmes' (*beleidsprogramma's*): democracy, individual freedom, autonomy and personal development, equality and tolerance (D66 1979: 3–5). In the eyes of many observers, as well as some party members, the Democrats were social liberals, combining liberal and social-democratic ideas (Van Doorn 1994; Lucardie and Voerman 2001). What distinguished the Democrats most clearly from other parties, however, was not so much their mixture of social–democratic and liberal ideas, but their pursuit of radical democracy, in the political system as well as in society at large – and in their own party (Wagenveld 1999). One could consider this democratic radicalism or republicanism an ideology, too, even if not a full-fledged one. Unlike socialism and liberalism (but like conservatism), radicalism does not contain clear ideas about social and economic policies. It does chime in with a certain view of man (and woman) as a rational, autonomous individual embedded in a (voluntary) community. 'Let the people decide' applies to the collective as well as to the individual level. Thus individuals should be free to use drugs, buy pornography, procure euthanasia, or to have an abortion or a divorce. As a collective, the people should be able to elect their representatives and leaders; not indirectly, with party elites acting as powerful intermediaries, as was (and is) the case in the Netherlands, but directly. In other words, the voters should elect a prime minister as well as a member of parliament (in their district), and a mayor in their city. These demands distinguish D66 from other parties, even if some have been taken up later by PvdA, PPR, Green Left and LPF.

One way to answer the question of whether D66 softened its ideology before or after entering government is to investigate if subsequent party programmes contain these demands for democratic reforms and individual autonomy or moral freedom in a pure form, in a diluted (compromised) form or not at all (Table 4.2). No significant differences were found between the election platforms of 1967 and 1971. In the anticipated elections of 1972, D66 presented a common platform

Table 4.1 Dutch election results: distribution of seats (1946–2003)

(a) 1946–67

Party	1946	1948	1952	1956	1959	1963	1967
KVP	**32**	**32**	**30**	**49**	**49**	**50**	**42**
ARP	13	13	12	**15**	**14**	**13**	**15**
CHU	8	9	9	**13**	**12**	**13**	**12**
CDA							
SGP	2	2	2	3	3	3	3
PvdA	**29**	27	**30**	**50**	48	43	37
CPN	10	8	6	7	3	4	5
VVD	**6ᵃ**	**8**	9	13	**19**	**16**	**17**
KNP		1	2				
GPV						1	1
PSP					2	4	4
BP						3	7
D66							7
Total	100	100	100	150	150	150	150

Notes

Figures printed in **bold** indicate that the party joined the government in this year.

a In 1946 the Party of Freedom (*Partij van de Vrijheid*)

(b) 1971–2003

Party	1971	1972	1977	1981	1982	1986	1989	1994	1998	2002	2003
KVP	35	27									
ARP	13	14									
CHU	10	7									
CDA			**49ᵃ**	48	45	54	54	34	29	43	44
SGP	3	3	3	3	3	3	3	2	3	2	2

PvdA	39	43	53	44	47	52	49	37	45	23	42
CPN	6	7	2	3	3						
VVD	16	22	28	26	36	27	22	31	38	24	28
KNP											
GPV	2	2	1	1	1	1	2	2	2		
PSP	2	2	1	3	3	1					
BP	1	3	1								
D66	11	6	8	17	6	9	12	24	14	7	6
PPR	2	7	3	3	2	2					
DS'70	8	6	1								
NMP	2										
RKPN		1									
RPF				2	2	1	1	3	3		
EVP					1						
CP					1						
GL							6[b]	5	11	10	8
CD							1	3			
SP								2	5	9	9
AOV								6			
U 55+								1			
CU										4[c]	3
LN										2	
LPF										26	8
Total	150	150	150	150	150	150	150	150	150	150	150

Source: H. Daalder et al. (eds) *Compendium politiek en samenleving in Nederland*. Deventer: Kluwer 2003, A0600-32.

Notes

Figures printed in **bold** indicate that the party joined the government in this year.

a Merger of ARP, CHU and KVP
b Merger of CPN, EVP, PPR and PSP
c Confederation of GPV and RPF

Table 4.2 Participation in government and ideological 'softening' or 'toughening' of D66
on relevant issues (1966–2003)

Election	Government (G) or Opposition (O)	Elect prime minister	Electoral reform	Elect mayor	Referendum	Moral issues[a]
1967	O	+	+	+	0	+
1971	O	+	+	+	–	+
1972[b]	G	+	+	+	0	+
1977	O	–	0	–	–	+
1981	G	–	–	–	–	+
1982	O	–	–	–	0	+
1986	O	0	+	0	+	0
1989	O	+	+	0	+	+
1994	G	+	+	+	+	+
1998	G	+	0	+	+	–
2002	O	+	+	+	+	+
2003	G	+	+	+	+	+

Source: Election platforms D66 1967–2003

Notes
a In 1967 and 1971: facilitate divorce, abolish censorship, allow contraceptives; from 1977 to 1982:
   allow abortion; from 1977 to 2003: legalize soft drugs; from 1981 to 1998: legalise euthanasia.
b Common platform of D66, PvdA and PPR
+ Tough: clear-cut position in favour of reforms
0 Ambiguous position, compromise, deferment of reforms
– Soft: the issue is ignored or the position reversed, reforms are rejected

Note on method
This table is based on a rough analysis of party programmes; coding not sentences (as in the
Comparative Manifesto Project) but issue positions. This method is obviously less rigorously
quantifiable and less reliable, less time-consuming but possibly as valid, at least with respect to
parties that advocate clear positions on the issues they own (or try to own).

with PvdA and PPR. Of course it had to make compromises now, but not on
constitutional reforms or on moral issues (D66, PvdA and PPR 1972). This can be
attributed not only to clever negotiations, but also to the sympathy among many
radicals and social democrats for democratic radicalism. However, in spite of this
support and the leading role of the three parties in the government that was constituted after the elections, the political reform proposals were not implemented.
After all, the three parties failed to muster a majority in parliament, let alone the
two-thirds majority required for constitutional changes.

Partly due to this frustrating experience in government, D66 did not articulate
constitutional demands in its election platform of 1977, though it still favoured a
different electoral system: 'In view of the defeat of recent government proposals
to reform the electoral system, it is useless to give any priority to this issue now'
(D66 1977: 19). With respect to moral issues, the 1977 platform seemed as radical
as the preceding ones: women should be able to decide on abortion; the use of
drugs should no longer be punished. In the policy programme that was adopted a
little later, the Democrats continued to argue for a more democratic society and

polity, involving citizens in decision-making. But they failed to specify this; the programme did not even contain a chapter on constitutional questions or political reforms (D66 1979: 3–5, 11). Therefore, one might be tempted to conclude that D66 did soften its ideology, at least with respect to the political system, after it had joined a government in 1973. Yet as important as participation in government may have been the change in leadership. The democratic radical Van Mierlo was replaced by Terlouw, who identified much more with liberalism, albeit a 'post-socialist liberalism' that would accept the socialist contribution to the welfare state (Van der Land 2003: 114–21, 141). In the eyes of the voters, the party moved a little closer to the centre (Van der Eijk and Niemöller 1983: 249–50).

By way of epilogue, we have to add that the ideological 'softening' of 1977 proved temporary. In 1985 Van Mierlo returned as leader of the party and inspired a return to the radical–democratic roots (Table 4.3). When he retired again in 1998 – this time because of old age – his successors accepted his legacy and continued to press for democratic reforms, so far, however, without much success. Only with respect to moral issues did D66 prove successful: abortion had been legalized in the 1980s, euthanasia was practically legalized in 2000. The programme of 2002 contained all the classical constitutional demands – election of the prime minister and of mayors, introduction of a referendum and a citizen's initiative. It had even

Table 4.3 Participation in government and ideological 'softening' or 'toughening' of PPR on relevant issues (1968–89)

Election platform	Government (G) or Opposition (O)	Economic democracy	State planning	Basic Income	NATO exit	Nuclear power	Elect mayor by council
1968[a]	O	+	−	−	−	−	+
1971	O	+	0	−	0	−	0
1972[b]	G	+	+	−	0	+	+
1977	O	+	+	+	+	+	+
1981	O	+	+	+	+	+	+
1986	O	+	0	+	0	+	+
1989[c]	O	+	0	+	0	+	0

Source: Election (draft) platforms PPR 1968–1989

Notes
a Strictly speaking not an election platform, but a manifesto voted at the founding congress.
b A draft platform, the official programme was *Keerpunt*, the common platform of D66, PvdA and PPR.
c A draft platform, before the common platform of GreenLeft was approved.
+ Tough: clear-cut position in favour of reforms.
0 Ambiguous position, compromise, deferment of reforms.
− Soft: the issue is ignored or the position reversed, reforms are rejected.

Note on method
This table is based on a rough analysis of party programmes; coding not sentences (as in the Comparative Manifesto Project) but issue positions. This method is obviously less rigorously quantifiable and less reliable, less time-consuming but possibly as valid, at least with respect to parties that advocate clear positions on the issues they own (or try to own).

revived the call for a different electoral system. Individual autonomy should extend to the use of soft drugs, which should be formally legalized (D66 2002).

Thus one may conclude that the Democrats have hardly changed their ideology when they were in government. When change did occur (as in the 1970s and again around 1985), it could be explained by a change in leadership, rather than by experience in government. Even the approval of a declaration of principles in 2000 was not a substantial change, but meant that the liberals had finally come out of the (pragmatic) closet.

PPR: the radicalization of the Radicals

In 1968 progressive Catholics, worried about the prospect of the KVP merging with Protestant parties into a conservative Christian Democratic party, founded the Radical Party (*Politieke Partij Radikalen*, PPR) with the help of a small group of like-minded Protestants (mainly from the ARP). In 1973 it joined a centre-left coalition government. Soon the PPR turned into a secular and Greenish New Left party. In 1990 it would merge with Communists, Pacifist Socialists and others in Green Left (*GroenLinks*).

Like the Democrats, the Radicals did not want to embrace an ideology when they broke away from the KVP or the ARP. They felt inspired by the Gospel to try and change the world, without creating a new system of beliefs (Gaay Fortman 1967: 10; Van Ginneken 1975: 108–9). In their election programmes they did not refer to ideologies – at least not until the 1980s. The programmes did mention certain principles, however: democracy, solidarity with the poor at home and abroad, peace, individual self-development (*zelf-ontplooiing*) and environmental concern. These may reflect Christian values, but this was rarely made explicit. In fact, the party welcomed non-Christian members from the start and became more and more secular as time went by.

The PPR became also more radical. This was a gradual process, without dramatic breaks. Even the very first programme, approved by the founding congress in 1968, contained radical demands for economic and political democracy, nuclear disarmament and foreign aid. The Netherlands should continue its membership in NATO, but push for more peaceful policies (Politieke Partij Radikalen 1970).

The very short 1971 election platform did not go any further (Politieke Partij Radikalen 1971). Yet in 1972 a more radical platform was drafted – but subsequently shelved, as the party congress decided on a common platform with D66 and PvdA. After the 1972 elections, the PPR joined the government – with some reservations, however. Soon, a rift appeared in the party ranks between loyal supporters and critics of the government. The former were often former members of ARP or KVP, the latter younger and recently recruited members without a confessional background. Their growing number weighed on the election programme voted in 1977 (Politieke Partij Radikalen 1977). It was more radical, as well as more elaborate, than the previous ones. It called for workers' self-management, planning of the economy by the state (without abolishing the market economy altogether), a basic income for all citizens, exit from NATO, social defence (instead of military defence), no nuclear power stations and selective economic growth. Even the PvdA felt uneasy about these demands of their ally, while the Christian Democrats refused to have anything to do with them. This rejection was reciprocal. The left wing of the party felt almost relieved that government participation could not be continued. Yet the party paid a heavy price in the elections: four of its seven seats were lost (Van Egdom 1991: 19–22).

The loss exacerbated a crisis within the party. In the debate about ideology and strategy, which would last for several years, three positions emerged, defined by colours. Older party members defended a 'blue' position: an alliance with the PvdA, continuing to challenge the Christian Democrats, willing to join a centre-left government. The left wing favoured a 'red' position: an alliance with Communists and Pacifist Socialists. A third option was called 'green': building a new ecologist party, in an alliance with new social movements. None of the three tendencies carried a majority, but when 'reds' and 'greens' formed an 'ecological–socialist' coalition, the 'blues' were defeated. In fact, many 'blues' had already bolted from the PPR and joined the PvdA before the factional struggle ended (Van Egdom 1991: 25–8; see also Waltmans 1983).

The election platforms of 1981 and 1986 reflected their defeat. However, in the 1980s the *Zeitgeist* seemed to work against the 'reds'. The 1986 platform was more cautious about state intervention in the economy than the 1981 and 1977 programmes (Politieke Partij Radikalen 1986; cf. Politieke Partij Radikalen 1981; Politieke Partij Radikalen 1977). Yet it referred explicitly to libertarian socialism and anarchism as sources of inspiration. In 1989 the PPR drafted a slightly more moderate programme, but shelved it when negotiations with CPN and PSP resulted in a common platform. The ideology of the new formation, which would become the Green Left, was as eclectic, and about as radical, as that of the PPR.

The gradual radicalisation of the Radical Party was noticed gradually by the voters. In their perception the party shifted slowly but steadily to the left. In 1968 it was placed not far from the centre, between D66 and ARP; in 1976 it had passed D66 and came close to the PvdA; in 1981 it had shifted to the left of the PvdA (Van der Eijk and Niemöller 1983: 249–50). Thus one might conclude that the PPR 'toughened', rather than 'softened', its main policy positions during (and after) its participation in government.

DS'70: the slow death of Democratic Socialism

Democratic Socialists '70 was founded in 1970 by members of the PvdA who were frustrated by the growing influence of the New Left (*Nieuw Links*) within that party, or, as they put it, the PvdA was increasingly dominated by 'anarchist, anti-parliamentarian and irreal pacifist tendencies' (Democratisch Socialisten '70 1971a: 318). Quite a few of them were also worried about the growing polarisation caused by the PvdA, at the national as well as at the local level. Yet not all of them wanted to return to the ideology of the Labour Party in the 1950s, which was not entirely coherent anyway. Moreover, soon the new party would be joined by people without any social democratic background. Thus, its ideology was even at the beginning a mixture of social democracy (more or less Fabian), liberalism and conservatism. On the one hand, DS'70 wanted to raise old age pensions, control prices and wages, build more cheap houses, promote public transport and take (modest) steps towards industrial democracy. On the other hand, it wanted to reduce taxes and government expenditure, yet maintain defence spending and fight Communism (Democratisch Socialisten '70 1971b).

Its political leader, Wim Drees – the highest civil servant at the Treasury, and the son of a very popular former prime minister – managed to 'sell' the programme quite well in the 1971 election campaign. The Democratic Socialists entered parliament with eight seats – the best results for a new party so far. Yet in the cabinet that was formed with Liberals and Christian Democrats, Drees failed to convince his colleagues with respect to financial policies. He felt obliged to resign after 12 months. The coalition collapsed, and new elections were called in 1972. As a result, Drees and his party were enjoying 'splendid isolation' in parliament, distrusted by both right- and left-wing parties (Schikhof 2002). DS'70 presented a new platform at the snap elections of 1972, perhaps slightly more leftist than the previous one, as it put more emphasis on industrial democracy and public transport.

The party lost two seats, and would not return to the seats of government. This upset many members, who had bolted from the PvdA precisely because they wanted to take part in (national or local) government rather than join the opposition. Waxing criticism of Drees's leadership and strategy led to a split in the party and its parliamentary group in 1975 (Drees 1991). The party would never recover. In the parliamentary elections of 1977 it was reduced to one seat, which it lost four years later. Ideologically, it seemed to shift from social democracy to social conservatism (Voerman 1991). Although it remained true to its original ideas about wage and price controls and an economizing government, it added more and more conservative issues to its programme: mayors should be appointed rather than elected; immigration should stop and immigrants should adapt to Dutch culture; unemployed workers should not refuse work that did not suit them; more funds should be reserved for the police and army; the comprehensive school (*middenschool*) should remain an experiment rather than become a universal model (Democratisch Socialisten '70 1977; Democratisch Socialisten '70 1981). In the eyes of the voters, the party also shifted to the right – though not very much (Van der Eijk and Niemöller 1983: 249–50). In 1982 the executive committee proposed to drop socialism formally as well, by changing the party name to the Democratic Social Party. To no avail: the next year the party congress (consisting of 62 delegates) decided to disband the party.

LPF: an ideology under construction?

The List Pim Fortuyn was set up in February 2002, three months before the general elections. Pim Fortuyn had belonged to the Marxist left wing of the PvdA, but shifted to the right in the 1980s and 1990s. In various publications he had criticized all established parties, particularly for neglecting urgent problems in

Dutch society like growing bureaucracy and the 'Islamisation' of Dutch culture (Fortuyn 1997). In November 2001 he was elected leader of *Leefbaar Nederland* (Liveable Netherlands). This was a populist party founded in 1999 by leaders of local parties which opposed technocratic urban renewal and claimed to represent the common people against professional political elites. Fortuyn agreed with this populist approach, but linked it to his critique of Dutch immigration policy. Other party leaders did not accept this link. In February 2002, Fortuyn's critical comments on immigrants and their 'backward Islam' caused a conflict with the executive committee of *Leefbaar Nederland*. Fortuyn was forced to leave the party and decided to present his own list of candidates at the parliamentary elections in May – still hoping to become prime minister.

In March, Fortuyn published a book which was presented as a party programme. The 186-page book was a rather idiosyncratic blend of autobiographical elements, dry statistics and political demands (Fortuyn 2002). It was demolished immediately by all other political leaders, but became a political bestseller – it was sold out within a few days.[1] In April, a very short and more moderate version of this programme was published on the website of the LPF. One could consider it a mixture of social conservatism, economic liberalism, populism and nationalism (Lucardie and Voerman 2002; see also Pels 2003). Priority was given to security, integration of immigrants and restriction of immigration, reduction of bureaucracy by returning to smaller scale (hospitals, schools, municipalities) and election of mayors and of the prime minister (List Pim Fortuyn 2003a).

With his outgoing, even exhibitionist personality and lively, theatrical style, Fortuyn dominated the election campaign from the very beginning. In March he led a new local party in Rotterdam to a surprising victory at the municipal elections. Journalists and established politicians who had ridiculed him before felt compelled to take him seriously now. So did his enemies. One of them, a fanatical animal rights activist, planned to assassinate him – and succeeded on 6 May 2002. Immediately, the election campaign came to a halt. Yet the elections, planned for 15 May, were not postponed – mainly out of fear of riots or other public upheaval. The LPF entered parliament with 26 (out of 150) seats, a unique electoral success in Dutch history. True to the Dutch consociational tradition, it was invited to join a coalition government.

Yet five months later the coalition of LPF, CDA and VVD fell apart and new elections were called. The LPF revised and expanded its platform. It did not deviate substantially from the earlier version, but spelled out measures to fight crime and to reduce immigration. With respect to some issues it might be considered more liberal or less conservative: it called for legalisation of soft drugs and cautioned against privatisation of public utilities, for example (List Pim Fortuyn 2003b). As analysed by Pennings and Keman, the 2003 programme turned out to be a bit less right-wing and less conservative than the 2002 platform (2003: 59). At the same time, almost all established parties had adopted more conservative and right-wing positions in their platforms, thus reducing the distance between them and the LPF. This may have contributed to the severe electoral defeat of the LPF (from 26 to 8 seats), quite apart from other factors such as its internal conflicts and lack of leadership. The ideology is, however, still 'under construction', as the head of the party's research office, Bert Snel, admitted (Du Pré 2004). However, the construction came grinding to a halt when the LPF lost all eight seats in 2006 and decided to disband in August 2007.

Government participation and organisational change

Gauging organisational change may be more complicated than analysing ideological change. It is not enough to study written documents like party constitutions and by-laws, one should also observe party culture, the way party members interact, socialize and clash with each other. For the purpose of this chapter, however, analysis of party documents should suffice.

D66: change is discussed all the time

The Democrats applied their democratic principles to their own organisation. All important decisions should be taken by rank-and-file members, either by a postal ballot (e.g. regarding the list of candidates for parliament) or by a general members' assembly. In other Dutch parties, party congress would consist of delegates from local branches. In D66, every member could attend, speak and vote at the congress (or general members' assembly). When the congress discussed the party programme or election platform, every member could propose amendments. Quite often, this led to chaos and confusion. Communication between members, and between the executive committee and the rank-and-file, was always a problem (Lucardie and Schikhof 2001: 6–9). Very often, task forces proposed changes to make the organisation more efficient and more professional. Yet very little was done about it.

The internal problems contributed to the crisis that developed in the early 1970s. Party leader Van Mierlo had used his charisma to engage his party in a close alliance with PvdA and PPR, but exhausted it in the process. Soon after D66 joined the coalition government led by Den Uyl (PvdA), Van Mierlo resigned. In the coalition, D66 seemed to lose its visibility. Its ministers maintained few contacts with the party, and did little to improve its image. Provincial elections in 1974 proved a disaster: only 1 per cent of the electorate still voted for D66. Internal conflicts erupted, even between members of parliament. In September 1974, the party congress voted in favour of dissolution of the party, with a majority of 242 against 188 votes. As a two-thirds majority was required for this kind of decision, the party survived – like a patient in coma. Practically all activities ceased. Yet a year later, the party was brought back to life. One man played a vital role here: Jan Glastra van Loon, who after he lost his position as state secretary (deputy minister) after a conflict with the minister, found time and energy to give inspiring speeches at local meetings all over the country. He inspired also Jan Terlouw, the disillusioned successor of Van Mierlo. Terlouw promised to lead the party if 1666 new members could be recruited and 66,666 supporters signed a petition. This campaign filled the languishing party with new energy. In the 1977 elections the party won eight seats, and membership increased to 4410 (Van der Land 2003: 105–23, 129–52).

However, the resurrected party organisation differed very little from the old one. Procedures of decision-making continued to be very democratic (major decisions were still taken by a general members'assembly or by a postal ballot). The formal role of members remained the same. The party-in-parliament and the party-in-government, which had already dominated the extra-parliamentary party organisation before 1973, became even more powerful when the party organisation started to decline. Yet this effect was not permanent and cannot be attributed directly to participation in government. Perhaps the only significant change concerned the party culture. The distrust of institutions, which seems typical of all radical democratic organisations, waned considerably after 1973. Yet again, this change was caused more by the internal crisis of the party than by its participation in government.

Modest changes did take place. In 1978 an Advisory Council was introduced, elected by postal ballot (region by region), that would give advice and information to the executive committee and to members of parliament (D66 1978: 7–8). The executive committee would include representatives from regional branches, mainly in order to improve vertical communication. As membership increased, new institutions were set up: a research office, a political education and training institute, a youth organisation (Van der Land 2003: 146–7, 165–8, 226–7). Perhaps even more important was the 'voting advice committee' (*stemadviescommissie*) that would produce a draft list of candidates before parliamentary elections in order to provide for more coherence in the parliamentary group. Though the draft list was only an 'advice' to the rank-and-file members (who still had the final vote), it would become influential, even decisive, in the years to come (Hillebrand 1992: 122–5). It was introduced in 1985, three years after a second and very brief stay in government.

During the third period in government (1994–2002), the organisation was changed again – yet not in the expected direction of professionalisation and centralisation. The Advisory Council was abolished, and the executive committee reduced in size, without regional representatives. Yet rank-and-file members received more powers: a membership vote (referendum) could be held if 3 per cent of the members (or the party congress or the executive committee) so desired (D66 2003; see also Van der Land 2003: 351–71). After the rather disappointing election results of 2002, the party congress decided to abolish the 'voting advice committee'. Now primaries would help members decide on the ranking order of the candidates on the list. All members can present themselves as candidates at regional meetings. Members in the region will rank order the candidates. The results of the primaries will be weighed by the number of inhabitants of the region and aggregated at the national level, before members can vote on the definitive list (D66 2003: 31–32).

Looking back at 40 years of organisational development of D66, we cannot conclude that the party has become much more professional and centralized. Though some institutionalisation took place, it seems still to be a party controlled by amateurs.

PPR: becoming a normal party?

The Radical Party was founded in the spirit of the New Left. Direct action was considered as important as participation in elections and governments. Hence local branches were called 'action centres'(*actiecentra*). The action centres could send 10 per cent of their members to a party congress – which meant (in practice) that all activists could attend. In between congresses, decisions could be taken by the 'core group' (*kerngroep*), elected by provincial or local branch meetings – other parties would call this a party council (Politieke Partij Radikalen 1974a,b).

Constitution and by-laws of the party were adapted only marginally after participation in government (1973–77). In 1979, the party congress was granted the right to recall members of parliament (Politieke Partij Radikalen 1980). Yet at the same time, institutionalisation took place: like established parties, the PPR set up a youth organisation, a women's organisation, and a research and training office. In 1988, it became almost a normal party: action centres were renamed local branches (*afdelingen*), the core group was called a party council (*partijraad*), the executive committee reduced in size and the party bureau modernized (Politieke Partij Radikalen 1988). However, the changes were hardly implemented when the PPR decided to merge with others into a new formation, Green Left, and to dissolve its just modernized party organisation.

DS'70: decline and stability

When the Democratic Socialists '70 left the PvdA, they took its organisational model with them. DS'70 was set up like a social democratic mass party, even though it probably never had many more than 2,000 members. Local branches would send a number of delegates to both party congress and party council, depending on the size of the branch. The congress would decide on the party programme and elect the national executive committee, while the party council would nominate candidates for parliamentary elections (Democratisch Socialisten '70 1970).

After the party had taken part in the government, it adapted its constitution – though only marginally. Larger branches were allowed more delegates to congress and party council; the executive committee was expanded (from 14 to 17 members) and only three members of parliament could be on the executive committee (Democratisch Socialisten '70 1973). In 1979, again a few alterations were decided upon (the executive committee was reduced again to 14 members). Yet the only dramatic change came in 1983, when the party dissolved its organisation.

LPF: a fellowship tries to develop into a party

When the LPF entered parliament with 26 seats in May 2002, it did not have a formal organisation, only an executive committee consisting of three friends of Fortuyn, a small office and a handful of volunteers who had collected the signatures required for participation in the election. It was a fellowship of friends, fans and opportunists, rather than a real party.

It lacked also political leadership – or a 'strategic centre', which every party in government needs, as argued by Joachim Raschke in his critical study of the German Greens (2001: 24–34). The very day after its founding father and president had died, the other members of the executive committee started quarreling about his succession. They were individualistic entrepreneurs, who knew each other mainly through Fortuyn. As a result, one of them resigned at once, but continued to play a role in the background. Under considerable pressure, a second ceased his activities as well, leaving only one man in charge of the party apparatus (still a very modest affair). The parliamentary party confirmed the latter in his position as party president. Yet a few days later the third man resigned as well, after a controversial interview where he had said, about the assassination, 'the bullet came from the Left' (Schulte 2002). Now a provisional executive committee led by real estate dealer Ed Maas was to direct and stimulate the development of a party organisation (Chorus and De Galan 2002: 214–15).

Yet in a strict sense, it did not have any legal status. When it organized a party congress in July, in order to decide on participation in government, some members questioned the status of the congress. The parliamentary party, however, went ahead and approved the government agreement. Soon, quarrels would break out within the parliamentary group, and even worse, among the members of the cabinet that had just joined the LPF – and did not know each other, coming from quite different backgrounds. These conflicts led to the collapse of the government in October.

Meanwhile, the provisional executive tried to build up a party organisation, along traditional lines of provincial and local branches. On 19 October it organized the first formal party congress of the LPF at Utrecht. According to the party constitution, all members were allowed to attend and vote, as with D66 (List Pim Fortuyn 2002: Article 15). The almost 700 attending members elected the executive committee as recommended by Maas – following a procedure that was not quite democratic, according to some critics. Two critics went to court, and won their case. Another meeting was held on 3 December in Rotterdam. Again, Maas was elected, with 665 out of 685 votes. The two critics were expelled from the party and thrown out of the building immediately. Four days later, the party congress met again in Rotterdam to elect candidates for parliament.

In the elections of January 2003, the parliamentary group was reduced from 26 to 8 members. In the second legislative period it managed to avoid the intense conflicts of the first period, though in 2005 one member, former Minister of Integration Hilbrand Nawijn, broke away and became an independent MP. Conflicts continued within the party on the ground, however, and led in September 2003 to the resignation of Maas and other members of the executive committee. Yet their successors did not achieve more stability. Membership dropped considerably, to about 1200 by 2006. In 2007 the organisation was dissolved. One might conclude that the LPF tried to adapt its party organisation in the expected direction – to become a normal party – with only limited success.

Conclusions

Why do some new parties join government whilst others remain in opposition forever? In the Dutch case, three conditions need to be met. The project of the party should be either 'pragmatic' reform of the political system or to challenge an established party. It should win at least 6 (out of 150) seats in parliament. And it should have luck: relevant established parties should feel unable to form a stable coalition without it.

Do new parties adapt their ideology once they take part in government (in a more pragmatic, 'realistic' direction)? The historical evidence is ambiguous here. D66 did 'soften' its ideology after its first participation in government, but this could be interpreted as adaptation to its new leadership rather than to its political environment. When the old leader returned, the party 'toughened' its ideology again. The PPR 'toughened' its ideology during its stay in government. DS'70 adapted its ideology (in a conservative direction), not immediately after it left the government, but much later. The LPF 'softened' its programme, but not in a very substantial way.

Do new parties adapt their organisation (institutionalisation, centralisation, professionalisation) after they join a government? To some extent, all new parties try to institutionalize, setting up branches, youth organisations etc. The impact of government participation seems to have been minimal, if not negligible, in our sample of four parties.

Thus, all hypotheses have to be qualified, to say the least. And perhaps we might add a fourth hypothesis, *post-hoc*: new parties in the Netherlands join government often only a few years after they enter parliament. Too soon, perhaps: they often face defeat in the next elections and face a long and arduous struggle to win back their supporters. In other words, the road to power may be often short, but the way back can be very long.

Note

1   It would be reprinted very soon; altogether about 170,000 copies were sold in 2002 (email from the publisher, 11 August 2003).

List of parties

AOV   *Algemene Ouderen Verbond* (General Association of Old Aged People)
ARP   *Anti-Revolutionaire Partij* (Anti Revolutionary Party) merged into CDA in 1980
BP   *Boerenpartij* (Farmer's Party)
CD   *Centrumdemocraten* (Centre Democrats): split from CP in 1984
CDA   *Christen Democratisch Appèl* (Christian Democratic Appeal): resulted from the merger of ARP, CHU and KVP in 1980
CHU   *Christelijk Historische Unie* (Christian Historical Union): merged into CDA in 1980

CP   *Centrumpartij* (Centre Party): founded in 1980, broke into two parts in 1984 – the CD and the more radical *Centrumpartij '86* (Centre Party '86); the latter was not represented in parliament and banned in 1998

CPN   *Communistische Partij Nederland* (Communist Party of the Netherlands): joined GL in 1990

CU   *Christen Unie* (Christian Union): confederation of GPV and RPF.

D66   *Democraten 66* (Democrats 66)

DS'70   *Democratisch Socialisten '70* (Democratic Socialists '70)

EVP   *Evangelische Volkspartij* (Evangelical People's Party): joined GL in 1990

GL   *Groen Links* (Green Left): merger between CPN, EVP, PPR and PSP in 1990

GPV   *Gereformeerd Politiek Verbond* (Reformed Political Association)

KNP   *Katholieke Nationale Partij* (Catholic National Party) rejoined KVP in 1955

KVP   *Katholieke Volkspartij* (Catholic People's Party): merged into CDA in 1980

LN   *Leefbaar Nederland* (Liveable Netherlands)

LPF   *Lijst Pim Fortuyn* (List Pim Fortuyn)

NMP   *Nederlandse Middenstandspartij* (Dutch Middle Class Party)

PPR   *Politieke Partij Radikalen* (Political Party of Radicals) joined GL in 1990

PSP   *Pacifistisch Socialistische Partij* (Pacifist Socialist Party): joined GL in 1990

PvdA   *Partij van de Arbeid* (Labour Party)

RKPN   *Rooms-Katholieke Partij Nederland* (Roman Catholic Party of the Netherlands)

RPF   *Reformatorische Politieke Federatie* (Reformed Political Federation)

SGP   *Staatkundig Gereformeerde Partij* (Political Reformed Party)

SP   *Socialistische Partij* (Socialist Party)

U 55+   *Unie 55+* (Union 55+)

VVD   *Volkspartij voor Vrijheid en Democratie* (People's Party for Freedom and Democracy)

Bibliography

Andeweg, R.B. and Irwin, G.A. (2005) *Governance and Politics of the Netherlands*, 2nd edn, Basingstoke: Palgrave Macmillan.

Buelens, J. and Lucardie, A.P.M. (1998) 'Ook nieuwe partijen worden oud: Een verken-nend onderzoek naar de levensloop van nieuwe partijen in Nederland en België', *Jaarboek 1997 DNPP*, Groningen: Documentatiecentrum Nederlandse Politieke Partijen, 118–52.

Chorus, J. and De Galan, M. (2002) *In de Ban van Fortuyn, Reconstructie van een Politieke Aardschok*, Amsterdam: Mets and Schilt.

D66 (1977) *'Het redelijk alternatief' Verkiezingsprogramma 1977–1981*, The Hague: D66.

82   Lucardie and Ghillebaert

D66 (1978) *Statuten en Huishoudelijk Reglement van de Politieke Partij Democraten '66*, The Hague: Democraten 66.

D66 (1979), *Beleidsprogram 1977–1981*, The Hague: D66.

D66 (2002) *Toekomst in eigen hand: Verkiezingsprogramma 2002–2006*, The Hague: D66; also in J. van Holsteyn, T. van der Meer, H. Pellikaan, H. Ijsbrandy and G. Voerman (eds) *Verkiezingsprogramma's: Verkiezingen van de Tweede Kamer 15 Mei 2002 en 22 Januari 2003*, Amsterdam: Rozenberg, pp. 151–80.

D66 (2003) *Statuten en Huishoudelijk Reglement*, The Hague: Democraten 66.

D66, PvdA and PPR (1972) *Keerpunt: Regeerakkoord van de Progressieve Drie*, Amsterdam: 1972.

Democratisch Socialisten '70 (1970) *Statuten DS'70, Vastgesteld op het Huishoudelijk Congres op 14 November 1970*, Amsterdam: DS'70.

Democratisch Socialisten '70 (1971a) 'Beginselverklaring van de politieke partij Democratisch Socialisten '70', *Parlement en Kiezer*, The Hague: Martinus Nijhoff, pp. 318–320.

Democratisch Socialisten '70 (1971b) 'Verkiezingsprogramma 1971', *Parlement en Kiezer*, The Hague: Martinus Nijhoff, pp. 320–6.

Democratisch Socialisten '70 (1972) *Werkprogramma voor Nederland '73–'77*, Amsterdam: DS'70.

Democratisch Socialisten '70 (1973) *Statuten DS'70, Vastgesteld op het Huishoudelijk Congres op 6 en 7 April 1973*, Amsterdam: DS'70.

Democratisch Socialisten '70 (1977) *Verkiezingsprogramma 1977: Vrijheid en Solidariteit in Redelijkheid*, Amsterdam: DS'70.

Democratisch Socialisten '70 (1981) *'Morgen is Nu': Verkiezingsprogram 1981*, Amsterdam: DS'70.

Drees, W. (1991) '"Vleugellam": het conflict in DS'70', *Jaarboek 1990 DNPP*, Groningen: Documentatiecentrum Nederlandse Politieke Partijen, pp. 58–91.

Du Pré, R. (2004) 'Wat fortuynisme precies is, weet eigenlijk nog niemand', *De Volkskrant*, 23 February 2004, p. 2.

Fortuyn, P. (1997) *Tegen de Islamisering van Onze Cultuur: Nederlandse Identiteit als Fundament*, Utrecht: Bruna.

Fortuyn, P. (2002) *De Puinhopen van Acht Jaar Paars*, Uithoorn: Karakter.

de Gaay Fortman, B. (1967) 'Het Christen-radicaal congres', in B. de Gaay Fortman and W. Veld (eds) *Christen-radicaal*, Hilversum: Paul Brand.

Godschalk, J.J. (1970) 'Enige politieke en sociale kenmerken van de oprichters van D'66', *Acta Politica*, 5(1): 62–74.

Gruijters, J.P.A. (1967) *Daarom D'66*, Amsterdam: De Bezige Bij.

Hillebrand, R. (1992) *De Antichambre van het Parlement: Kandidaatstelling in Nederlandse Politieke Partijen*, Leiden: DSWO Press.

Hug, S. (2000) 'Studying the electoral success of new political parties', *Party Politics*, 6(2): 187–97.

Ignazi, P. (1996) 'The crisis of parties and the rise of new political parties', *Party Politics*, 2(4): 549–66.

List Pim Fortuyn (2002) *Statuten Lijst Pim Fortuyn*, on-line: www.pimfortuyn.nl/party99f8.html (accessed via archipol archive service, 22 March 2004).

List Pim Fortuyn (2003a) '"Zakelijk met een hart": Verkiezingsprogramma 2002', in J. Van Holsteyn, T. van der Meer, H. Pellikaan, H. Ijsbrandy and G. Voerman *Verkiezingsprogramma's: Verkiezingen van de Tweede Kamer 15 Mei 2002 en 22 Januari 2003*, Amsterdam: Rozenberg, pp. 361–7.

List Pim Fortuyn (2003b) ' "Politiek is passie": Verkiezingsprogramma 2003', in J. van Holsteyn, T. van der Meer, H. Pellikaan, H. Ijsbrandy and G. Voerman (eds) *Verkiezingsprogramma's: Verkiezingen van de Tweede Kamer 15 Mei 2002 en 22 Januari 2003*, Amsterdam: Rozenberg, pp. 368–91.

Lucardie, P. (2000) 'Prophets, purifiers and prolocutors: towards a theory on the emergence of new parties', *Party Politics*, 6(2): 175–85.

Lucardie, P. and Schikhof, M. (2001) 'Organizational and ideological effects of government participation: the case of D66', paper presented at the workshop 'New Parties in Government', Free University of Brussels, 7–8 December 2001.

Lucardie, P. and Voerman, G. (2001) 'Liberalisme met een rode rand', in J. Veldhuizen, B. Aris, P. Harms, M. van der Land, S. Pieters and S. Verbeeck (eds) *D66: een Blijvend Appèl: 35 Jaar Werken aan Vernieuwing*, Den Haag: D66, pp. 108–11.

Lucardie, P. and Voerman, G. (2002) 'Liberaal patriot of nationaal populist? Het gedachtegoed van Pim Fortuyn', *Socialisme and Democratie*, 59(4): 32–42.

Pels, D. (2003) *De Geest van Pim: Het Gedachtegoed van een Politieke Dandy*, Amsterdam: Anthos.

Pennings, P. and Keman, H. (2003) 'The Dutch parliamentary elections in 2002 and 2003: the rise and decline of the Fortuyn Movement', *Acta Politica*, 38: 1, 51–68.

Politieke Partij Radikalen (1970) 'Program P.P.R.', in *Parlement en Kiezer*, The Hague: Martinus Nijhoff, pp. 283–93.

Politieke Partij Radikalen (1971) 'Verkiezingsprogram P.P.R.', in *Parlement en Kiezer*, The Hague: Martinus Nijhoff, pp. 454–9.

Politieke Partij Radikalen (1974a) 'Statuten 1969', *PPRAK*, 51: 5–7 (*Bijlage*).

Politieke Partij Radikalen (1974b) 'Huishoudelijk Reglement', *PPRAK*, 51: 1–5 (*Bijlage*).

Politieke Partij Radikalen (1977) *Vrede, Macht, Milieu, Welzijn: Verkiezingsprogramma 1977/1981 van de PPR*, Amsterdam: PPR.

Politieke Partij Radikalen (1980) 'Huishoudelijk reglement', *PPRAktiekrant*, 150: 16–18 (*Bijlage*).

Politieke Partij Radikalen (1981) *Programma 1981–1986*, Amsterdam: PPR.

Politieke Partij Radikalen (1986) *Verzet en Vernieuwing: PPR Programma 1986–1990*, Amsterdam: PPR.

Politieke Partij Radikalen (1988) *Handboek PPR*, Amsterdam: PPR.

Raschke, Joachim (2001) *Die Zukunft der Grünen: 'So Kann Man Nicht Regieren'*, Frankfurt: Campus Verlag.

Rijksvoorlichtingsdienst [Government Information Service] (2003) *Het Kabinet-Balkenende II: Meedoen, Meer Werk, Minder Regels*, The Hague: Quantes.

Schikhof, M. (2002) 'Opkomst, ontvangst en "uitburgering" van een nieuwe partij en een nieuwe politicus. DS'70 en Drees Jr.', *Jaarboek Parlementaire Geschiedenis 2002*, Nijmegen: Centrum voor Parlementaire Geschiedenis, pp. 29–38.

Schulte, A. (2002) 'Leider LPF volhardt: de kogel kwam van links', *Het Parool*, 13 May 2002, 1.

Terlouw, J.C. (1983) *Naar Zeventien Zetels en Terug: Politiek Dagboek 9 Maart 1981 – 5 November 1982*, Utrecht/Antwerpen: Het Spectrum.

Van Doorn, J.A.A. (1994) 'Democratisch pragmatisme: de vierde stroming in de Nederlandse politiek', *Beleid en Maatschappij*, 21: 1–2, 15–21.

Van der Eijk, C. and B. Niemöller (1983) *Electoral Change in the Netherlands: Empirical Results and Methods of Measurement*, Amsterdam: CT Press.

Van Egdom, H. (1991) *Er Werd een Commissie Ingesteld: Lief en Leed in 23 Jaar PPR*, Amsterdam: PPR.

Van Ginneken, F. (1975) *De P.P.R. van 1968 tot en met 1971*, Breda: 1975.

Van der Land, M. (2003) *Tussen Ideaal en Illusie: De Geschiedenis van D66, 1966–2003*, The Hague: Sdu.

Voerman, G. (1991) 'Een geval van politieke schizofrenie: het gespleten gedachtengoed van DS'70', *Jaarboek 1990 DNPP*, Groningen: Documentatiecentrum Nederlandse Politieke Partijen, pp. 92–114.

Wagenveld, M. (1999), 'Wat vindt men van sociaal-liberaal? Van Mierlo: verlies van uniciteit', *Idee*, 20: 2, 23.

Waltmans, H. (1983) *Niet bij rood alleen*, Groningen: Xeno.

5 Close but no cigar?

Newly governing and nearly governing parties in Sweden and New Zealand

Tim Bale and Magnus Blomgren

Introduction

In polities where minority administrations are common and may even be the norm, we should adopt a broader definition of what constitutes participation in government and examine 'new' parties that have provided legislative support to, as well as actually joined, coalitions. New Zealand and Sweden have both developed innovative contractual forms of handling minority administration and can therefore provide us with case studies of both newly governing and 'nearly governing' parties. Interrogating their experiences suggests that the organisational, ideological and electoral risks are not currently perceived as high enough to put such parties off bargaining for office. The benefits of coaliton and cooperation may not be large in policy terms, but in the long run they may lead to more opportunities to play a more consistent role in government.

Contexts

New Zealand

New Zealand switched in the mid 1990s from a first past the post (FPP) to a mixed member proportional system (MMP). Pressure for change came about not only because both main parties – Labour and National – were felt by voters to have betrayed their trust but also because, for some time, New Zealand had been really a two party system in name only. The economic populist party Social Credit regularly took close to 10 per cent of the vote in the fifties and sixties, rising to double that in 1981. Labour's surprise neo-liberal turn following its victory in 1984, and National's refusal (despite its promises in opposition) to pause its progress when elected to office in 1990, had also combined with personality clashes to produce two splinter parties. The first, 'NewLabour', had been founded by the charismatic Labour MP, Jim Anderton, and quickly attracted support from disgruntled left-wingers. Meanwhile, the even more charismatic National MP, Winston Peters, set up 'New Zealand First' in July 1993.

After it became clear that New Zealand would adopt an electoral system that would facilitate a few smaller parties, more political entrepreneurs entered the fray. Most of their ventures ended in failure, but one that stood some chance of success was the avowedly centrist 'United New Zealand', formed in 1995. This was because, like the parties founded by Anderton and Peters, it was able to count on a politician – Peter Dunne MP – with a seemingly impregnable majority in his own district (or electorate as it is called in New Zealand). New Zealand's mixed system, modelled on Germany's, guaranteed representation to parties able to win just one electorate seat even if they fell short of the 5 per cent threshold nationwide. Dunne believed that there should be room in New Zealand for an equivalent of the FDP – a supposedly centrist party able to use its pivotal position to maintain a practically permanent place in coalition governments formed by whichever of the two big parties emerged as the winner of the election. In fact, things were complicated by the fact that Peters, although more than willing to use anti-immigration rhetoric to appeal to both white Europeans and Maori, was careful to insist that NZ First's social and economic policies put it slap bang in between National (now in government) and Labour (which by that time was reconverting itself to social democracy).

Anderton (who predictably insisted that any such reconversion was too little too late) had no interest in the centre ground, believing that it might be possible to replace Labour as the mainstream alternative on the left. Yet he, too, faced some competition. Sneaking onto his territory – via the latent post-materialist– materialist dimension – were the Greens, who were attracting sufficient interest, especially among young, urban voters, to worry NewLabour: indeed, at the 1990 election, fought under FPP, the Greens had scored 6.8 per cent. Anderton's solution was to persuade them to join what became the Alliance – an electoral and parliamentary coalition, founded in late 1991, which also included Mana Motuhake (a Maori party) and the Democrats (the successor party to Social Credit).

By the time of the country's first election fought under MMP, then, it was clear that Labour and National were going to be joined in parliament by several newcomers: indeed, even before the election, the pre-PR manoeuvrings had left National without a clear majority, obliging it to sign a coalition agreement with United Future whereby its leader not only made it into the Cabinet but was allowed a clear run in his Wellington electorate – a fortunate decision, it turned out, since his party won less than 1 per cent in October 1996, leaving him its sole survivor in parliament. The obvious victor among the small parties was NZ First, which scored over 13 per cent. But the process by which it ended up parlaying that result into a place in the first coalition of the MMP era was by no means a simple one.

NZ First had done well in the election by fighting on a platform that was economically centrist but also economically nationalist to the point of xenophobia. Many of its supporters, especially among Maori, were traditionally Labour voters and had expected the new party to go into coalition with their first love. However Labour, having lost so many votes to NZ First, was not in a position to offer the latter participation in a majority coalition: a three-way deal involving the Alliance (which had slipped disappointingly from the 18 per cent scored under FPP to just 10 per cent under MMP) was ruled out because of the difficult relationships between the potential partners. Labour was also reluctant to offer NZ First its pick of the ministerial posts and in particular the post of finance minister to its leader, Winston Peters, who, after nearly two months of parallel negotiations with both Labour and National, decided to go with the latter.

The National–NZ First coalition that followed lasted only eighteen months, and it is hard not to see the enterprise as doomed from the outset. National had made too many concessions to win over Winston (as he is invariably known) and soon deposed its leader in favour of Jenny Shipley, who became the country's first woman prime minister. Even before the knock-on effect of the Asian financial crisis threatened to make a nonsense of its spending plans, NZ First's support had plummeted as many of its voters felt betrayed and distinctly unimpressed with a bunch of newcomers with little or no parliamentary and/or executive experience, and little sense of shared ideology or *esprit de corps*. The ensuing break-up of the coalition was a messy affair with several of Peters' NZ First colleagues deciding to leave the party and stay as ministers in what would now be a National-led minority government supported on confidence and supply by the small, ultra-market liberal ACT party and by Dunne, still the sole parliamentary representative of his United party. Meanwhile, spurred on in part by the possibility that this cobbled-together administration might suddenly collapse, the Alliance and Labour were able to overcome their mutual antipathy and declare that they would work to form a coalition after the next election, though this would not include the Greens since that party – which was growing in strength – had decided to quit the Alliance and fight the contest under its own banner.

When, at last, the election did come in November 1999, the putative coalition won less than half the seats in parliament but, so locked in was it to its plans, that it nevertheless formed a minority government, supported rather than joined by the Greens (see Bale *et al.* 2005). However, as the next election, due in late 2002, loomed, internal arguments with the Alliance over the leadership's supposedly supine stance towards its senior coalition partner spilled out into the open, whereupon the Alliance's leader promptly jumped ship and formed his own party, the 'Progressive Coalition'. In the meantime, a still-popular Labour Party had begun to take precautions by courting a closer relationship with the Greens. Just before the election, however, its best laid plans were blown apart when the two parties fell out after the Greens insisted that a moratorium on GM crops was a pre-condition of their co-operation with a Labour-led government.

While playing hardball may have done the Greens no great harm electorally (the party went from 5.2 per cent in 1999 to 7 per cent in 2002), it made it almost certain that Labour would look elsewhere for support. And cometh the hour, cometh the man: a strong performance by Peter Dunne during the main leaders' debate on television saw his party, now called United Future following a merger with a small (but highly organised) Christian Party, came out of nowhere to win nearly 7 per cent and eight seats, the majority of which went to a bunch of unknown (and thoroughly surprised!) candidates apparently brought together by little more than a shared commitment to 'family values'. Partly because he had no wish to repeat the experience of NZ First, Dunne made no attempt to take his party into coalition. Instead, he negotiated a written support agreement with a minority government led by Labour, along with the two Progressive Coalition MPs who were the only survivors of the Alliance debacle, the Alliance proper scoring only 1 per cent (down from nearly 8 per cent in 1999). Interestingly, however, after securing a contractual arrangement with United Future, Labour took out an insurance policy by signing a very similar document with the Greens, who, somewhat chastened by their experience but now with two additional MPs, decided their future did indeed lie in some kind of centre-left co-operation.

This 'contract parliamentarism' (see Bale and Bergman 2006a) saw the Labour-led government safely through to the next election in 2005, though not without the party losing one of its MPs (and some of its voters) to the newly formed Maori Party. On the other side, a revivified National made capital out of Labour's 'politically correct' attitude to minorities and immigrants while promising sweeping tax cuts – a populist turn that saw it gain an incredible 18 percentage points, mainly by cannibalizing the votes of smaller parties on the right (including NZ First, whose 5.7 per cent vote share, however, was just enough to ensure that it could still enter parliament despite its leader finally losing his precious electorate seat). Yet the initiative still lay with Labour. It had no intention of relying on the splinter Maori Party, but could rely on the continued, if sometimes grudging, support of the Greens, who were disappointed to lose three seats. United Future had fared even worse, dropping to three seats in total on a vote share of just 2.7 per cent, but it was still in a strong position because of its location in the centre of the socio-economic left–right spectrum. The same could be said of NZ First – although its leader had slightly less room for manoeuvre, having promised during the campaign to tolerate a government formed by the largest party, which was Labour (just).

Labour's response to the parliamentary arithmetic facing it was creative to say the least. Once again, it chose to lead a minority government: all Labour with the exception of Jim Anderton, who once again clung on to his seat but this time as the sole representative of a party which existed in little more than name only. Once again, Labour arranged contracts with smaller parties, adding NZ First to United Future and the Greens. The innovation came in what the leaders of the first two of the three parties were offered. Although their parties were outside government, both Peters and Dunne were made ministers – foreign minister and minister of revenue respectively. Both would be bound by collective responsibility in areas touching on their portfolios, but would otherwise be free (within the boundaries mentioned in their support agreements) to criticise the government. Their attendance at cabinet would depend on the matters to be dealt with at each meeting.

New Zealand, then, has in little more than a decade gone from being 'more Westminster than Westminster' to a country employing government formation solutions so unusual that they routinely amaze political analysts unfamiliar with them. That it has done so is a testament both to the breakthroughs and to the mistakes made by the new parties. MMP politics, in short, has not turned out to be an easy ride for New Zealand's newly governing parties, whether they have been full-blown coalition partners or instead providers of essential parliamentary support for the minority administrations that after 1998 have been the Kiwi norm.

Sweden

Until environmental issues forced their way onto the political agenda in the late 1970s, the Swedish party system had been remarkably stable since the 1930s: five largely united parties were aligned from left to right into two almost equally strong blocs, with the balance tilting slightly to the left. However, if voter volatility *between* the blocs has decreased (Holmberg and Oscarsson 2004: 87), volatility *within* the blocs – particularly (though not exclusively) within the so-called socialist (as opposed to the 'bourgeois') bloc – has increased enormously since the 1960s, reaching 30 per cent in 2002. This less settled situation has brought with it new entrants into parliament and offered more parties than ever the chance to get into, or at least close to, government.

From the 1920s, the socialist bloc was dominated by the Social Democrats, but included a smaller Communist (now Left) Party – an organisation more prone to internal conflict than most Swedish parties. Even though these conflicts are far from over – and often revolve around the extent to which the party should act 'responsibly' or take a more radical, even oppositional, stance – they have not (or not yet, at least) prevented the party from playing an important role in the government formation process by supporting, though never being invited to actually join, Social Democratic minority administrations – a pattern facilitated by Sweden's 'negative parliamentarism' whereby (as in New Zealand) governments have to be defeated on confidence and supply, rather than actively supported by the majority of MPs. Consequently, the Social Democrats have played a more or less hegemonic role during the whole post-war period and governed for 51 out of 61 years between 1945 and 2005. But if this meant that, traditionally, the Social Democrats were able to take the Left Party for granted, things began to change in 1990 when the Social Democratic government launched a far-reaching programme to deal with a growing budget deficit. The rejection of the programme by the Left Party obliged the government to resign before being reinstalled just eleven days later with a programme that excluded some of the original reforms that upset its erstwhile supporter.

The dark horse of the 1990 crisis was the Green Party. Created in 1981 by those on the losing side of the previous year's referendum on nuclear power, and reflecting growing interest in environmental issues as well as increased criticism of the political establishment (see Wörlund 2005: 241), the Greens also claimed to do politics in a radically different, more democratic way, entering parliament in 1988. This was perhaps why, when the Social Democratic government was unable to count on Left Party support for its 1990 programme and turned to the Greens for help, they demanded too much in return for their support, forcing the Social Democrats to go back to the Left Party. Although this is a minor event in Swedish political history, it was the first time a genuine newcomer found itself in a position to be a saviour or executioner of a Swedish government.

Although the Social Democratic government eventually succeeded in creating a majority for various reforms, the financial problems were not solved and the popularity of the socialist bloc fell considerably, encouraging parties within the bourgeois bloc to form tighter relations in order to take power in the 1991 election. At the time, the bloc consisted of just three parties. The strongest party, the Moderates, were traditionally a conservative party, but since the 1970s had made moves toward neo-liberalism (Widfeldt 2005: 115). The second party, the Liberals, emphasised social liberal values, arguing for a developed welfare state while advocating market solutions (Pierre and Widfeldt 1992). Notwithstanding its coalitions with the Social Democrats in the 1930s and 1950s, the third party in the bourgeois bloc was the rural-based Centre Party, mobilising along the centre–periphery divide rather than the left–right cleavage.

Since their last experience of governing together between 1976 and 1982 had been less than positive, the three centre-right parties realised they had to be better prepared in 1991. As it turned out, they managed exceptionally well – at least initially. The 1991 election ended in the largest shift towards the right in Swedish modern history: the Social Democrats suffered their worst election since 1937; the Left Party ended up dangerously close to the threshold of 4 per cent; the Greens fell below it. The election also saw the entry of two parties new to parliament: the Christian Democrats and New Democracy – both clearly positioned within the bourgeois bloc, but with very different characteristics.

The Christian Democrats were formed as early as 1964 and had been trying to reach the Riksdag ever since. The party was created as a reaction against secularisation. It stressed the nuclear family as the most important entity of society and criticised the negative effects of urbanisation (Bäck and Möller 1997: 86). Even though Christian values are important elements in the party's ideological heritage, today the division between religion and politics is emphasised as a strategy to broaden the electoral base of the party. In the 1991 election the Christian Democrats mainly gathered votes from the Liberals and the Centre Party (Gilljam and Holmberg 1993: 72).

If the Christian Democrats were an established party on the Swedish political scene, albeit outside parliament, this did not apply to the other newcomer, New Democracy. It was formed in Spring 1991, just nine months before the election. The party was created by a director of a record company and an earl. This seemingly incompatible mix of political inexperience and weak political organisation was initially considered a joke. However, its right-wing populist programme, with clearly xenophobic elements and an anti-establishment rhetoric, clearly touched a nerve and it was able to gather votes both from the left and right, especially from the Social Democrats and Moderates, as well as attracting previous non-voters (Gilljam and Holmberg 1993:72).

The two newcomers were welcomed very differently into parliamentary politics. The bourgeois bloc won the election, but the three established three right-wing parties did not by themselves obtain a majority in parliament. And including the Christian Democrats still left them short. Consequently, New Democracy ended up in a similar situation to that which the Left Party traditionally has done. Under negative parliamentarism, minor parties positioned on either end of the left–right divide are practically obliged either to tolerate a government closer to its ideological position, or to revolt and thus risk ending up with a government based on parties from the opposite bloc. Unwilling to invite the populist party into its now four-way coalition, the government was a minority administration supported at the outset by New Democracy.

The years that followed the 1991 election were exceptional in many respects. Sweden found itself in the worst financial crisis in decades: the Swedish currency dropped dramatically and the crisis went so far that Swedish interest rates increased briefly to an astronomical 500 per cent. In this chaotic situation, some argued that the government needed more stable support – even if it meant a closer relationship with New Democracy. Even though the Moderates were open to such a dialogue, the Liberals in particular were reluctant to turn to the populist right for firm and ongoing support: having campaigned heavily against New Democracy, they feared co-operation between the two would be frowned on by voters. Instead, the government ended up turning to the Social Democrats with deals done that crossed the left–right divide. Perhaps not surprisingly, the bourgeois government was defeated at the next election in 1994 – a contest that saw New Democracy, which had already lost its founding leaders, take just 1 per cent. The Christian Democrats, however, narrowly survived, while on the other side the Greens broke back into parliament.

But all was not plain sailing on the left. The Social Democrats returned to government, but as usual needed legislative support. With memories of being let down by the Left Party in 1990 still strong, they instead turned to the Centre Party a year after the election. Since the Centre Party had a stronger bargaining ground because of its pivotal position, an arrangement was developed that was qualitatively different to those negotiated with the Left Party in earlier periods. Earlier, there were few if any public statements on the common ground between the government and the supporting party. Such statements were made after the 1994 election and, furthermore, the Centre Party had representatives in a number of ministerial departments.

After the following election, in 1998, the Left Party and the Greens were forgiven their earlier sins by a Social Democratic party chastened by the loss of some its more radical supporters to its smaller rivals. Indeed, the Left Party and the Greens together obtained 16.5 per cent, and were therefore not so easily dismissed. The type of arrangement that had been developed between the Social Democrats and the Centre Party was once again adopted, but also developed. A 'contract' was written between the governing party and the two supporting parties, as well as the supporting parties being allowed to place advisors in some ministerial departments. After the 2002 election, this arrangement between the three parties was repeated and further developed, with promises to work together on certain key areas such as the economy, employment policy, income distribution, gender equality and environmental progress included in the contract. The parties also 'agreed to disagree' on certain policy areas, such as EU policy and foreign policy. Thus, the supporting parties were able to have an impact on important policy areas, without being responsible in areas where they disagreed with the government, in exchange for granting the minority government greater stability.

In the last ten years, then, two important changes have taken place in Swedish politics. First, the traditional five-party system has been transformed into a seven-party system, although the dividing line between the two blocs remains, notwithstanding an ultimately unconvincing attempt by the Greens to straddle it to try to increase their bargaining strength in the wake of the 2002 election. Second, a kind of 'contract parliamentarism' has developed, in which the minority government and supporting parties agree on a mutual agenda and assume mutual obligations but without forming a formal coalition.

Experiences

New Zealand

United (Future)

United has been kept in play by its leader's astute policy of merger and affiliation – the first with Future New Zealand, a self-styled Christian Democratic party; the second (which lasted only two years between 2003 and 2005) with Outdoor Recreation, the Kiwi equivalent of the French *Chasse, Pêche, Nature, Traditions*. In so doing, Dunne gained an element of national organisation and a fresh supply of candidates in return for a say on policy and an all-but-guaranteed voice in parliament. What he did not surrender, however, was his highly centralised control of the party, which, notwithstanding his being joined by a handful of fellow MPs and the establishment of a party board, continues to be rooted in and run from the leader's office. Certainly, tactics in the volatile post-election environment are decided by the leader. Since the party is so centralised, the question of how that part of the party that is in government is integrated into the wider party organisation effectively does not arise.

As for ideology and policy, participation in or near government has had relatively little effect on United. Not only rhetorically but also in the eyes of voters, the party has, on the socio-economic dimension, maintained its position just to the right of centre: United emphasises what it calls 'common sense' (low inflation, debt reduction and macro-economic stability, as well as some reduction in company tax and regulation) but at the same time rejects calls to seriously slim down the country's already lean welfare state. If anything, the party's 2005 support arrangement with the Labour-led minority government (which included a ministerial place for United's leader) has seen it emphasise its business-friendliness in order to signal both its continued independence and its availability for coalition with National next time around. Indeed, in mid-2006 it made clear its support for a private member's bill which would impose a 90-day probation period for new employees, during which time they could be dismissed with virtually no questions asked. The party – and especially its leader – also takes a particularly vituperative stance against the Green Party, refusing in 2005 (as in 2002) to support a Labour government if that went into coalition with the party.

Indeed, the most notable ideological development during United's short lifespan is the hardening of its moral and social conservativism – a development that owes much to its merger with the evangelical Future New Zealand and has occured in spite of its involvment with Labour in government. Aware of its strong, albeit niche, appeal to the country's small community of churchgoers, United has since 2002 been vociferous in branding itself the party of 'family values' (see Aimer 2003), with some of its more openly religious MPs leading the charge against the Labour government-sponsored bills to grant civil unions to same sex couples and to liberalise the law on prostitution. Whether, though, the party's inability to prevent the legislation going through was partly responsible for its loss of support between the 2002 and 2005 elections is a moot point. One MP who lost his seat in 2005, for instance, suggested (along with Outdoor Recreation, which has now disaffiliated) that it was United's links to Christian fundamentalists, rather than its failure to deliver to them, that had harmed it. Regardless, the two MPs who did make it back into parliament alongside their leader (solely by virtue of his once again winning his electorate) are both active Christians, so, in as much as the party can be said to have links with civil society, then those links may persist. Whether the party itself will survive in the long term, though, once Dunne retires from (or perhaps even loses) his electorate seat is by no means certain. Being in or near to government has not encouraged United Future to institutionalise and build its membership: at heart, it remains a one man band.

New Zealand First

The very same could be said – in spades – of NZ First, which, despite its bigger following amongst voters, has likewise failed to institutionalise, leaving it heavily reliant on its mercurial leader. Indeed, some observers argue that, notwithstanding evidence that it has loyal support and is not simply a repository of protest, Winston Peters' outfit is a perfect example of a 'personality-driven party' (Miller 2005: 114) – a vehicle whose wheels will fall off once the charismatic populist who founded it decides to call it a day. There can be no doubt that Peters has always been in the driving seat: the party's campaigning, its policy, and its positions on joining the government (in 1996 and in 2005) and leaving it (in 1998) are his; anyone who has opposed him has either resigned from their office or left the party completely. Although the parliamentary party sanctioned the confidence and supply agreement with Labour – and they were, note, the only party body that needed to do so – some MPs were unhappy and would clearly have preferred (like some of their United Future counterparts, in fact) to deal with National rather than Labour. But most of the criticism was directed at what was generally thought to be a lacklustre election campaign – a campaign that those replying to the criticisms confessed was run entirely out of the leader's office in parliament with little input or even supervision from the board that supposedly helps run the party.

The extent to which government participation 'tames' populist parties is very much a live issue all over Europe, with Jörg Heider's FPÖ the obvious case in point. NZ First's period as a full-blown coalition partner between 1996 and 1998 provides another. So keen were the two main parties to have it on board that both offered considerable policy concessions, and NZ First was able to persuade its final choice, National, to spend more on education and health, to grant a referendum on compulsory superannuation, and not to pursue further privatisation; however, it did little to force the pace on two of its signature issues – a clampdown on immigration and on foreign investment in New Zealand firms. Whether the fact that the coalition broke up ostensibly over state asset sales indicated that the party was sticking to its economically nationalist guns is, however, questionable: many observers believed Peters – freefalling in the polls – was by that stage looking for a reason to go and hoped, by picking that one, to morally oblige his increasingly wayward ministerial team to walk out with him. This, of course, he failed to do.

In the long term, however, participation appeared to have no softening impact on the party's key populist positions. True the emphasis on economic nationalism has declined, not least because Labour-led governments have not sought further sell-offs. And the party's anti-corruption stance is not quite as high up in the mix as it was in the early 1990s. On the other hand, the party has moved even further in an authoritarian and xenophobic direction (Miller 2006). From 1999 onwards the themes have been harsher prison sentences, no special privileges for Maori and, above all, immigration: after all, in the wake of 9/11, claimed Peters (Clifton 2002), 'We have an obligation to our own people, our own emerging culture and our own creeds . . . before that of any Tom, Dick, Harry, Mustaq or bin Laden who wants to come here'.

This sort of stuff goes down well, of course, with what has become NZ First's core vote, namely the middle-aged and elderly and low to low-middle income earners wanting to reduce immigration and reintroduce the death penalty (see Miller 2006). But there is little evidence that this increasing *fidélisation* at the level of the voter has, however, translated into a solid membership that persists over time. Nor – and not perhaps surprisingly given part of a populist party's raison d'être is to recapture the state from 'special interests' – is there any evidence that NZ First has embedded itself in civil society: at the 2005 election the party campaigned for a 'golden age card' that would raise pensions and offer subsidies and discounts on healthcare, transport and utility bills, all of which went down well with the lobby group for older Kiwis, Grey Power; but so, too, did the goodies offered them by the other parties, and the group (at least in public) maintains its independence from all of those seeking to win its favour.

At the parliamentary level, of course, it is NZ First that the other parties have had to woo, particularly because Peters has resisted any pressure to lean toward Labour or (more obviously) National. NZ First is thus a right-wing populist party that, unusually, has managed to avoid becoming trapped on one side of the bipolar divide. Pulling off this rare trick has only proved possible, of course, because the Labour prime minister, Helen Clark, has been prepared to do deals with a party whose views she has described as 'deeply offensive'. The advent of a less flexible Labour leader might in effect call NZ First's bluff, forcing it into National's increasingly 'big tent'. If that were to happen, the party's survival would be at risk, since National's economic and social policy at last appears headed in a more centrist direction, while its line on immigration and minorities has hardened considerably. In such a situation, NZ First's only remaining unique selling point would be its leader. Yet 'Winston' may well be a wasting asset: he has finally lost the electorate seat that was his party's guarantee of legislative representation whether it reached the 5 per cent threshold or not; moreover, his acceptance of the post of foreign minister can not only be spun as a betrayal of his claim not to be interested in 'the baubles of office' but might also indicate that his horizons have widened beyond party and parliamentary politics.

The Alliance

When the Alliance joined Labour in a minority coalition in 1999, it had at least an inkling of the risks involved, particularly when it came to the need to maintain party unity and identity in the face of the inevitable compromises of government and the need to communicate that it was adding value, not simply a handful of cabinet and parliamentary seats, to Labour's efforts. The party's mistake was that it chose to achieve the latter not through a conventional coalition agreement promising policy wins for ministers in key departments, but via an 'agree to disagree' clause in what was otherwise an incredibly vague, virtually policy-free, one-and-a-half-page document signed by the partners just a few days after the election. That it did so was due to the authority of the party's charismatic founder, Jim Anderton, who argued that to hold out for more was, first, inconsistent with the party's stress on the relationship of trust that it had re-built with Labour and, second, risked re-evoking memories of the long-drawn-out negotiations and 72-page coalition agreement between National and NZ First – a process that did nothing to hold their government together when the chips were down. The Alliance was also concerned lest 'playing hard to get' might encourage Labour to turn a two-way coalition into a three-way arrangement including the Greens. Finally, the Alliance – or at least its leader – believed that ultimately voters would reward the party for being a responsible part of a centre-left government pursuing policies that would bring a badly needed dose of stability as well as tangible benefits to its low-income constituents.

It soon became apparent, however, that, inasmuch as they were grateful, voters (and the trade unionists that had flirted with the party as an alternative to Labour) were grateful to Labour rather than the Alliance – understandably so given that the latter had already dumped almost all its distinctive policies as part of its unofficial pre-electoral pact with Labour which, once in government, was careful not to renege on its left-ish promises. Consequently, the Alliance began (to coin a phrase) polling 'beneath the margin of error'. This would have been bad enough, but when combined with the government's decision to send military assistance for the invasion of Afghanistan, it created considerable internal disquiet, with some critics on the party's council apparently claiming that it should have had a veto over Alliance ministers' support for the decision – a sign that the party had never really resolved the institutional relationship between the party in public and in central office. But there was disquiet, too, within the parliamentary party and even amongst the Alliance's cabinet ministers. Some of the latter shared the view of the party's (extra-parliamentary) party president that the Alliance had to begin throwing what little weight it had around, thus creating some brand differentiation.

Yet it was not immediately obvious what any claim to differentiation could be based on: the Alliance was not so much ideologically 'tamed' by Labour as gradually denuded of all purpose as the latter returned to reclaim the social democratic flame which the Alliance (or at least its leader) had kept burning in the dark days of neo-liberalism. In any case, as soon as it became evident to the leader, now the deputy prime minister, that his rock-solid electorate majority and his force of personality would not be enough to persuade others to sit tight and wait for the rewards of responsibility, he simply founded his own party, taking half the Alliance's contingent of ten MPs with him. He, of course, was re-elected at the 2002 general election called shortly thereafter, managing to bring in (on a party vote of just 1.7 per cent) another 'Progressive Coalition' MP; the rump of the Alliance, with an even smaller share of the vote and no electorate winners, dropped out of parliament, lost its high-profile members (some of whom ended up in the recently founded Maori Party), and scored a derisory 0.7 per cent in 2005. For all its left-wing, democratically controlled and quasi-federal credentials, then, the Alliance fell prey to a general failure among the newly governing parties in New Zealand to wean themselves off their dependence on their leader – a dependence institutionally reinforced (possibly even locked in) by the fateful decision to subvert the 5 per cent threshold by granting proportional representation to any party capable of winning an electorate seat.

The Greens

Like their counterparts in Europe, the Greens have had to seek a blend between their preference for grass-roots, participative democracy and their need to function in a fast-moving, media-saturated political world that revolves around the legislature and the executive. It is fair to say that, up until now at least, the Green Party in New Zealand has managed this as well if not better than most. Although the parliamentary party and leadership is allowed considerable discretion in campaigning, policy development and presentation, legislative tactics and dealing with government, the wider party continues, via an AGM, to have virtually the final word on policy and on candidate selection (Bale and Wilson 2006). Accordingly, the Greens have avoided the serious public spats that have dogged their sister parties in, say, Germany, France, Belgium and Finland. To some extent this has been because, in absolute if not in relative terms, its membership is so small and, at the middle and upper levels, so stable, that there is still regular and friendship-based contact from top to bottom among those who are active, be it at local or parliamentary level. But the other big difference is that Green parties in the countries mentioned have managed to work their way into full-blown coalitions. In New Zealand, despite the best efforts and fondest wishes of most of their MPs, the Greens have so far only been taken on as a support party, albeit with increasingly sophisticated written agreements.

This involvement in governance rather than government has meant that there has been little direct pressure on the Greens to moderate ideologically, even if contract parliamentarism has forced them to focus on those policies that stand most chance of being taken up (and funded) by the Labour minority governments they have supported. The party continues to argue against military entanglements abroad, unless they are focused on peace-keeping. It keeps up the pressure for New Zealand to live up to its 'clean and green' image by prioritising public transport and alternative energy and agriculture, cutting pollution and resisting non-sustainable development. It takes Maori and women's rights very seriously. It stresses its commitment to social justice by fighting for the pay and protection of lower-paid workers. And it speaks out against what it perceives as the evils of globalisation, resisting New Zealand's ongoing efforts to secure free trade agreements with economic powerhouses such as the US and China, and even urging citizens to 'buy Kiwi-made'. The only obvious 'taming' that has occurred has been the party's reluctance to make a moratorium on GM crops a non-negotiable 'bottom-line' – a hard-line stance that wrecked whatever chance it had of joining Labour in coalition in 2002. It has also attempted – not very successfully it must be said – to explore contacts with the business sector, which (even outside the biotech industry) has taken a predictably hysterical view of what Green involvement in government might mean. That said, the party remains close to the anti-GM groups that sprang up in the mid 1990s, as well as to the range of new social movements from whose ranks many members, at both the top and bottom of the party, sprang.

Out of all New Zealand's new parties, the Greens (along, possibly, with the Maori Party) probably stands the best chance of long-term survival. It has a genuine membership base, even if it is older and more passive than it would like. It mobilises along a cleavage that is (and very likely will continue to be) sufficiently important to get it over the 5 per cent threshold – an achievement made all the more likely by the feeling among many Labour supporters that the Greens are a useful way of ensuring that their party does not drift too far right. Added to this is the feeling, even amongst Labour's leadership, that the Green Party is good for a few parliamentary seats that Labour might not win otherwise, that might make the difference between holding onto or losing power, and that can continue to be 'purchased' via a support contract rather than a more costly coalition agreement. But this is the Green's dilemma: their best hope of full participation in government would seem to be a coalition with Labour; yet the only way of making that happen, assuming the continued existence of United, NZ First and voters' (and Labour's) seeming reluctance to reward the party for a more aggressively leftist stance, is somehow to leapfrog Labour into the centre and open up the possibility of a deal with National, thereby ending the party's captive status.

To do that, however, would require not only some kind of conversion by National (which still seems sceptical even on climate change) but also junking precisely those policies which make the party distinctive and worth voting for and belonging to. Even if the parliamentary party and its advisors wanted to trade policy for office, and believed they could do it without losing votes, their so-far acquiescent activist base not only would but could prevent them. The events of June 2006, when the Greens chose as their new co-leader someone who (although he has a PhD in political science!) was neither an MP nor associated with any mooted move to the centre, suggests that any such move is unlikely.

Sweden

New Democracy

New Democracy may not have lasted long, but it helped break up the solid five party system and expanded political debate. Yet as a fundamentally populist party, it not only faced a familiar dilemma between preserving its identity as an outsider and wanting a share of power, it also lacked a basic ideological compass that might have guided its decisions on policy and organisation. The two founders of the party, Ian Wachtmeister and Bert Karlsson, had very different views on what the party should accomplish and how it should be run (Holck-Bergman 1995: 17). And they disagreed on New Democracy's relationship with the government: either the party should proclaim that it would always support a bourgeois government (Wachtmeister), or it should position itself in the middle and act as a thorn in the side of both blocks (Karlsson).

New Democracy was a new party in every sense – the product of two political entrepreneurs catching the moment rather than an organised institution. The fact that, on entering parliament, the party lacked formal statutes (Holck-Bergman 1995: 25) obviously gave the two founders immense influence over the organisation. At the same time, the party had a very vulnerable membership base, recruited during its rapid expansion and with very little experience of politics. Some, indeed, were eccentrics who soon became a burden rather than a resource: one MP, for instance, argued that foreign aid was counterproductive because Africa would become too crowded even though lions did a good job of keeping down the population.

But the issue that eventually marked the end of party unity was more prosaic. The centre-right minority coalition that to begin with relied on New Democracy's legislative support proposed family subsidies as an alternative to publicly financed kindergarten places for younger children, prompting accusations that it was trying to bring back the traditional housewife. New Democracy effectively split into three on the issue, with one group supporting the proposal, one group abstaining from voting (Wachtmeister) and one group maintaining the original party line and voting against (Karlsson).

Since New Democracy's existence very much depended on the two founders of the party, when they started to disagree, it immediately started to implode. And when public support bled away, the party lost members as quickly as it had attracted them and its organisation collapsed amid internal disputes, some of which led to legal battles. Yet, although New Democracy came to grief while supporting a government, it is hard to argue that that support was the reason for its downfall: more important were the internal contradictions that were there at its conception.

The Christian Democrats

The Christian Democrats were a coalition partner in the 1991–94 bourgeois government and have survived in parliament since then. The party had the same party leader, Alf Svensson, for 30 years and in the public's eyes he more or less was the party. Even though the party has had a pretty strong core of members over the years, the almost hegemonic role of the leader guaranteed a relatively centralised party organisation: nothing got through without being signed off by Svensson and being in government made little or no difference.

During its period in government, the Christian Democrats were very loyal towards their coalition partners, preferring pragmatism to obstinacy. This cooperative stance contributed to a solid platform for the government within parliament, but the party paid a price for its unselfishness. An electoral backlash in the election in 1994 (where the party dropped from 7.1 per cent to 4.1 per cent) was arguably the result of lack of a clear political profile within the coalition. To some extent, this was a result of securing only what some saw as essentially lightweight ministries, with Svensson, for instance, becoming minister of foreign aid and deputy foreign minister. In the wake of the election, the relative invisibility was criticised and there were even mumblings about Svensson himself, although his dominance was such that it took another ten years before the party got round to electing a replacement.

Even though the Christian Democrats have emphasised the division between politics and religion, the party consists of what many would see as Christian fundamentalists. Some of its members are active members in a widely criticised non-conformist church. In political terms, this means an internal debate on, for example, women's right to abortion, on homosexuality and on religious education. In order to be accepted by other parties, the leadership was obliged to tone down these tendencies and demands. For example, the founder of the anti-abortion movement (*Ja till livet*), Mikael Oscarsson, was elected as an MP for the Christian Democrats in 1998 and was controversially asked to choose between his chairmanship and his parliamentary position. Oscarsson, who was not alone in the party in taking a conservative Christian position, remained in parliament but the discussion on these fundamental issues continues.

With a focus on family values (and financial support) and religiously inspired morality (especially in education), the Christian Democrats have found their niche within the political spectrum but, as a consequence, are very much bound into the bourgeois bloc, of which they are electorally one of the weakest members. If the party should stumble on the line between fundamentalism and pragmatism, this would certainly threaten its parliamentary survival. Since 2004, it has also had to adjust to life after Svensson. Its new leader, Göran Hägglund, has sought to fashion a new, modern and younger, image of the party, although this does not include any fundamental change in its political position. Since the Achilles heal of the bourgeois block has always been its disunity, its component parties are understandably reluctant to emphasise issues that would threaten a post-2006 election coalition. But this means that the Christian Democrats could find it difficult both before and after the contest to differentiate themselves from their allies – something which, no less than an overly fundamentalist stance, could threaten the party in the long term.

The Greens

In addition to convincing Swedes about the importance of environmental issues, the Greens wanted to build a different kind of political party – one with a flatter organisational structure, with a stronger say for rank-and-file members, with less hierarchical decision-making and a gender-balanced leadership. But although they continue to have one male and one female spokesperson and a relatively open candidate selection process, they have had to make some compromises in other areas in order to keep a tighter grip on issues and speed up the decision process. A stronger, centralised leadership has proved a necessity in order to get the most out of what is a difficult role as a support party (Bale and Bergman, 2006b).

A second important principle for the Greens was the emphasis on not belonging to either the left or the right in the political spectrum. Over time, however, the leftist nature of the party's position has become more obvious, although this has probably been due as much to developments within the party as to its co-operation with Social Democratic governments. Green views on, among other things, economic growth, international trade, and military intervention are not compatible with standard right-wing positions and it has become increasingly difficult for the Greens to maintain their 'neither left nor right' stance. That said, the latter probably did facilitate the party's attempt, in the aftermath of the 2002 election, to start negotiations with some of the bourgeois parties with the ostensible purpose of creating a centre-right government but also of enhancing the Greens' bargaining power vis-à-vis the Social Democrats. Whether, after so many years of close co-operation with the Social Democrats and the Left Party, their move was a credible one is a moot point.

The Swedish Greens have not been completely untouched by the *realo-fundi* conflict familiar to their counterparts in other countries. However, since the party today has substantial experience in making compromises with the Social Democrats and Left Party on both national and local levels, it is obvious that it is the more pragmatic view that characterises the Greens. This means that the party has been forced to accept a less progressive political agenda than it otherwise would opt for – even if, for the most part, this implies not so much a different direction of travel but simply a slower pace of change, with the decommissioning of nuclear power and a move towards eco-taxes (and away from employment taxes) as obvious examples. Unfortunately for the party, where there is a more fundamental difference (for instance, the Greens' support for private solutions in welfare and schooling), there is also strong consensus between the Social Democrats and the Left Party, which results in the Greens ending up in a rather weak bargaining position. At the same time, it is important to remember that the Greens do not work in a vacuum: within the Social Democrats there are people that would like to emphasise a sustainable environment, and they are helped by co-operation with the Greens. Reforms that otherwise would have been more or less impossible, because of conflicting views within the Social Democrats, could be implemented on the grounds that they are necessary in order to maintain support in parliament.

The Left Party

Since the mid 1960s, the Left Party has struggled with internal conflicts between a more pragmatic socialist position and a more fundamentalist leftist position – conflicts which are both ideological and organisational, and which have been made all the more pressing by the party's decision on more than one occasion to support Social Democratic governments. For a while, however, those conflicts could be elided via the charismatic leadership – and the emphasis on gender politics – provided by Gudrun Schyman between 1993 and 2003. Under Schyman, the party tolerated a degree of centralisation and ideological–policy compromise that otherwise it might not have countenanced.

The strategy of the Left Party during the 1990s seemed successful. However, even before Schyman was obliged to resign the leadership after a financial scandal, the Left Party seemed unable to sustain the electoral gains made in opposition, largely at the expense of the Social Democrats: its high-water mark of 12 per cent in 1998 was reduced to 8.4 per cent in 2002 after four years providing confidence and supply to the minority government – despite the fact that co-operation has provided both stability and economic growth. Even if the conflicts in the party revolved mainly around more fundamental ideological positions, they were nonetheless fuelled by a sense of frustration about the compromises inherent in supporting the government.

All in all, the Left Party has been less visible as a support party than the Greens, who have arguably been more successful in negotiations – possibly because the party's claim not to be a captive of the Social Democrats has been even less convincing than that of the Greens. On the other hand, it is important to remember two things. First, both parties' aim has been essentially to drag or at least anchor the Social Democrats to the left and/or towards greater focus on the environment: the Left Party – even if it cannot lay claim to huge advances towards socialism – can claim that it has gone some way to stopping the rot. Second, the co-operation between the two support parties and the government has not included foreign policy and EU policies. To some extent, these are the areas in which the differences between the Social Democrats and the Left Party are most marked. By keeping these outside their co-operation agreements, the Left Party has been able to remain in opposition on areas that are important for the identity of the party.

Yet this – and the more Marxist tone of the party's new leader since 2004, Lars Ohly – has not been enough. Several MPs have publicly stated their disquiet and branches on the local level have left the party and created local alternatives. The general picture was of a party in serious decline. In response, Ohly publicly stated that his party was not prepared to support a Social Democratic minority government that did not include the Left Party after the election in 2006. This represented a major shift in the party's strategy but did not rescue it electorally. Many believed the Left Party remained more prepared to bark than to bite, although the night's victory left the question unanswered.

Conclusion

With one obvious exception (the Alliance, which actually fell apart under the strain), the actual experience of joining or supporting governments does not, in and of itself, appear to have fundamentally changed the organisation of those parties under consideration. Those parties which were highly centralised – some of them, indeed, depending on dominant leaders – remained so. Inasmuch as parties that were less centralised became more so, this was already under way as an adaptation to the demands of parliamentary life in a fast-moving, mediatised environment rather than constituting a response to gaining power. In parties where the exercise of authority and discipline has always been questionable – those on the radical left (including the Greens) – have not made some kind of step-change and left those questions behind. The impact on membership is harder to gauge: participation does not seem to boost membership, but (with the possible exception of the Swedish Left Party) neither does it result it widespread departures – although in some cases (especially in New Zealand) membership is so low and figures so hard to come by that detecting any such movement would be next to impossible anyway. Likewise, links with civil society are either so attenuated or tentative as to make no difference or, where they do exist (for example, in Christian and Green parties), they are apparently not unduly jeopardised by participation.

Nor has the impact of supporting or joining government on parties' ideology been very significant – at least beyond the short-term policy compromises inevitably (though, for supporters, often problematically) involved. Even when those compromises are made, most parties make strenuous (though not always successful) efforts to remind voters that they retain their distinctive aspirations, arguing (more or less convincingly) that even if the pace of change is not what they would like, they are broadly happy with the overall direction of travel. This has become – and has had to become – the mantra for the Greens and for other parties on the left, but it also applies to others. Once out of the government loop, parties soon start singing the same old songs: parties inspired by Christianity bang the drum for family and traditional values; populists seem to forget how they were sucked into 'politics as usual' – and so, to an extent, do voters, some of whom appear ready to believe that next time around such parties really will be able to sweep away the cobwebs, the corruption and the compromises and return the country to 'the people'.

The electoral consequences of getting into or getting near to government, however, are clear. Though rarely fatal, participation means a loss of votes above and beyond the incumbency penalty paid by most governing parties – at least in the short term. And, contrary to what is sometimes said to be one of the potential advantages of supporting rather than actually joining a government, occupying that intermediate position seems to offer no protection against such losses. On the other hand, losses can generally be recouped after one or two terms in opposition, which in New Zealand could be as little as three to six years. In the eternal triangle of policy, office and votes, and the trade-off between them, time-horizons and discounting play a big part. At least for the 'newly governing' and 'nearly governing' parties examined here, and notwithstanding the supposedly greater influence opposition parties can wield in one country (Sweden) compared to the other (New Zealand), the short term (and sometimes paltry) policy gains that result from participation are so far seen to outweigh the hopefully temporary costs incurred. This may be because – even when the contract involved does not constitute a full-blown coalition agreement – it at least offers relative newcomers the chance to demonstrate that they can act responsibly at the highest level and are therefore good bets for government in the future. Were such a wager taken up, both by voters and by bigger, older parties, it could fundamentally alter the political map of both countries.

Bibliography

Aimer, P. (2003) 'United Future', in R. Miller (ed.) *New Zealand Government and Politics*, 3rd edition, Auckland: Oxford University Press.

Bäck, M. and Möller, T. (1997) *Partier och Organisationer*, Stockholm: Norstedts Juridik AB.

Bale, T. and Bergman, T. (2006a) 'Captives no longer, but servants still? Contract Parliamentarism and the new minority governance in Sweden and New Zealand', *Government and Opposition*, 41 (3): 422–49.

Bale, T. and Bergman, T. (2006b) 'A taste of honey is worse than none at all? Coping with the generic challenges of support party status in Sweden and New Zealand', *Party Politics*, 12(2): 189–209.

Bale, T. and Wilson, J. (2006) 'The Greens', in R. Miller (ed.) *New Zealand Government and Politics*, 4th edition, Auckland: Oxford University Press.

Bale, T., Boston, J. and Church, S. (2005) '"Natural because it had become just that." Path dependence in pre-electoral pacts and government formation: a New Zealand case study', *Australian Journal of Political Science*, 40 (4): 481–98.

Clifton, J. (2002) 'Immigrant song', *New Zealand Listener* 21-28 September, 18–22.

Gilljam, M. and Holmberg, S. (1993) *Väljarna inför 90-talet*, Stockholm: Norstedts Juridik.

Holck-Bergman, J. (1995) *Kannibalerna (Nyd)*, Simrishamn: Tant Gredelin AB.

Holmberg, S. and Oscarsson, H. (2004) *Väljare: Svenskt Väljarbeteende under 50 år*, Stockholm: Norstedts.

Miller, R. (2005) *Party Politics in New Zealand*, Melbourne: Oxford University Press.

Miller, R. (2006) 'New Zealand First' in Miller (ed.) *New Zealand Government and Politics*, Auckland: Oxford University Press.

Pierre, J. and Widfeldt, A. (1992) 'Sweden', in R. S. Katz and P. Mair (eds) *Party Organizations: A Data Handbook*, London: Sage.

Widfeldt, A. (2005) 'De konservativa partierna i Norge och Sverige: Høyre och Höger/ Moderata samlingspartiet', in M. Demker and L. Svåsand (eds) *Partiernas Århundrade: Fempartimodellens Uppgång och fall i Norge och Sverige*, Stockholm: Santérus Förlag.

Wörlund, I. (2005) 'Miljöpartiet i Norge och Sverige', in M. Demker and L. Svåsand (eds) *Partiernas Århundrade: Fempartimodellens Uppgång och fall i Norge och Sverige*, Stockholm: Santérus Förlag.

6 Greens in a rainbow

The impact of participation in government of the Green parties in Belgium

Pascal Delwit and Emilie van Haute

Introduction

The Belgian party system has been fairly fragmented and open to new parties. However, the integration of new parties into national-federal governments has been limited. The Belgian political system, characterised by pillarisation and consociationalism (Delwit *et al.* 1999), encourages the three traditional party families (Christian Democrats, Socialists and Liberals) to share power amongst them, and to limit the access of new parties to power. Consequently, welcoming new parties in government is relatively rare. Nevertheless, consociationalism as *crisis management* has sometimes encouraged the traditional parties to incorporate new parties into the old ones in order to solve a crisis, or to stabilise the political system after the emergence of a new cleavage (Deschouwer 2002). Three cases of this can be found since the end of the Second World War (Magnette 2000): *neo-unionist coalitions*,[1] the *regionalist coalitions*,[2] and the *rainbow coalition*.[3]

This chapter deals with the third case, the entry of the French-speaking Green party (Ecolo) into the Belgian federal, Walloon and French Community governments in 1999. Green parties have been widely analysed during the last decades, but the focus has been on the emergence and the development of these new parties (Müller-Rommel 1989; Poguntke 1989; Richardson and Rootes 1995; O'Neill 1997), their ideological corpus and organisational rules (Poguntke 1987, 1990), or their electoral success (Kitschelt 1988; Müller-Rommel 1994; Vialatte 1996; Delwit and De Waele 1999). The analysis of the meaning (Rüdig and Rihoux 2006) and the consequences of their first participation in power is only just beginning to be made (Müller-Rommel 2002).

This contribution examines how Greens have been affected by being in power. More precisely, it analyses the changes that have occurred in their internal organisation rather than those that have taken place in the electorate or in their ideological profiles (Rüdig and Rihoux 2006). The chapter focuses on potential transformations in the membership of the party. Analysing participation through this perspective is particularly relevant because grass-roots democracy is an essential feature of Green parties. Participation in government has led to membership growth, and we will try to see whether this has also meant a qualitative change in the membership.

The road to power

The road to representation was fairly easy for Ecolo when compared to other Green parties in Europe. Ecolo was born as a party in March 1980, but its roots go back to the early seventies (Deschouwer 1989; Delwit and De Waele 1996). It can be found in several ecologist movements (*Les Amis de la Terre*), but also in former political parties (RW, *Démocratie Nouvelle, Combat pour l'Ecologie et l'Autogestion, Ecolog, Wallonie-Ecologie, Europe-Ecologie*). This legacy made it easy to move past the stages of authorisation and representation (Pedersen 1982; Buelens 2001). Participation in elections was not a real problem for the party.

Its early years were characterized by a direct electoral takeoff, followed by stagnation during the second half of the 1980s. The step from representation to coalition potential was, however, crossed rapidly at the local level (Table 6.1). By 1982 the party had already taken part in four local governments, including the city of Liège (second largest city in Wallonia).

Yet reaching coalition potential and governmental power was more difficult at other levels of power. In 1985, Ecolo accepted an offer to participate in the Walloon regional government by a small majority (50.7 per cent). This caused great tension and an internal crisis. The questions of whether the party had to be a movement or a real party, and whether it could also be office-seeking, were quite divisive. Many 'fundamentalist' members and figureheads left the party. In the end, the support proposal was rejected by the Liberals (PRL). This clearly shows that being in government still had to become more or less acceptable not only for Ecolo, but also for the other parties.

Table 6.1 Electoral results of Ecolo, 1981–2004

		Wallonia	*Brussels*
Legislative Elections (Lower House)	1981	6.1	2.2
	1985	6.4	4.3
	1987	6.5	4.3
	1991	13.6	7.1
	1995	10.3	6.5
	1999	18.3	21.3
	2003	7.5	9.5
European Elections	1979	5.1	
	1984	9.4	6.8
	1989	16.0	10.6
	1994	12.6	8.3
	1999	21.5	15.6
	2004	9.2	7.3
Regional Elections	1995	10.4	9.0
	1999	18.2	18.3
	2004	8.5	8.4

Source: Cevipol, http://www.ulb.ac.be/soco/cevipol

By the end of the 1980s, Ecolo had begun to score higher in elections thanks to a number of factors. The departure of the 'fundamentalist' group had pacified the party. Moreover, the Socialists (PS) had gained power at the federal level in 1987, leaving the Greens almost alone as an opposition party on the left of the political spectrum. And the re-emergence of environmental issues after Chernobyl benefited the party (Delwit 2003: 73). Ecolo achieved good electoral results in the local elections in 1988, but also in the 1989 European elections and the 1991 federal elections (Hooghe 1992).

As a consequence, the party now explicitly expressed its desire to participate in the Walloon government, but the Christian Democrats (PSC) and the Socialists (PS) remained deaf to its claim. However, in 1992, they had to call the Greens back to help them to reach the two-thirds majority necessary for a constitutional change, as the Liberals had refused to give them this support. The Greens thus found a good opportunity of testing their political relevance. The two Belgian Green parties (Ecolo and Agalev) negotiated some compromises, including ecological taxes that were, however, never implemented. This episode left the Greens disappointed.

Ecolo subsequently faced its first electoral defeat in the 1994 European elections, followed by gloomy results at the 1995 federal, regional and European elections (Hooghe 1995). The party then faced its second period of internal crisis (Buelens and Deschouwer 2002). Two wings confronted each other: one more 'fundamentalist–environmentalist', and one more 'generalist–social'. They disagreed on both the project (single issue versus full society project), and the strategy (opposition versus participation). The second wing got the better of both.

This was confirmed by a survey conducted among party members in 1994 (Delwit and De Waele 1996). It revealed a high degree of consensus for participation in government. A large majority was ready for their party to fulfil its responsibilities at all levels – even if approval was more noticeable for the local level: 97.5 per cent of the respondents (fully) agreed with the statement 'Ecolo has a vocation to exercise power at the local level', whereas 90.4 per cent of them (fully) agreed for the federal level.[4] If attitudes towards participation were controversial during the party's first years, the survey shows that in 1994, the debate had been left behind. Ecolo was ready for government.

Ecolo experienced its biggest electoral growth and victory in its (short) life in 1999. The party almost doubled its electoral result. From 243,362 votes (4.01 per cent, 6 seats out of 150 in Parliament), it climbed to 457,281 votes (7.43 per cent, 11 seats in Parliament), a growth rate of 187 per cent.

Several factors can be invoked to explain this huge victory. First, the 1995–99 coalition partners (Christian Democrats and Socialists) had been implementing a painful budgetary policy to reach the requirements for entering the euro zone (Delwit 2003: 84). In the second place, during the 1990s, Ecolo had positioned itself as the defender of the schools and teachers during the long-lasting financial conflict with the French Community government (Christian Democrats and Socialists). The party had also used its time in opposition to organize the '*Etats généraux de l'écologie politique*', a series of meetings with civil society groups.

It allowed Ecolo to gain sympathy but also to listen carefully to societal demands. Moreover, the party was able to win the protest votes connected to the 'Dutroux' case, the White March (Rihoux and Walgrave 1997), and the condemnation of the death of Semira Adamu, an illegal refugee who had been killed by Belgian police officers trying to escort her back to her country of birth. Finally, the campaign for the 1999 elections was focusing on a very ecological topic: the presence of dioxins in poultry and in a series of by-products. The real impact of that issue on the vote is still in dispute by scholars (Hooghe and Rihoux 2000; Baudewijns and Dumont 2003; Rihoux 2003), but all agree that it played a role – even if marginal – in the Green Party's electoral success.

Following its electoral victory, the party decided to enter the federal government in an original coalition of Liberals, Socialists, and the Flemish Green party Agalev (now Groen!). The origins of this coalition lie in a pre-election agreement between the French-speaking Socialists and Liberals. Both parties wanted to exclude the Christian Democrats – in power since 1958 – from government. In Flanders, the CVP lost its leadership for the first time since universal suffrage.

Ecolo was mathematically not needed to create an alternative majority on the French-speaking side of the political spectrum. Nevertheless, negotiations were open to the whole Green family, including Ecolo. First, the unexpectedly huge electoral victory of the Greens drove the Socialists and Liberals to revise their pre-election agreement so as to partly match the voters' choice. Moreover, Agalev votes were needed to form a coalition without the Christian Democrats in Flanders (Delwit and Hellings 2004). And Belgian federal coalitions are traditionally built on a symmetrical basis (parties from the same family on both sides of the linguistic divide). For all the above-mentioned reasons, Ecolo was included in the negotiations. The rainbow coalition was thus neither a *minimal winning coalition* (Riker 1962), nor a *minimal connected winning coalition* (Swaan 1973).

Negotiations for federal government were coupled with negotiations for regional and community governments. The fact that Ecolo was arithmetically not necessary is essential to the understanding of its subsequent small influence on the other parties in the coalition. The Greens failed to stand out during the negotiations. Despite its victory, Ecolo got only small and not very visible portfolios.[5]

As a result, many members were critical of these negotiations. The party statutes stipulate that participation in government must be approved by a vote of the *Assemblée Générale* (AG). Such an AG was called on July 11, 1999. Participation in three levels of power was approved with difficulty by the *Assemblée Générale*.[6] The members even rejected participation in the Brussels majority (53.9 per cent against, 44.5 per cent in favour and 1.6 per cent abstention). This internal division affected the life of the party and the conditions of its participation in government. Ecolo had been ready for power, but suddenly faced the consequences of being a small surplus partner in the coalitions.

Between 1999 and 2003, four different teams succeeded each other at the head of the party. After the difficult negotiations in 1999, the leading team of three resigned. It was succeeded by an 'anti-participationist' team that won by 56.0 per cent against the team supported by the Green MPs and Ministers. For three years the party was therefore led by anti-participationists while in government. This fairly awkward position was labelled '*participposition*'.

The situation was at the very least uncomfortable. This team resigned in July 2002, after having negotiated an agreement with the PS, stipulating that on certain issues both parties would defend the same positions.[7] For some of the activists, this agreement made Ecolo appear as the minor partner, as it only 'greened' the socialist programme. They feared that it would diminish Ecolo's strategic relevance and political pertinence within the party system (a prediction that turned out to be accurate). Again, the team that negotiated the agreement resigned. It was replaced by another trio, elected with 93.6 per cent of the votes. They also resigned after the electoral defeat of 2003.

The external context also changed between 1999 and 2003 (Delwit and Hellings 2004). In the first place, Ecolo's rivals (Socialists, Christian Democrats, and Liberals) initiated a programme of successful internal reform. The French-speaking Socialists (PS) and Liberals (MR) appeared as the serious partners in the coalition, achieving results on significant issues. In addition, the international context benefited parties holding portfolios linked to international questions. In this sense, the war in Iraq put the minister of foreign affairs, Louis Michel (MR), under the eye of the media. It also favoured the apparently serious, reliable, traditional parties. And, 15 days before the 2003 elections, a crisis emerged on the issue of night flights over Brussels. Ecolo's federal ministers isolated themselves from the rest of the government and were forced to resign, again displaying an image of amateurism and lack of reliability.

At the local elections of 2000 that followed soon after the joining of the federal and regional coalitions, Ecolo had still managed to achieve good results. In Brussels, it confirmed its excellent 1999 results, with 16.46 per cent of the votes. Ecolo entered 11 municipal executives out of 19. In Wallonia, the Green Party captured 10.74 per cent of the votes. Ecolo joined 24 local executives, and got three mayor's seats. By the end of the twentieth century, the Green Party had reached its peak in terms of participation in power. Having got into federal, regional and French Community governments, the party began to strengthen its local base. But a few years later the conclusion had to be that the first participation in regional and federal government had been paid in full at the polls. At the federal elections of May 2003, Ecolo only won 3.06 per cent, which meant a loss of more than half of its 1999 voters. In the Lower House, the party kept only four of its 11 seats.

It is interesting to note that former new parties in Belgian government have experienced the same difficulties with their first participation in coalitions. The example of the involvement of regionalist parties in government in the seventies reveals great similarities to our case study. After they participated in government, both the RW and the VU suffered enormous defeats (respectively in 1974–77[8] and in 1977–78[9]).

After the 2003 defeat and exit from the federal government, Ecolo decided to remain part of the regional and community governments until the end of the legislature in 2004. The 2004 European and regional elections, however, largely confirmed the disastrous 2003 federal election. In Wallonia, Ecolo lost half of its

1999 voters. The party fell to fourth place, just above the Front National (FN), but with fewer seats (FN 4; Ecolo 3). It was not even able to form a parliamentary group. Paradoxically, Ecolo retained good visibility in Brussels and became part of the regional government within an 'olive tree coalition' (PS, CDH, Ecolo). With lower electoral results, Ecolo was nevertheless in a better position than in 1999, considering that they were this time essential in forming the coalition.

Membership development

Green parties seem to have difficulties in recruiting members. They have one of the lowest voter/member ratios (Poguntke 1990: 246). According to Poguntke, Green grass-roots members suffer from a lack of feeling of attachment because of their high educational level; they have weak relationships with political parties, feeling loyalty to policy rather than to political organisations (Poguntke 1990: 253). Ecolo fits this pattern well (Table 6.2).

The development of the membership figures also illustrates the crises and successes that the party experienced. Its development could be split into four phases. During the first years after its foundation (1980–1988), the party was unable to recruit members. Its size remained comparable to a 'party movement', with a membership : electorate ratio of 0.39 per cent, which is totally insignificant com-

Table 6.2 The evolution of membership of Ecolo

Year	Members	Growth (%)
1984	808	
1985	959	+18.7
1986	836	−12.8
1987	617	−26.2
1988	891	+44.4
1989	1,403	+57.5
1990	1,212	−13.6
1991	1,360	+12.2
1992	1,876	+37.9
1993	1,934	+3.1
1994	2,347	+21.3
1995	2,488	+6.0
1996	2,058	−17.3
1997	2,321	+12.8
1998	2,721	+17.2
1999	2,903	+6.7
2000	4,050	+39.5
2001	4,008	−1.0
2002	4,463	+11.3

Source: Maes (1988), Delwit and De Waele (1996), Biondi *et al.* (2000).

pared with traditional parties. After the first proposal to participate in regional government in 1985, and the subsequent internal crisis, the party even lost some of its figureheads and 'fundamentalist' members. The second stage began when the electoral successes of the end of the 1980s and beginning of the 1990s were reflected in membership figures. Between 1988 and 1995, the party almost trebled its membership (from 891 to 2,488; +279.2 per cent). But as its electorate also grew proportionally, the membership/electorate ratio remained constant. In the same way, the 1995 electoral decline was mirrored in the membership figures, with a drop in 1996. The third stage of development began after the '*Etat généraux de l'écologie politique*' in 1996. This certainly had a positive impact on membership recruitment, with a growth in membership in 1997 and 1998. But more decisively, this positive trend was reinforced by the decision of the party to participate in power at different levels. This corresponds to the fourth and last stage (1999 and after). As also experienced by other Green parties, participation in government attracted plenty of new members (Biorci 2002; Boy 2002). In four years (1999–2002), party membership grew from 2,903 to 4,463 members (+153.7 per cent). Participation in power and membership growth certainly corresponded to a new developmental stage for the party.

The arrival of new members was a necessity (Poguntke 1990: 244). First, Greens are dependent on a high rate of internal participation. But the need became more pressing after participation in government, as the party statutes stipulate the separation of administrative positions and mandates, the rotation principle and collective leadership. All these internal rules increased the need for staff to hold mandates while keeping the intra-party organisation alive.

Intra-party changes

Hypotheses and data

The influx of new members was a necessity when participating in government. The party had to fill a large number of positions. Its undersized membership did not provide the party with a sufficiently large reserve. The post-1999 membership growth could be interpreted as an attempt to meet this challenge. But this influx may have had consequences. This section investigates the effects of this new development on the party's internal cohesion.

According to Rüdig and Rihoux (2006), one could expect two consequences of participation in government on membership. The first consequence expected is that members who joined the party before participation in government may feel alienated from the party. This idea derives from the constraints arising from participation in government. As single-issue parties, Green parties enter government without a full social project. Participation forces them to position themselves on new issues, and members may not recognize their party in this new positioning. Participation in government also implies compromises. Members may feel angry or frustrated by the party's behaviour while in power.

The second consequence of participation in power could be that Green parties become more attractive from an elite recruitment perspective. In this view, Green parties are expected to professionalise their recruitment (Norris 1997), i.e. attracting new members with a different sociological (more professional) and attitudinal (less radical) profile.

Two hypotheses can be derived from these expectations. The first hypothesis is that *members who joined after participation in government may have a different sociological and attitudinal profile* from their predecessors. The second hypothesis is that *members who joined the party before the 1999 participation in government may feel more alienated from the party* than members who joined after the entry in the rainbow coalition.

These hypotheses are tested with the results of a survey conducted among party members in March 2004, between the federal electoral defeat of May 2003 and the regional electoral defeat of June 2004. A total of 3,200 questionnaires were sent to party members, together with the *Quinzaine*, one of the party's internal publications. 1,029 questionnaires were returned, which represents a low (32.2 per cent) return rate. Geographical and gender distributions do, however, confirm the sample as being representative. Respondents were divided according to their year of entry to the party. Two categories were created, one of members who joined before 1999 ('pre-1999 members'), and one of members who joined in 1999 and after ('post-1999 members'). Among the respondents, 649 belonged to the first category (63.1 per cent), and 380 to the second (26.9 per cent).

Findings

According to the first hypothesis, we should find differences in the socio-demographic profile of grass-roots members according to the membership generation to which they belong (pre-1999 or post-1999 members; Table 6.3). Yet the proportion of women remains relatively constant between the generations (around one third, 34.77 per cent among pre-1999 members and 37.47 per cent among post-1999 members). There is however a change in the age distribution. The proportion of members above 50 years old is much lower among post-1999 members (38.9 per cent) than among their predecessors (53.4 per cent). Conversely, the younger generation (under 40 years of age) is better represented among the post-1999 generation (32.4 per cent) than among their counterparts (14.1 per cent). Nevertheless, the middle category (40–49 years old) remains constant across the generations. The party retains a pool of about 30.0 per cent of its members in their 40s. This means that the party recruited new members in their forties, and not just young people.

The level of education also remains constant across the generations. About 70 per cent of the Green members have higher education (respectively, 72.4 per cent among pre-1999 members and 71.8 per cent among post-1999), which is a high proportion. Given this, the party did not have to increase the level of education after participation – the level was already quite high.

An analysis of the degree of pillarisation[10] of the grass-roots members reveals an interesting development. The proportion of members strongly linked to the

Table 6.3 Socio-demographic and attitudinal profile of the pre- and post-1999 members of Ecolo

		Pre-1999 Members		Post-1999 Members		Total	
		N	%	N	%	N	%
Gender	F	226	34.77	142	37.47	368	35.76
	M	423	65.08	237	62.53	660	64.14
	Total	649	100.00	379	100.00	1028	100.00
Age	<40	90	14.11	120	32.43	210	20.83
	40-49	207	32.45	106	28.65	313	31.05
	≥50	341	53.45	144	38.92	485	48.12
	Total	638	100.00	370	100.00	1008	100.00
Education	No/Primary	17	2.62	6	1.58	23	2.24
	Secondary	162	24.96	101	26.65	263	25.58
	Superior	470	72.42	272	71.77	742	72.18
	Total	649	100.00	379	100.00	1028	100.00
Pillar	Weak (1)	175	28.18	117	32.77	292	29.86
	Mid (2)	183	29.47	115	32.21	298	30.47
	Strong (3)	263	42.35	125	35.01	388	39.67
	Total	621	100.00	357	100.00	978	100.00
	Mean (1–3)		2.14		2.02		2.10
Self-positioning left–right	Left	588	93.33	350	93.33	938	93.33
	Right	42	6.67	25	6.67	67	6.67
	Total	630	100.00	375	100.00	1005	100.00
	Mean (1–4)		1.86		1.82		1.85
Positioning left–right	Left	593	94.13	357	94.95	950	94.43
	Right	37	5.87	19	5.05	56	5.57
	Total	630	100.00	376	100.00	1006	100.00
	Mean (1–4)		1.96		1.96		1.96
Socio-economic	Left	472	84.59	271	86.03	743	85.11
	Right	86	15.41	44	13.97	130	14.89
	Total	558	100.00	315	100.00	873	100.00
	Mean (1–4)		1.76		1.76		1.76

Category		n	%	n	%	n	%
Universalism–particularism	Universalism	466	91.02	256	89.20	722	90.36
	Particularism	46	8.98	31	10.80	77	9.64
	Total	512	100.00	287	100.00	799	100.00
	Mean (1–4)		1.43		1.51		1.46
Libertarism–authoritarism	Libertarism	244	47.47	115	38.08	359	44.00
	Authoritarism	270	52.23	187	61.92	457	56.00
	Total	514	100.00	302	100.00	816	100.00
	Mean (1–4)		2.57		2.72		2.62
Progressism–conservatism	Progressism	400	86.02	234	83.27	634	84.99
	Conservatism	65	13.98	47	16.73	112	15.01
	Total	465	100.00	281	100.00	746	100.00
	Mean (1–4)		1.61		1.64		1.62
External participation	Negative attitudes	56	9.76	25	7.37	81	8.87
	Positive attitudes	518	90.24	314	92.63	832	91.13
	Total	574	100.00	339	100.00	913	100.00
	Mean (1–4)		3.45		3.53		3.48
Intra-party functioning	Negative attitudes	358	71.46	226	78.20	584	73.92
	Positive attitudes	143	28.54	63	21.80	206	26.08
	Total	501	100.00	289	100.00	790	100.00
	Mean (1–4)		2.18		2.04		2.13
First goal	Socio-economic	192	30.00	119	31.60	311	30.60
	Environmental	402	62.80	228	60.50	630	61.90
	Other	46	7.20	30	8.00	76	7.50
	Total	640	100.00	377	100.00	1017	100.00
Re-centre environment	In favour	193	47.50	207	56.40	500	50.80
	Against	324	52.50	160	43.60	484	49.20
	Total	617	100.00	367	100.00	984	100.0

Catholic pillar drops in the post-1999 generation (–7.3 per cent). Ecolo historically defines itself as a party outside the traditional Belgian pillars. Nevertheless, it had clear roots in the Christian Democratic movement (Delwit and De Waele 1996). The profile of the pre-1999 members confirms this (42.3 per cent of the members strongly integrated into the Catholic pillar). But after participation in government, membership diversified. There is a clear expansion and opening towards a new sociological stratum, i.e. people linked to the Socialist pillar. Nevertheless, if the developments in question are examined in greater detail, it appears that the opening up has been steady and gradual since the founding of the party rather than sudden, after participation. The first hypothesis also predicted differences in the attitudes of the members depending on the membership generation to which they belong (less radical attitudes among post-1999 members).

The first indicator of this relates to socio-economic attitudes.[11] The results indicate very coherent 'centre-left' attitudes within and across generations (an average of about 85 per cent of the respondents positioning themselves on the left of the scale, with an average positioning of 1.76 on the 1–4 scale for both generations). This is confirmed by the self-positioning of the respondents on the left–right scale (1–4 scale). An obvious majority of the members position themselves on the left of the scale (93.3 per cent), no matter which generation they belong to. The centre-left positioning is corroborated by the average positioning of 1.86 (pre-1999 members) and 1.82 (post-1999 members). In the same way, 94 per cent of them position their party on the left on a similar scale (average position of 1.94).

A second indicator measures libertarian–authoritarian attitudes.[12] Members position themselves closer to the centre on this scale. This average position varies somewhat across generations. Post-access to power members adopt more authoritarian attitudes than their older counterparts (61.9 per cent as against 52.2 per cent).

The third indicator – universalist–particularist attitudes[13] – reveals a clear radical positioning. About 90 per cent of the respondents position themselves on the universalist side of the scale. The average position on the scale is 1.43 for the pre-1999 members and 1.51 for the post-1999 members, which means a slight fall over the generations.

A fourth indicator measures the positioning of the respondents on a progressive–conservative scale.[14] Again, the majority of the members position themselves on the progressive side of the scale (about 85 per cent), with few variations over the two generations.

The first hypothesis (professionalisation of the members after participation) was thus not confirmed. The socio-demographic profile of the members remained quite constant across the generations, except for the age distribution. An opening-up in terms of socio-cultural background (pillarisation) was emphasised, but the development noted is progressive rather than subsequent to participation. In terms of attitudes, members also show a high level of cohesion, no matter which generation they belong to.

The second hypothesis states that members who joined the party before participation may feel more alienated from the party than members who joined after participation. This hypothesis can be linked to the *fundis–realos* cleavage emphasised by Poguntke (1989) or O'Neill (1997). According to these authors, fundamentalists and realists differ on two axes. The first axis is the 'radical dilemma', i.e. extremists versus moderates in terms of principles and organisational strategy. The second axis is the 'pure green versus watermelons' axis, i.e. environmentalism versus a greater openness towards other social issues. The hypothesis would then be that the pre-1999 members would correspond to the 'extremist' and 'pure green' axes, and the post-1999 more to the 'moderate' and 'watermelon' axes.

In order to test the divisions between the generations on the first axis (moderates versus extremists), two scales can be used. The first scale measures the members' view of the first participation in power.[15] On this scale, members show a great 'realo' consensus, no matter which generation they belong to. The opinion of the grass-roots towards the performances of their party in government is on the whole positive. Pre-1999 members do not have a worse view of their party's participation in power than the post-1999 members. Conversely, on intra-party issues,[16] members adopt moderate 'fundis' scores. About three quarters of the respondents take a negative view of intra-party functioning. Post-1999 members seem to have a slightly more sceptical view of intra-party functioning than their predecessors (averages of 2.18 and 2.04).

As far as the second axis is concerned (policy priorities), about two-thirds of the respondents placed environmental issues as the top priority for the party, whereas one third of the respondents chose socio-economic issues. This proportion does not vary across the generations. But on the question 'should the party re-centre itself on environmental issues?', the picture is more contrasting. The respondents are clearly divided in and between generations. This division crosses the generations: 50.8 per cent of the respondents agree with the idea, whereas 49.2 per cent are against. Nevertheless, the majorities are reversed if the generations of the members are taken into account. Among pre-1999 members, a small majority is against this proposal (52.5 per cent), whereas a small majority of the post-1999 members is in favour (56.4 per cent).

The analysis can be refined by means of logistic regression. This method allows for the testing of the likelihood of being a post-1999 member, as a function of socio-demographic and attitudinal variables (Table 6.4). The results reveal which characteristics and attitudes differentiate post-1999 members from pre-1999 members. Four characteristics unequivocally differentiate post-1999 members from pre-1999 members: age, pillarisation, authoritarian attitudes and opinions regarding intra-party functioning. This tallies with the conclusions of the first part of our analysis and confirms some of our previous findings. Members who joined the party after the 1999 reform are on average younger, less pillarised, adopt more authoritarian attitudes and take a more sceptical view of intra-party functioning. The impact of all other attitudes is not statistically significant. These results are very interesting because they also mean that differences in attitudes can mainly be explained by differences in the age structure of pre- and post-1999 members.

Table 6.4 The difference between the two generations of members: regression analysis

	B	Exp(B)
Gender	0.212	1.236
Age	− 0.421**	0.656
Education	0.106	1.112
Pillar	− 0.398**	0.671
Socio-Economic	− 0.146	0.864
Particularism	0.204	1.227
Conservatism	0.025	1.025
Autoritarism	0.387*	1.472
External Participation	0.267	1.306
Internal Participation	− 0.383*	0.682

Notes
$*P < 0.05$; $**P < 0.01$.

Conclusion

This contribution examined how the French-speaking Belgian Greens have been affected by participation to power. It first described Ecolo's road to power and membership developments. We emphasised the fact that participation in government went hand in hand with membership growth. Participation in power and membership growth certainly corresponded to a new stage for the party. The second section then investigated the effects of this new stage on the organisation of the party, and more precisely the potential changes in the membership. The underlying idea was that participation would reinforce membership recruitment, and that new members may have a specific profile and specific attitudes. Two hypotheses were tested. The first hypothesis was that members who joined after participation in government may have a different sociological and attitudinal profile from their predecessors. The second hypothesis was that members who joined the party before the 1999 participation in government may feel more alienated from the party than members who joined after entry to the rainbow coalition.

The first hypothesis (professionalisation) was not confirmed. Testing of the second hypothesis revealed a more sceptical view of intra-party operations among post-1999 members, as well as a clear division on the need for the party to refocus on environmental issues. This division crosses the respondents regardless of the year of their joining the party.

The logistic regression partly confirmed these findings, and highlighted four characteristics that explicitly distinguish the post-1999 members from pre-1999 members. Members who joined the party after the 1999 reform are, on average, younger, less pillarised, adopt more authoritarian attitudes and have a more sceptical view of intra-party functioning.

Participation in power did not lead to a profound reorientation of party recruitment. The profile and attitudes of post-1999 members hardly differ from that of their predecessors. Nevertheless, the findings show that members, regardless of the year they joined the party, are divided on the need for Ecolo to refocus on environmental issues. This reveals that members are divided on the strategy they want their party to adopt. Future decisions on whether or not to join again a federal or regional government are likely to bring again to the front the crucial questions about identity and strategy of Ecolo.

Notes

1 Coalitions including the Communists, the Christian Democrats, the Socialists and the Liberals, from 27 September 1944 until 12 March 1947, in order to stabilise the political system after the war.

2 Coalitions including regionalist parties that emerged from the centre-periphery split in order to implement the reform of the State: 25 April 1974 to 18 April 1977 (RW; Christian Democrats and Liberals); 3 June 1979 to 13 October 1978 (FDF; VU; Christian Democrats and Socialists); 3 April 1979 – 24 January 1980 (FDF; Christian Democrats and Socialists).

3 Coalition including the Green parties (Ecolo, Agalev), together with the Socialists and the Liberals, from 13 June 1999 until 18 May 2003.

4 As regards the regional level, the agreement covers 90.4 per cent of the respondents; the proportion reaches 91.2 per cent for the French Community.

5 This was revealed in the distribution of the portfolios. In federal government, Ecolo was assigned one deputy prime minister and the minister of mobility and transport; in the Walloon government, it got the minister of social affairs and health, and the minister of transport, energy and mobility; in the French-speaking community government, the party got the minister of primary education, and the minister of social affairs; finally, in the German community government, Ecolo got the minister of youth, family, social affairs and historic buildings.

6 Federal government: 58.5 per cent in favour, 38.5 per cent against and 3.0 per cent abstention; French community government: 71.6 per cent for, 22.6 per cent against and 5.8 per cent abstention; Walloon government: 68.7 per cent for, 28.3 per cent against and 3.0 per cent abstention.

7 *Convergences à gauche. Engagements communs des socialistes et des écologistes*, Plate-forme du 28 Septembre 2002.

8 In 1977, the RW lost half its votes and 8 seats out of 13.

9 In 1978, the VU lost 180,000 votes and 6 seats out of 20.

10 The 'Pillar' index varies from 1 to 3, 1 corresponding to a weak integration in the Catholic pillar (as opposed to the Socialist pillar), and 3 to a strong integration in the Catholic pillar. It sums up three indicators. The first indicator relates to the educational network. The Belgian educational network is divided across the State–Church division. The two main networks (Official and Free denominational) historically each belong to one side of the division and to one pillar (Christian Democrat versus Socialist and Liberal), and are associated with the matching pillar parties. Nowadays, the educational network is also divided across the community split, between Flemish and French-speaking networks. The second relates to membership of a mutual insurance company. In Belgium, the State itself does not run health insurance. It transfers the money received in taxes to semi-private health insurance companies. Citizens are obliged to register with one of these companies. Again, each pillar has developed its own health insurance company. Finally, the index takes into account the positioning of the members on the 'belief' item.

11 The index sums up the average position of members on four items: attitudes towards privatization, the role of unions in economic decisions, the role of the state in economic decisions and the individualisation of the social security services. Answers were coded and range from 1 (left) to 4 (right).

12 The index sums up the average positions of members on three items: decriminalisation of cannabis consumption, learning discipline at school and police funding. Answers were coded and range from 1 (libertarian attitudes) to 4 (authoritarian attitudes).
13 The index sums up the average positions of members on four items: expulsion of asylum seekers, voting rights for foreigners, enlargement of European Union, and feeling at home in Belgium. Answers were coded and range from 1 (universalist attitudes) to 4 (particularist attitudes).
14 The index sums up the average positions of members on four items: attitudes towards abortion, homosexual relationships, having children outside marriage and the distribution of condoms in schools. Answers were coded and range from 1 (progressive attitudes) to 4 (conservative attitudes).
15 The external participation index sums up four items: participation in power as a good opportunity, vocation for power, contribution of the party during office and work of the ministers in office. Answers were coded and range from 1 (positive vision of participation) to 4 (negative vision of participation).
16 The internal index sums up two items: intra-party tensions and weight of the members inside the party. Answers were coded and range from 1 (negative vision of intra-party operations) to 4 (positive vision of intra-party operations).

List of parties

CDH (ex-PSC)	*Centre Démocrate Humaniste* (French-speaking Christian Democrats)
CD&V (ex-CVP)	*Christen Democratisch en Vlaams* (Flemish Christian Democrats)
Ecolo	*Ecologistes Confédérés pour l'Organisation de Luttes Originales* (French-speaking Greens)
FDF	*Front Démocratique des Francophones* (French-speaking Regionalists)
FN	*Front National* (French-speaking extreme right)
Groen! (ex-Agalev)	*Anders gaan Leven* (Flemish Greens)
MR (ex- PRL-FDF-MCC)	*Mouvement Réformateur* (French-speaking Liberals)
PS	*Parti Socialiste* (French-speaking Socialists)
RW	*Rassemblement Wallon* (Walloon Regionalists)
SP.A (ex-SP)	*Socialistische Partij Anders* (Flemish Socialists)
VB	*Vlaams Blok* (Flemish extreme right)
VLD	*Vlaamse Liberalen en Democraten* (Flemish Liberals)
VU	*Volksunie* (Flemish Regionalists)

Bibliography

Baudewyns, P. and Dumont, P. (2003) 'L'affaire Dutroux et la crise de la dioxine: quel effet sur le vote en 1999 ?' in A.-P. Frognier and A.-M. Aish (eds) *Elections, la Rupture? Le Comportement des Belges face aux Élections de 1999*, Bruxelles: De Boeck.
Bauduin, J. (1999) 'Ecolo: après un raccourci', *La Revue Nouvelle*, 110(9): 20–37.

Biondi, P., Dewachter, W., Fiers, S. and Wauters, B. (2000) 'Tableau statistique synoptique', *Res Publica*, 42(1): 119–63.

Biorcio, R. (2002) 'Italy', in F. Müller-Rommel and T. Poguntke (eds) *Green Parties in National Governments*, London: Frank Cass.

Boy, D. (2002) 'France', in F. Müller-Rommel and T. Poguntke (eds) *Green Parties in National Governments*, London: Frank Cass.

Buelens, J. (1996) 'To change or not to change', paper presented at the ECPR Joint Sessions, Oslo, March–April 1996.

Buelens, J. (2001) 'Greens in Belgium: from local to governmental participation to power', paper presented at the ECPR Joint Sessions, Grenoble, April 2005.

Buelens, J. and Deschouwer, K. (2002) 'Belgium' in F. Muller-Rommel and T. Poguntke (eds) *Green Parties in National Government*, London: Frank Cass.

Delwit, P. (2003) *Composition, Décomposition et Recomposition du paysage Politique en Belgique*, Bruxelles: Labor.

Delwit, P. and De Waele, J.-M. (1996) *Ecolo: Les Verts en Politique*, Bruxelles: De Boeck Université.

Delwit, P. and De Waele, J.-M. (eds) (1999) *Les Partis Verts en Europe*, Bruxelles: Complexe.

Delwit, P. and van Haute, E. (2004) 'Les élections fédérales du 18 mai 2003: un scrutin de "défragmentation"', *L'Année Sociale 2003: Revue de l'Institut de Sociologie*, pp. 11–24.

Delwit, P. and Hellings, B. (2004) 'Ecolo et l'élection du 18 mai 2003: Du paradis au purgatoire ou à l'enfer?', *L'Année Sociale 2003: Revue de l'Institut de Sociologie*, pp. 38–49.

Delwit, P. and Pilet, J.-B. (2005) 'Regional and European election in Belgium: the Greens still at low tide', *Environmental Politics*, 14(1): 112–17.

Delwit, P., De Waele, J.-M. and Magnette, P. (eds) (1999) *Gouverner la Belgique: Clivages et Compromis dans une Société Complexe*, Paris: PUF.

Deschouwer, K. (1989) 'Belgium: The "ecologists" and "Agalev"', in F. Müller-Rommel (ed.) *New Politics in Western Europe: The Rise and the Success of Green Parties and Alternative Lists*, London: Westview Press.

Deschouwer, K. (2002) 'Falling apart together: the changing nature of Belgian consociationalism, 1961–2001', *Acta Politica*, 37(1–2): 68–85.

Deschouwer, K. and Buelens, J. (2002) 'The lifespan and the political performance of Green parties in Western Europe: Belgium', *Environmental Politics*, 11(1): 112–32.

Hooghe, M. (1992) 'The Green parties in the Belgian general elections of 24 November 1991', *Environmental Politics*, 1(2): 287–92.

Hooghe, M. (1995) 'The Greens in the Belgian elections of 21 May 1995', *Environmental Politics*, 4(4): 253–7.

Hooghe, M. and Rihoux, B. (2000) 'The Green breakthrough in the Belgian general election of June 1999', *Environmental Politics*, 9(2): 129–36.

Hooghe, M. and Rihoux, B. (2003) 'The harder the fall: the Greens in the Belgian general elections of May 2003', *Environmental Politics*, 12(4): 120–6.

Kitschelt, H. (1988) 'Organisation and strategy in Belgian and West German Ecology parties: a new dynamic of party politics in Western Europe?', *Comparative Politics*, 20: 127–54.

Kitschelt, H. (1989) *The Logics of Party Formation: Ecological Politics in Belgium and Germany*, Ithaca: Cornell University Press.

Laakso, M. and Taagepera, R. (1979) 'Effective number of parties: a measure with application to Western Europe', *Comparative Political Studies*, 12: 3–27.

Maes, M. (1988) *De Ledenaantallen van de Politieke Partijen in België 1945–1987: een Documentaire Studie*, Leuven: Afdeling Politologie K.U. Leuven.

Magnette, P. (2000) 'Un siècle de gouvernement proportionnel', in P. Delwit and J.-M. De Waele (eds) *Le Mode de Scrutin fait-il l'Élection?*, Bruxelles: Editions de l'Université de Bruxelles.

Müller, C.W. and Ström, K. (eds) (2000) *Coalition governments in Western Europe*, Oxford University Press, Oxford.

Müller-Rommel, F. (ed.) (1989) *New Politics in Western Europe: The Rise and the Success of Green Parties and Alternative Lists*, London: Westview Press.

Müller-Rommel, F. (1994) *Green Parties under Comparative Perspective*, Barcelona: Institut de Ciències Polítiques i Socials.

Müller-Rommel, F. (2002) *Green Parties in National Governments*, London: Frank Cass.

Norris, P. (1997) *Passages to Power: Legislative Recruitment in Advanced Democracies*, Cambridge: Cambridge University Press.

O'Neill, M. (1997) *Green Parties and Political Change in Contemporary Europe: New Politics, Old Predicaments*, Ashgate, Aldershot.

Pedersen, M. (1982) 'Towards a new typology of party lifespans and minor parties', *Scandinavian Political Studies*, 5(1): 1–16.

Poguntke, T. (1987) 'The organization of a participatory party: the German Greens', *European Journal of Political Research*, 15: 609–33.

Poguntke, T. (1989) 'The "New Politics Dimension" in European Green Parties' in F. Müller-Rommel (ed.) *New Politics in Western Europe: The Rise and the Success of Green Parties and Alternative Lists*, London: Westview Press.

Poguntke, T. (1990) 'Party activists versus voters: are the German Greens losing touch with the electorate?' in W. Rüdig (ed.) *Green Politics One*, Edinburgh: Edinburgh University Press.

Rae, D. (1968) 'A note on the fractionalization of some European party systems', *Comparative Political Studies*, 3: 413–18.

Richardson, D. and Rootes C. (eds) (1995) *The Green Challenge: The Development of Green Parties in Europe*, London: Routledge.

Rihoux, B. (2003) 'La percée d'Ecolo au 13 juin 1999: un effet dioxine, et des électeurs moins "verts"?', in A.-P. Frognier and A.-M. Aish (eds) *Elections, la Rupture? Le Comportement des Belges face aux Élections de 1999*, Bruxelles: De Boeck.

Rihoux, B. and Walgrave, S. (1997) *L'Année Blanche: Un Million de Citoyens Blancs, qui Sont-ils, que Veulent-ils?*, Bruxelles: E.V.O.

Riker, W.H. (1962) *The Theory of Political Coalitions*, Yale University Press, New Haven.

Rüdig, W. and Rihoux, B. (2006) 'Analysing Greens in Power: Setting the Agenda', *European Journal of Political Research*, 45(S1): S1–33.

Sartori, G. (1976) *Parties and Party Systems: A Framework for Analysis*, Cambridge: Cambridge University Press.

Swaan, A de. (1973) *Coalition Theories and Cabinet Formation: A Study of Formal Theories of Coalition Formation applied to Nine European Parliaments after 1918*, Amsterdam: Elsevier.

Vialatte, J. (1996) *Les Partis Verts en Europe Occidentale*, Paris: Economica.

7 Moving from movement to government

The transformation of the Finnish Greens

Jan Sundberg and Niklas Wilhelmsson

Introduction

Most new parties in Finland are small and have a limited influence. Only the Christian League and the Greens have been successful during the past decades. Others, like the populist Finnish Rural Party (now True Finns), have vanished after two successful elections in 1970 and 1983. As a result, the effective number of parties has only modestly increased. The number of parties in parliament has increased from six to ten, between the first general election in 1907 and 1999, and the effective number of parties in parliament from 3.57 to 5.15 during the same period (Sundberg 2002: 85–7). Eighteen parties contested the 1999 election, and nine of them were successful. The tenth party MP mandate is represented by the autonomous Åland, which is a one-member constituency.

One of these successes is the Finnish Greens. The party was founded in 1988, won its first parliamentary seats in 1983 while still a movement, and joined the government coalition after the 1995 election. Four years later, after the 1999 election, the Green Party prolonged its membership in government. Its career in the coalition ended abruptly when the party resigned from government in late May 2002. The decision to leave was taken by the party Council and the Parliamentary Party in protest against the Cabinet amendment accepted by the majority of the Parliament favouring the building of a fifth nuclear plant. As a result, the Greens joined the opposition in Parliament and managed in the 2003 election to win more votes and seats. However, the party was not accepted in the new coalition cabinet. However, after the 2007 election the Greens joined the new non-socialist cabinet.

The framework

We know that new and small parties succeed better in some political systems than in others. Small party votes are larger in proportional systems. Small parties also tend to take advantage of electoral volatility and high turnout (Mair 1991: 41–70). Margit Tavits' (2006) study of 358 new parties in national elections from 1960 to 2002 in 22 OECD democracies gives support for this theory of 'strategic entry'. The emergence of new parties is indeed related to the costs of registering a party, access to public funding, benefits from electoral office, the probability of electoral support and the probability of getting elected on the entry calculations (Tavits 2006: 99–119). However, earlier studies have found that strategic entry is especially true for contender parties. Promoter parties, whose major objective is to use the party as a vehicle for bringing attention to a particular issue (Harmel and Robertson 1985: 501–23) tend to contest elections in electoral systems that are least likely to reward new parties with votes and seats.

Mogens Pedersen has pointed out that small parties are mortal organisations, although they seldom totally disappear. Small and new parties tend to fluctuate in strength from one election to another, and in this process they have to pass or try to avoid some important thresholds. First parties have to pass the threshold of declaration, that is, when a political group declares its intention to participate in elections. Second, parties have to pass the threshold of authorisation, that is, legal regulations on what requirements have to be met to participate in electoral campaigns, elections and to nominate candidates. Thirdly, parties have to pass the threshold of representation, that is, to cross barriers to obtain seats in the legislature. It defines the 'ins' and 'outs' in the party system. Fourthly, parties have to pass the threshold of relevance, that is, when parties have impact and become influential, at best as a ruling party in government (Pedersen 1982: 1–16, 1991: 95–114).

Pedersen gives a heuristic explanation, taking into account institutional and political conditions for understanding the persistence of small parties. The thresholds emphasised by Pedersen are useful if combined with the factors related to strategic entry, which is indeed what we will do in this chapter. The discussion starts with an overview of all new parties who have contested parliamentary elections from the 1960s onwards. Following this, we focus on the Green Party's success in moving from one threshold to another.

The success of new parties in the Finnish party system

The effective threshold for parties to get seats in Parliament in 1995 was 12.5 per cent in the smallest constituency and 3.1 per cent in the largest (Sundberg 2002: 67–99). However, as parties have the option to enter electoral alliances, small and new parties may well be successful in getting their candidates elected. Since the early 1960s as many as 23 new parties have contested parliamentary elections (Table 7.1).

When the Greens contested elections for the first time in the 1980s, many predicted for them a similar fate as for the Union for Democracy, the Private Entrepreneur's Party and the Constitutional Party: some success in the beginning and then disappearing again. In fact, after the entrance of the Greens in the electoral arena, 15 new parties have tried to do the same. In 1991 no less than six new parties contested elections for the first time. In 1995 three newcomers nominated candidates; in 1999 one party, and in the 2003 election four newcomers, did the same. Very few of all 23 parties have a good long-term record of electoral support.

Table 7.1 The support for new parties contesting parliamentary elections in Finland since 1962

Parties	1962	1966	1970	1972	1975	1979	1983	1987	1991	1995	1999	2003
True Finns[a]	2.2	1.0	10.5	9.2	3.6	4.6	9.7	6.3	4.8	1.3	1.0	1.6
Christian Democrats[b]		0.4	1.1	2.5	3.3	4.8	3.0	2.6	3.1	3.0	4.2	5.3
Union for Democracy[c]					1.7	0.3	0.1					
Private Entrepreneurs' Party					0.4	0.0						
Constitutional Party					1.6	1.2	0.4	0.1	0.3			
Greens							**1.4**	**4.0**	**6.8**	**6.5**	**7.3**	**8.0**
Democratic Alternative								4.2				
Pensioners' Party								1.2	0.4	0.1	0.2	
Women's Party									0.5	0.3		
Communist Workers' Party									0.2	0.2	0.1	0.1
Pensioners for the People[d]									0.2	0.2	0.2	0.2
Ecological Party									0.1	0.3	0.4	0.2
Humanity Party									0.1			

Continued overleaf.

Table 7.1 Continued.

Parties	1962	1966	1970	1972	1975	1979	1983	1987	1991	1995	1999	2003
Joint Responsibility Party[e]									0.1	0.1		0.0
Progressive Finnish Party										2.8	1.0	
Alliance for Free Finland										1.0	0.4	
Natural Law Party										0.2	0.1	
Reform Group											1.1	
Forces for Change in Finland												0.4
For the Poor												0.1
Finland Rises												0.1
Finnish People's Blue-Whites												0.2
United People in Great Finland												0.1

Notes

a Rural Party before 1995, and Small Holders Party before 1966.
b Christian League before 1999.
c Unification Party of the Finnish People before 1983.
d Independent Pensioners before 1995.
e Party for Pensioners' and Green Mutual Responsibility before 1995.

Most of the parties appear only twice and sometimes only once. Others try several times with poor results. The True Finns and its predecessors have the longest record with sharp ups and downs. Only the Christian Democrats and the Greens have managed to establish a stable electoral base. Of these two, only the Greens have managed to increase their share of votes from one election to another, except for the 1995 election when the support was unchanged.

Nine of the new parties have managed to win seats in parliament, of which four have won seats more than once (Table 7.2). One of these parties has passed the threshold to parliament only twice, whereas the three others have done it permanently from the early beginning of their career. In addition, all these successful new parties have passed the threshold to become a cabinet party. The True Finns was first to be adopted in a coalition in 1983. Before that it had spent five election periods in parliament with varying numbers of MPs. The seventh election they contested in 1983 gave them 17 seats in parliament and two seats in cabinet. In the following election the party lost eight seats and won only one seat in cabinet. When their single minister resigned the party lost even more credibility in elections. Since then the True Finns have played only a marginal role in parliament. The Christian Democrats spent six periods in parliament. After eight contested elections the party was offered a cabinet seat in 1991. As in the former case, the Christian Democrat minister resigned during the cabinet period. The party has, however, managed to keep its position in parliament without any significant losses.

In contrast to the two other new parties, the Greens had only spent two terms in parliament when the party was given access to cabinet. Yet the Greens turned down the offer. Four years later the Greens were again offered one seat after the 1995 election, and this time they accepted. After the 1999 election they were offered one and a half seats in cabinet, which they accepted as well. As in the two former cases the Green ministers left the cabinet. Yet this has not negatively affected the party in elections. The number of seats in parliament even continued to increase at a steady rate.

The threshold of forming the Green Party

Founding a party in Finland is not only a matter of organising people; it is also affected by formal institutional constrains. The formal threshold to found a party in Finland is higher than in most other democracies. From 1919 political organisations in Finland have been regulated by an Act of Associations, and in 1969 these regulations were completed in a new Party Act. When the law came into force, a party register was established by the Ministry of Justice, with the task of dealing with party applications and ensuring that the regulations in the party law are followed. To be accepted as a party, an application must include a list of 5,000 enfranchised adherents. In addition, the party is obliged to have written rules following democratic principles of internal decision-making. The party is also obliged to have a written program (Partilag 10/1969). All foreigners were prohibited from membership in parties until 1989 when the right was extended to

Table 7.2 New party seats in the Finnish Parliament (time of entering cabinet shown in bold)

Parties	1962	1966	1970	1972	1975	1979	1983	1987	1991	1995	1999	2003
True Finns	0	1	18	18	7	7	17	9	7	1	1	3
Christian Democrats		0	1	4	9	9	3	5	8	7	10	7
Union for Democracy					1	0	0					
Constitutional Party					1	0	1	0	0			
Greens							2	4	10	**9**	**11**	14
Democratic Alternative								4				
Ecological Party									0	1	0	0
Progressive Finnish Party										2	0	
Reform Group											1	

cover Nordic citizens living in Finland (Lag om föreningar 1/1919; Föreningslag 503/1989). Changes in party rules and party programs are not enforced before the formal acceptance and registration in the party register. A party will be struck off the register if it fails to get at least one candidate elected in two subsequent parliamentary elections. A court may dissolve a registered party if it acts against the law (also the party law) or against the intentions of its own rules. Before 1990 the Ministry of the Interior could issue a complaint to the court; since then the right has been extended to the general prosecutor and a single party member (Lag om föreningar 1/1919; Föreningslag 503/1989). Finally, a party is given the right, after application to the Ministry of Justice, to be deleted from the party register.

The regulations in the Party Act include the central party organisation whereas the Act of Associations applies to the central party organisation, as well as all membership associations on the sub national and local level. The Act of Associations thus also affects the ancillary and affiliated organisations. All party branches, municipal organisations, and subnational organisations are registered in a public register of associations administered by the Ministry of Justice. To be accepted in the register, the association has to make a detailed application including information on its purpose, forms of activity, and the rules of the organisation. According to regulations in the Act of Associations, every organisation must be run on the principle of majority rule and democratic representation. An organisation can be deleted from the register of associations on the same basis as a party from the party register (Lag om föreningar 1/1919; Föreningslag 503/1989).

Registering a party in Finland thus involves a lot of costs in terms of signatures, a common program, detailed rules, and much paperwork to get the party registered. As a result of these regulations, parties in Finland are closely controlled by the state. In addition, the introduction of public subsidies in 1967 also strengthened the parties' dependency of the state.

It took many years before the Greens could find an agreement on the transformation from a movement to a party. The party was finally registered in 1988, but already in 1983 the Green movement had nominated candidates in eight constituencies. Of the 46 candidates, two were elected. Indeed, the Election Act gives the opportunity for voters' associations to nominate candidates. These associations must be registered and 100 signatures are required for every candidate. This paperwork must be done before every election. Established parties have no need to go through the process of signatures once the party is founded. On the other hand, the Election Act regulates that the nomination process must follow a democratic process, which includes a popular vote among the members. If a party lacks rules of how to nominate, it is obliged to follow the rules stipulated in detail in the law (Vallag 1998/714).

In 1983, the Green voting associations that nominated Green candidates won 1.4 per cent of all national votes, and two candidates were elected. In the election of 1987, the Green voters' associations won 4 per cent of the votes and four candidates were elected. As the voters' associations operated independently without any organisational and financial support from a national campaign machine, these results were impressive.

The Electoral Law allows parties to enter electoral alliances with other parties. Small parties use this to obtain the help of larger parties or to enter alliances with several small parties. This is the reason that some new and small parties have managed to win seats in Parliament. The Ecological party won a seat in 1995 with an electoral support of only 0.3 per cent. All new parties who have managed to win seats in Parliament have used the option of electoral alliances, either in all constituencies or in a selected number of constituencies. The Greens are different, as they have avoided bargaining with other parties. The Greens made it clear to their voters that every vote goes to them and not to any other party. This policy was changed in the 1999 election when the Greens joined electoral alliances in four out of 14 constituencies with different parties ranging from the Left Wing Alliance (former communists) on the left, to the Progressive Finnish Party on the right. In the 2003 election the Greens joined electoral alliances in two constituencies, one with the Left-Wing Alliance and the Social Democrats, in the other with the Centre Party.

An electoral alliance is technical since voters can't tell from the candidate list whether the party in the constituency is a member of an alliance or not. Forming an electoral alliance requires lengthy negotiations and hard bargaining. If two or more parties form an electoral alliance, careful calculations must be done, and the weaker party will in most cases find it advisable not to nominate more candidates than they can reasonably expect to be elected (Törnudd 1968: 88–101; Sundberg 2002: 67–99). In addition, voters are urged to concentrate their votes, if more candidates are nominated than the weaker party expects to be elected. Otherwise the stronger party may take full advantage of the greater comparison figure if none of the small party candidates are elected.

It was under expectations of even better electoral success that the pressure increased for the Greens to found a party. The process was also reinforced by the fact that the four Green MPs did not receive any public subsidy because this is only given to party organisations. However, founding a party was not an easy decision. Internal conflicts had divided the Green activists during the years before and even soon after the foundation of the Green Party. First there was a strong antipathy against becoming a party since they were seen as relics from the past, only rarely discussing important matters (Paastela 1987: 26–37). In addition, the formal rules in the Party Law were seen as an instrument to institutionalise and integrate the Greens into the public order. Of all organisational solutions discussed and quarrelled over, the foundation of a party was only one alternative. And even among those who might prefer a party, there was much discussion about its form and content. One proposal was to found an ecological party, the other was to found a broader Green alternative party.

The first proposal to found an ecological party was made by the fisherman and former urban intellectual Pertti Linkola. He predicted an imminent ecological catastrophe and the end of human life. He advocated terrorism, urging the killing of factory leaders before they killed us with pollution. He defended Hitler and his concentration camps as an acceptable demographic policy (Harakka 1998: 116–119). He published a pamphlet with a programme in which he defended a totalitarian state, including population reduction and the necessity of returning to small-scale agricultural production using horses and human energy (Paastela 1987: 37–46). His vision of an eco-fascist party did of course not receive much support, but during a couple of years no other Green program existed apart from Linkola's.

When the more moderate supporters around Linkola aimed at founding an eco-logical party, the Green association of movements had to react. A Green Party was founded. Before that, a Green League was founded to assemble different Green and alternative movements under one umbrella. This alternative form of organisa-tion did not work, and after a year the Green Party was founded. By this move, the Green Party for the first time received public subsidies and it became possible to write a programme, hire party bureaucrats, build up the organisation and make it an efficient campaign machine. In contrast to these advantages, only a very small number of activists joined the party.

The maximisation of Green votes

The Green Party was founded during an election year. In the 1988 municipal elec-tions, two Green parties competed, one of which later took the name 'Ecological Party the Greens'. The voters' choice was further complicated as different green voters' associations nominated candidates. The Greens lost votes and managed only to get 2.2 per cent. The Ecological party got only 0.2 per cent of the votes. It was a disappointment for the Greens who until now had been pushed forward by polls and media. It was also a reminder that the Greens had to organise and act more efficiently in elections. To cope with the next national and local elections the party had to widen its narrow ecological profile, and to reorganise according to common party principles.

In 1991, the Greens contested Parliament elections as a registered party for the first time. Its programme was based on five pillars: (1) ecological balance in economy; (2) partnership between nature and human beings; (3) partnership be-tween people (4) non-violence; and (5) government by the people (Vihreä Lanka 1990). A chairman who could not be a Member of Parliament ran the party. The executive power was in the hands of the party meeting. With this, still narrow, ecological programme and egalitarian organisation, the forecasts were not the best for the Greens in the coming election. However, the 1991 election was a victory: 6.8 per cent of the votes. It won 10 seats in Parliament (5 female and 5 male MPs). In the 1992 municipal elections the success continued and the party won 6.9 per cent of the votes, quite a dramatic increase compared with the 1988 municipal elections.

After the parliamentary election the Greens were invited to negotiate with the Centre party about the formation of a new cabinet coalition. They requested environmental taxes and insisted on an annual 2 per cent reduction of energy consumption. As the Greens left no room for negotiations, a cabinet coalition membership was never seriously considered.

The rule which prevented an MP from becoming party chairman was changed in 1992. Egalitarian intentions did not work well in a context where all competing party leaders combined these functions. By the end of 1993, the party was organised in three tiers: national, subnational, and local. At the national level an executive was introduced, led by the chairman. Its members are elected according to a quota rule, which balances the share of women and men. To support the executive, a party council was introduced, following the same quota rule as the executive. Formally, the highest party unit is the annual party meeting, and between these meetings the party is run by the council and the executive (http://www.vihreat.fi/saannot – accessed 26 May 2006). With this change in rules, the Greens lost parts of their former egalitarian character (Sundberg 1997: 97–117), and moved towards a more hierarchical organisation, similar to that of the established parties.

During the early 1990s, the party programme retained its original ecological image, but it was widened to cover a much broader spectrum of issues. The ten parliamentary party members put pressure on the party to do so. In addition, in 1994 the issue of EU membership divided citizens' opinions in the referendum. The Greens were also deeply divided, and the party could only give its adherents a free choice, although the party in principle was against membership. It was agreed, however, to accept the results of the referendum. In contrast to the more sceptic Greens in other European democracies, the Finnish Greens became supporters of the European Union.

One important part in the integration process was the active Green opposition politics, which in form and content resembled the tactics of other opposition parties. The party had to come with an alternative budget; it had to concern itself with social, cultural and a wide range of other matters in the legislative process. This process was like a school for the Greens, who could no longer continue to discuss their illusions and criticise the government without formulating tangible alternatives. In the 1995 election campaign the party had to be concrete and defend its EU membership decision. And that led to the loss of votes and of one seat in Parliament.

The threshold of relevance: in and out

After the 1995 parliamentary election, the Greens were not satisfied with the previous period in opposition. During this four-year period they had concretised their view on agriculture, economy, social policy, and environmental protection. Being more open now for compromise, these views could be better used in government than in opposition. The coming Social Democratic prime minister, Lipponen, offered a minister post in the grand coalition. The Greens accepted with a relatively low profile. Lipponen's five party cabinet included the former communists Left-Wing Alliance, the Social Democratic Party, the Greens, the Swedish People's Party, and the conservative National Coalition. As the coalition included parties from the left to the right, it was labelled the 'rainbow cabinet'. In the cabinet programme the parties agreed among other things to cut at least 3.3 billion euros from the budget during the coming four years, and to join the European Monetary Union. As compensation the Greens were assigned the post of minister of the environment, which according to their view gave them a real chance to implement a green environment policy.

The party leadership had few real problems in defending the Green cabinet policy to its members and adherents. Some of the members did want the Greens to move back to their original roots, as the party in government too much resembled the other established parties. Yet the Green minister and the party leadership defended their cabinet membership as being successful in preventing the government from building new nuclear plants, and in spreading environmental consciousness among cabinet members. In 1996, more than one year after its entrance in the cabinet, the popularity of the Greens was tested in the combined municipal and European Parliament elections. The result from the municipal election was a slight loss of 0.6 per cent to 6.3 per cent of the votes. The results for the European Parliament election were more promising: the party won 7.6 per cent of the votes and one seat in the European Parliament.

After four years in cabinet the Greens contested for the first time parliamentary elections in the position of a government party. In the campaign the party had the role of defending the government and not the more familiar role (for them and for the voters) of criticising it. The campaign therefore started with more uncertainty than usual. Perhaps to insure against a defeat, the Greens entered for the first time into electoral alliances with other parties in four of their weaker constituencies. Although these four alliances did not pay off, the total outcome was a success. The Greens won 7.3 per cent of the votes, which gave them two new seats in Parliament. The total number rose to 11 seats.

The party profile of the Greens has clearly changed since the 1987 election. In 1987 40 per cent of the Green candidates were female; in 2003 it was 52 per cent. Female Green candidates got 47.9 per cent of the votes in 1987 and 66.6 per cent in 2003. In 1987 all elected Green MPs were male; in the 2003 election 78.6 percent were female (Statistics Finland 2003). The party has become a party for feminists and other female-dominated alternative movements such as peace activists, solidarity groups with developing countries, Attack, Amnesty International, and of course the environmental activists. As a result the party is popular among well-educated young urban people. The average age of Members of Parliament in 2003 was 47.9 years, whereas the average for the Greens was 41.8 years. Old age seems to be more prominent among the Green male MPs (average 51.3 years) than among the female MPs (39.2 years).

After the 1999 election the Greens accepted the offer to be again part of the cabinet without any hesitation. Now the party got one seat in cabinet (minister of the environment) and partially the ministry of health and social service, which the party shared with the Swedish People's Party following the principle of rotation. Soon after the cabinet investiture in April the European Parliament elections were held in June. Again the Greens scored well and increased their share of the votes by 5.8 per cent to 13.4 per cent, which meant a second seat in the European Parliament. Later in 1999 the Greens nominated for the first time a presidential candidate. Although the Greens did not succeed well in this election, it showed that the party was ready to compete for the highest elected mandate in the republic.

The biggest conflict facing the rainbow Cabinet and the Parliament during the period was in 2002, when a decision had to be taken whether or not to build a fifth nuclear plant. An amendment to build this fifth nuclear plant had already been issued in 1993. At that time it was rejected by the Parliament although the cabinet coalition should have won the vote. The amendment split most cabinet parties, and as a result the nuclear plant plans were taken off the agenda. However, representatives of the industry continued to defend it, pointing among others at the continuing increase of electric energy consumption. An amendment was raised again and against the protest from the Greens in cabinet, including the Left-Wing Alliance chairman.

The vote in Parliament took place on 24th of May and the amendment was accepted by 107 yes votes and 92 no votes. The vote split all the parties except the Greens, who all voted against. The result of the vote put the Greens into a problematic dilemma: whether to stay loyal to the cabinet or to exit. To stay loyal would be hard to explain to their electorate and to their Green sister parties in Europe. The choice for exit, on the other hand, had already been denounced by the prime minister as an act of disloyalty, which could be turned against the Greens in the next cabinet coalition negotiations after the 2003 Parliament election. Two days later the Green Party council and the Parliamentary party met to consider the situation. Few arguments were found to continue in cabinet and the overwhelming majority favoured an exit from the cabinet, against the will of the party chairman Osmo Soininvaara.

The Greens went on in opposition and contested the 2003 election with good results. They managed to increase their representation with three seats in Parliament. The Greens are now stronger than ever before. And after one term in opposition, they returned to power in 2007.

Who are the Greens' supporters?

One essential part of strategic entry is the probability of electoral support. Although Green parties in continental Europe had gained support in elections there was no guarantee that this would also happen in Finland. The experience from other Scandinavian countries was not very promising. Green parties are not represented in the Danish, Icelandic, or the Norwegian parliament. In 1988 the Greens managed to pass the 4 per cent threshold in Sweden, and since then have once failed to get representation and mostly pass the threshold narrowly. In addition, the big supply of contesting parties in Finland, new and old, gave not much room for one more competitor.

A solid social base can be a better guarantee for persistence of a political party than ideological consensus. If ideological issues dominate, the risk of internal disputes increases. The party will easily neglect changes in the societal environment and fail to adapt. Social loyalties maintain party cohesion even in times when the party faces political differences (Rose and Mackie 1988: 533–558). The Finnish Greens certainly maintain an ideology where environmentalism is a keystone. However, during the process from a movement to government party the Greens have been forced to formulate an opinion on a wide range of issues from social policy to foreign affairs. In this process the Greens have tried to find out a way that these different issues can be combined with an environmentalist ideology. Even in environment related issues the Greens have been forced to make compromises with other cabinet parties.

The Finnish Green Party is known for attracting young, urban, mainly female, and well educated voters. If this is indeed a stable phenomenon, it can explain why the party is able to attract a stable number of voters, irrespective of its position in or out of government. Table 7.3 compares the social base of the Greens with that of the other major parties. And that reveals immediately that the Green voters are predominantly female. Other parties like the Christian Democrats (KD) and the Swedish People's Party (SFP) are, however, even more female, but the proportion of female voters among the big established parties is clearly lower.

More than 80 percent of the Green voters are younger than 44. None of the other parties come close to that. Voters above the age of 65 are a substantial share of the social base in all parties except the Greens, who totally miss this category. The group of middle-aged voters is also much smaller among the Green voters than among the other party voters.

The educational level also shows a clear profile, with a very low proportion of voters with basic education and an overrepresentation of the voters with higher education. The distribution between types of profession does not show any distinctive pattern for the Greens, except for the high proportion of students who vote for them. But place of residence is very important. Only a minor proportion of the Green voters are residents of rural municipalities or country towns. Some 60 per cent of the votes are cast in the Helsinki region and in two other major cities in southern Finland. None of the established parties comes close to this concentration of urban votes. All of this confirms without any doubt that the Finnish Greens have indeed built a well-defined electoral base: urban, relatively young, predominantly female and better educated.

Conclusion

The entrance of the Greens into the Finnish party system is clearly strategic (Tavits 2006). It is a contender party that entered in order to become electorally successful.

The Greens won representation in Parliament without first passing the threshold of becoming a party. The institutional threshold to found a party in Finland is indeed quite high. And for the Greens it was even higher since they did not (immediately) want to become a party just like the others. Yet the absence of public subsidies while having four MPs was an important incentive to cross the threshold.

The threshold of relevance was passed when the party became a member of cabinet. Having resigned from cabinet, it certainly has not lost all influence. All established parties keep an extra eye on the Greens, knowing that they have the potential to attract categories of voters who have lost their confidence in party politics.

Table 7.3 Voter characteristics in the Finnish parliamentary elections of 2003

	KESK	SDP	KOK	Left	Greens	KD	SFP	PS	Other	Total (n)
Gender										
Men	50	50	53	55	**45**	32	44	44	73	456
Women	50	50	47	45	**55**	68	56	56	27	477
Total (%)	100	100	100	100	**100**	100	100	100	100	
Total (n)	194	235	128	83	**73**	68	121	9	22	933
Age										
18–24	11	6	16	10	**22**	18	11	22	9	108
25–44	35	27	33	27	**60**	32	31	56	41	313
45–64	37	46	34	51	**18**	27	36	11	41	352
65–	17	21	17	13	0	24	22	11	9	160
Total (%)	100	100	100	100	**100**	100	100	100	100	
Total (n)	194	235	128	83	**73**	68	121	9	22	933
Education										
Basic education	31	34	13	32	7	28	18	44	32	239
Intermediate level	53	54	55	55	66	56	47	56	46	502
Higher education	16	12	33	13	**27**	16	35	0	23	191
Total (%)	100	100	100	100	**100**	100	100	100	100	
Total (n)	194	235	128	82	**73**	68	121	9	22	932

Profession										
Farmer	12	0	2	0	0	4	3	0	0	33
Worker	26	35	20	35	22	28	14	33	9	51
Entrepreneur	6	3	9	4	4	2	11	11	0	31
Official	16	21	32	16	30	22	22	11	14	203
Leading position	3	4	3	1	3	2	6	0	0	31
Student	11	6	12	10	29	13	16	22	9	112
Other	26	31	23	35	12	29	29	22	23	252
Total (%)	100	100	100	100	100	100	100	100	100	
Total (n)	194	235	128	83	73	68	121	9	22	933
Place of residence										
Helsinki region	12	24	33	22	45	28	33	56	43	194
Other city	4	10	5	9	14	13	0	0	19	63
Countryside	84	66	62	68	41	58	67	44	38	501
Total (%)	100	100	100	100	100	100	100	100	100	100
Total (n)	184	215	119	76	71	60	3	9	21	758

Notes
KESK, Centre Party of Finland; SDP, Social Democratic Party of Finland; KOK, National Coalition Party; Left, Left Wing Alliance; Greens, Green League; KD, Christian Democrats in Finland; SFP, Swedish People's Party in Finland; PS, True Finns

In sum, the electoral success of the Finnish Greens seems not to be in danger, as the party has established itself among the bigger ones without losing its vitality. The party has not ceased to be influential, though the larger parties can well manage without the Greens in coming coalitions. This is because the barrier between socialist and non-socialist parties in Finnish politics is ambiguous. The situation can, however, change if the Greens continue to win elections. Winning parties cannot be neglected in the long run. In the capital, Helsinki, the Greens are now one of the major parties in the city government. The situation has changed in a similar direction in other larger urban areas as well.

Governing has thus changed the party. It has come a long way from a movement reluctant to become a party to a party with relevance and coalition potential. Unlike other new parties it has found itself a stable place in the party landscape and it has secured a well-defined electoral base. In a country like Finland, where coalitions can take many forms, this means that the party will not lose its relevance soon.

Bibliography

Harakka, T. (1998) *Viemärirotta*, Helsinki: Kustannusosakeythiö Otava.

Harmel, R. and Robertson, J.D. (1985) 'Formation and success of new parties: a cross-national analysis', *International Political Science Review*, 6: 501–23.

Kitchelt, H. (1997) 'European party systems: continuity and change', in M. Rhodes, P. Heywood and V. Wright (eds) *Developments in West European Politics*, London: Macmillan Press, pp. 131–49.

Lane, J.E. and Ersson, S. (1999) *Politics and Society in Western Europe*, London: Sage Publications.

Mair, P. (1991) 'The electoral universe of small parties in postwar Western Europe', in F. Müller-Rommel and G. Pridham (eds) *Small Parties in Western Europe*, London: Sage Publications.

Paastela, J. (1987) *Finland's New Social Movements*, University of Tampere, Research Reports 86.

Pedersen, M. (1982) 'Towards a new typology of party lifespans and minor parties', *Scandinavian Political Studies*, 5: 1–16.

Pedersen, M. (1991) 'The birth, life and death of small parties in the Netherlands', in F. Müller-Rommel and G. Pridham (eds) *Small Parties in Western Europe*, London: Sage Publications, pp. 95–114.

Rose, R. and Mackie, T. (1988) 'Do parties persist or fail? The big trade-off facing organizations', in K. Lawson and P.H. Merkl (eds) *When Parties Fail*, Princeton: Princeton University Press.

Statistics Finland (2003) Parliamentary Elections 1962–2003, Helsinki: Statistics Finland.

Sundberg, J. (1997) 'Compulsory party democracy: Finland as a deviant case in Scandinavia', *Party Politics*, 3: 97–118.

Sundberg, J. (2002) 'The electoral system of Finland: old, and working well', in B. Grofman and A. Lijphart (eds) *The Evolution of Electoral and Party Systems in the Nordic Countries*, New York: Agathon Press.

Tavits, M. (2006) 'Party system change: testing a model of new party entry', *Party Politics*, 12: 99–120.

Törnudd, K. (1968) *The Electoral System of Finland*, London: Hugh Evelyn.

Vihreä Lanka (1990) www.vihrealanka.fi

8 Independents in government
A sui generis model?

Liam Weeks

Introduction

New parties have been studied, analysed, and placed into different typologies, which include various residual groups ranging from personal vehicle parties to mobilising and challenging parties (Rochon 1985: 421, 425–426). The problem with these categories is that some of the parties are little more than glorified one-man bands, which have been forced to establish a party because of electoral laws not permitting non-party (i.e. Independent) candidates to stand. An example is the List Pym Fortuyn (LPF) in the Netherlands, which centred on the eponymous party leader, without whom the group fragmented.[1] The central argument of this chapter is that in Ireland, the only country in Western Europe where Independents are regularly elected (Mitchell 2001: 188), and where their representation in parliament is greater than the combined total in Western Europe (Weeks 2003: 221), some Independents with well-mobilised organisations do not differ greatly from some of these new parties, such as the aforementioned LPF. Indeed, it is a feasible hypothesis that, were a list electoral system introduced in Ireland whereby all candidates had to stand under a party name, many of the successful Independents could quite easily form a personalised list, and would henceforth be studied as new parties.

The first section of this chapter elaborates on this argument, using a number of empirical examples to demonstrate why, in many cases, Independents are not so different from new parties. The second section looks at the context that explains why Independents' electoral success is unmatched elsewhere in Western Europe, to the extent that they have played a decisive role in almost 40 per cent of government formations. The third section examines in detail what this role comprises, before going on to assess the consequences of their participation in government.

Independents: who are they?

Commonly known as Independents,[2] non-party candidates have been an ever-present feature of Irish elections, and along with the Labour Party, are the only grouping to have been elected to every Dáil[3] since independence was achieved in

1922. Given their collective title, Independents are sometimes treated as if they are a unitary body, and were even referred to as the 'Independent Party' in the early years of the party system (Chubb 1957: 134).[4] However, the number of Independent politicians has expanded since then, with the result that they are now in effect a heterogeneous residual category of all those falling outside of the party system.

The number of Independents elected to parliament regularly reached double figures until the 1950s, an impressive showing in a parliament ranging from 138 to 147 seats (Figure 8.1). Following these decades, Independents entered a period of decline, which contemporary writers predicted would spell the end of the non-party TD[5] (Chubb 1957). It was presumed at this stage that the flourish of Independents had simply been due to a new party system in a state of flux, a trend that is common in other newly emerging democracies, with the former Soviet Bloc countries in Eastern Europe being a comparative example in the 1990s. However, the phenomenon of the Irish Independent TD has not ended, having had a resurgence of support since the late 1970s. At the general election of 2002, Independents won 13 of 165 contested seats, receiving almost 10 percent of all first preference votes cast. The credibility of this performance is further accentuated when it is considered that this number of seats is far greater than the combined total won by Independents in all West European parliaments (Gallagher *et al.* 2003: 103).

Why are Independents like new parties?

Some readers may by now be querying the relevance of a chapter devoted to non-party candidates in a volume concerning new parties. Appreciating its significance requires an understanding of both the differences and similarities between an Independent and a party.

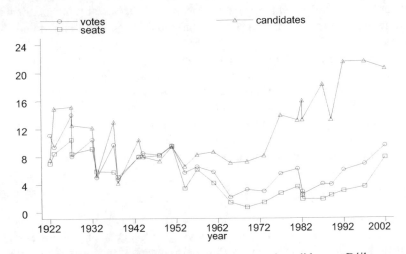

Figure 8.1   Independents' proportion of votes, seats and candidates at Dáil
         elections, 1922–2002.

Defining an Independent

Defining an Independent at first glance appears a relatively straightforward task; akin to a party label, an Independent is simply any candidate running under this title. However, since an Independent 'does not necessarily call himself an "Independent"' (Chubb 1957: 131), it is easier to define them according to what they are not, that is, party politicians. In other words, anyone who runs for election, and is not a party candidate, is an Independent. This explains why some prefer to use the descriptive term non-party, rather than Independent, for such politicians. It is easier to define Independents in this negative sense, because being 'independent' is a label that is difficult to pin down. For one thing, some party politicians like to call themselves 'independent' because it can also be a qualitative term that offers a positive description of their character. Within many parliamentary parties there are members who think of themselves as independent-minded and do not always toe the party line. Such 'independent' MPs are prevalent in systems where party discipline is relatively weak, examples being the US Congress and the Japanese Diet. For another, not all Independent MPs are necessarily truly 'independent', since they can be (1) the nominee of an interest group; (2) a disaffected party politician; or (3) members of an alliance of Independents. Recognising the ambiguity of the Independent label, one maverick party TD went so far as to claim in 2005 that he was the only true Independent in the Dáil (Kelly 2005).

In the light of such obstacles, Chubb defined a true Independent based on the possession of two necessary characteristics (1957: 132):

1   The candidate does not have the resources of a party behind him or her at election time.
2   The candidate does not take a party whip in the Dáil.

Since both these traits are essentially concerned with party membership, defining an Independent boils down to establishing what a party is, and any candidate who is standing for a group that cannot be considered a party is an Independent. While identifying a major party is fairly easy, distinguishing a minor party (which new parties usually are) from an Independent is not so clear-cut. The potential similarities between the two, as outlined in the next section, constitute the major reason to justify the inclusion of Independents in this volume.

Distinguishing a party from an Independent

While there is no problem in differentiating between a major party and an Independent, the predicament lies with minor parties whose definition is not so clear-cut. Pedersen's seminal study of minor parties defined a party as 'an organisation – however loosely or strongly organised – which either presents or nominates candidates for public elections, or which, at least, has the declared intention to do so' (Pedersen 1982: 5). The difficulty with this definition[6] is that there are a lot of examples of Independent candidates standing for election who were nominated by organisations, ranging from candidates nominated by regional farming associations to those chosen at selection conventions by Unionist organisations, who could all be included as parties according to Pedersen's definition. This ambiguity explains why Sinnott asserted that 'the category of "independents" is a residual and shifting one, its size depending on how much substance one attributes to ephemeral party labels' (1995: 64), and why Coakley claimed that 'it is not always obvious how a minor party is to be distinguished from a group of independents' (1990: 270).

A simple method of determining what constitutes a party would be to use the legal definition, but this in itself poses difficulties. For a start, until the 1963 Electoral Act, there was no official registry of parties, and party affiliations were not stated on ballot sheets, which leaves it open to subjective interpretation in deciding whether some groups are genuine parties or merely personalised organisations of Independents. These ambiguities were not cleared up with the introduction of an official Registry of Parties either, since the requirements to qualify as a party allow some Independents to attain party status. For example, any group with one TD (or three local authority members) and a set of written rules that provide for an annual conference and an executive can register as a party,[7] thus implying that virtually any Independent TD with a mobilised support group can form their own party label. These rules were exploited by two Independent TDs to form their own respective 'parties', the Socialist Labour Party in the 1970s, and the Democratic Socialist Party in the 1980s, both of which have been treated as parties by academics and political commentators alike.

Further evidence of the difficulty in distinguishing between minor parties and Independents lies with representatives of interest groups elected as Independents to parliament. A prominent example is the 'Independent Unionists' who were continuously present in the Dáil from 1922 up to the 1960s. These deputies were selected by Protestant associations that sought to represent their interests in a parliament which they feared would enact sectarian legislation that reflected the Catholic ethos of the country. The chosen nominees, if successful, were kept in constant reminder of their role as a representative of the Protestant community, and whenever an important issue arose, the TD consulted the local organisations to decide what stance to take in relation to the particular matter. If an Independent Unionist TD ignored the express wishes of his electorate, he was expected to stand down, and if he did not he would certainly be deselected at the next convention. Since such associations could easily have qualified for party status according to the aforementioned legal qualifications, the only difference between these groups and promoter parties (those concerned with promoting a particular issue or cause (Harmel and Robertson 1985: 517–518)) is that the latter had a party name.

Based on this evidence, it seems clear that when distinguishing between a minor party and an Independent, the only unambiguous difference is simply that the former calls itself a party while the latter does not. A striking example of this lies with two socialist-minded TDs in the 29th Dáil (2002–2007). Both represented left-wing working-class organisations that selected them to run for the Dáil and also have other political representatives elected at local level. The only difference between the two organisations is that one chooses to call itself the Socialist Party (and has official party status), while the other uses the label 'The Workers and Unemployed Action Group'.

The final similarity of note between new parties and Independents is that Independents are not necessarily isolated political units operating on their own. Besides having the support of mobilised organisations behind them, they sometimes work with other Independents in parliament to form a bargaining unit, details of which are provided in the later sections of this chapter. Indeed, based on this evidence one can go so far as to claim that there is no major difference between a small cadre party (such as the Progressive Democrats (PD), a new party that emerged on the Irish political scene in 1985) and a group of Independents working together in parliament. Within a cadre party, each MP is relatively independent, being almost entirely reliant on personal appeal and status as a 'local notable' to deliver votes at election time. Cadre parties usually have few members, with the bulk of their grass roots support comprising the personalised organisations of its individual TDs, just like those of Independents. These similarities were highlighted in the 1997–2002 government, when Fianna Fáil was dependent on the support of four PD TDs and four Independent TDs. Since the Independents worked closely together as a cohesive group, it can be argued that the only major difference between the PDs and the Independents was that the former called themselves a party while the latter did not.

The purpose of these various examples has been to demonstrate that the only significant distinction between many Independent TDs and new parties is the Independents' decision not to place a party label alongside their name on the ballot sheet. If such individuals were required to contest elections as a party, as occurs in most European list systems, most of them would qualify as a party, and these Independents would be analysed simply as minor or personal vehicle parties. It is therefore apt to study Independents alongside new parties, since many of them are in effect what Duverger defined as personality parties, that is, 'purely parliamentary groups having no real party organisation in the country . . . they are made up of deputies who chafe under the discipline imposed by major parties, or who consider that these are not capable of satisfying their ambitions' (1959: 290–291). Having established their suitability for analysis, the following sections look at the role of Independents in propping up minority administrations, and how this participation has affected their electoral performance, their policy, their strategy and their organisation. It also examines the effect of Independents on government policy, in order to assess what Independents gained in return for their support.

The nature of Independents' support status

A variety of terms, from 'legislative coalition' (Laver and Schofield 1990) to 'contract parliamentarism' (Aylott and Bergman 2004), to an 'executive coalition', have been coined to describe the nature of support offered to a minority government by parties not directly participating in office. With one exception, when

Independents were an equal government partner with a seat at the cabinet table, Independent participation has been limited to support status, a position that lies somewhere between opposition and government. This position, that is, the extent of their participation, has varied across administrations, ranging from simple external parliamentary support to formal arrangements that were not far removed from contract parliamentarism (a concept that relates to an explicit institutionalised relationship between a minority government and its support parties (Bale and Bergman 2006). The motivations and actions of the balance of power holders in minority governments have also been classified on two scales, based on (1) whether they were motivated by particularistic incentives or a desire to mount a challenge to the political system; and (2) whether they acted as individuals or collectively as a group (Moon 1995: 143–4). Adapting this model to Independents in Ireland, all were motivated by particularistic incentives, but some in addition also sought to challenge public policy. On two occasions they acted collectively, both of which constitute the cases when they extracted maximum concessions from the government. Moon has christened such arrangements 'ersatz coalitions', while the remaining cases where Independents acted individually are designated 'ersatz majoritarianism' when their motives were purely particularistic, and 'ad hoc minoritarianism' when some sought to influence government policy (ibid.).

Why are Independents involved in the government process?

Party motivations

The first reason that Independents are involved in the government process is that parties are willing to include them. For the first 26 years of the new state's existence (i.e. 1922 to 1948), even though Independents supported minority governments, they played no formal role in the government formation process. They were not courted by the parties, nor did they seek a role. This was because those Independents supporting the governments shared the same ideological beliefs as the parties in office, and were happy to support the administration's minority status without any form of compensation (largely because they preferred them to the alternative of the opposition being in power). However, the nature of Independents changed in the 1940s, as fewer 'establishment' Independents were elected to the Dáil. The new wave of Independents recognised the potential influence they could wield in a hung parliament, some of whom were determined to secure compensation for their support.

More importantly, the attitudes of the parties changed. After a period of 16 consecutive years in opposition, during which their vote had almost halved, the main opposition party, Fine Gael, was desperate to get back into power in 1948, and was thus willing to conduct negotiations with Independents as a co-equal government partner. However, since the dominant party, Fianna Fáil, was unwilling to share power with anyone, Independents could only participate in the government process if the main opposition parties, Fine Gael and Labour, won enough seats. Therefore, even though the Fianna Fáil minority governments of de Valera and Lemass in the 1950s and 1960s were dependent on the support of Independents, the latter received little to no explicit compensation for their support.[8] At times, they were even dared by Fianna Fáil to vote against their own administration, as the party correctly believed the last thing Independents wanted was an early election (Farrell 1987: 140).

All this changed in the 1980s with the tacit acceptance by Fianna Fáil that they would be unlikely to form a single-party majority government again for the foreseeable future. Desperate to cling to power, but unwilling to enter coalition with another party, they opened the way for Independents, who could now seek to extract policy concessions from a minority Fianna Fáil-led administration, which they have done in four of seven Fianna Fáil-led governments formed since 1982. The political parties now see Independents as real players to contend with, evidence of which is provided by Fianna Fáil's continuous meeting with Independents on a weekly basis since the party returned to power in 1997. Until 2002 they did so to ensure that their minority coalition with the Progressive Democrats retained majority support in parliament, while since then they have done so to ensure their remaining in power should the majority coalition fall apart.

This change in party attitudes has occurred because parties now realise the many rational advantages stemming from an arrangement formed with Independents. A party can retain all the benefits accruing from majority support in parliament, with none of the disadvantages brought by having to include an extra partner in coalition. They do not have to give up a ministerial position to Independents and do not have an extra potential dissenting voice when formulating government policy at cabinet level. Admittedly a minority government always has the potential for instability, but this has occurred when parties have chosen to ignore Independents and attempted to call their bluff during crucial votes in parliament.[9] When the parties do negotiate with Independents, even if only a token gesture to acknowledge their support, such governments can be just as stable as any majority administration. This explains why the 1997–2002 government, which negotiated separate deals with four Independents, all of whose support they were dependent upon, was the longest-serving government in peacetime history.

Party system

The lack of fluidity within the party system is a major reason why Independents are included in the government process. Traditionally, the Irish party system has been characterised as a 'two and a half' party system, where the two consist of the alternate ruling parties, Fianna Fáil and Fine Gael (who between them have led every government in the Dáil), and the half the relatively weak (from a comparative European perspective) Labour Party. Other small parties have occasionally flourished, but it is only these three, in various guises, (along with Independents) that have had a continuous presence in the Dáil. Because Fianna Fáil was ideologically opposed to the idea of coalition government until 1989, if either they or the Fine Gael–Labour combination failed to win a majority of seats, a potential stasis in parliament loomed. In such instances, Independents acted as a safety valve as the parties looked to their support to overcome an electoral deadlock by forming a minority government.

Even after Fianna Fáil broke with tradition by coalescing with the Progressive Democrats in 1989, the refusal of the two main parties to consider coalition with each other[10] has the consequence that the party system is still quite shackled, with the result that a hung parliament is a very feasible potential outcome at every election. For example, since the last single-party majority government was elected in 1977, eight of the ten governments formed have involved protracted negotiations. The nature of the party system and the potential difficulties it brings for the process of government formation gives Independents a disproportionate influence, and explains why they have often held the balance of power in parliament.

Electoral system

Of course, if Independents did not win any seats in parliament in the first place, they would not be able to play a role in government. An important institutional feature to consider in accounting for their presence is the electoral system, proportional representation by the single transferable vote (PR-STV), the influence of which has been referred to on numerous occasions in the relevant literature (see Carty 1981: 121; Mair 1987: 63–68; Chubb 1992: 94; Gallagher 2005: 523). The main thrust of the argument is that PR-STV allows localism and personalism, two features of the political culture that cultivate support for Independents, to persist. This relationship stems from the candidate-centred nature of the electoral system that fosters intra-party competition in multimember constituencies. Because candidates of the same party have to compete against each other, their electoral campaign has to offer something more than just a party label or party policy. They therefore choose to focus on their personal attributes and on what they can provide for the local constituency in terms of particularistic benefits. This personalistic style of campaigning is reinforced by the mechanics of the electoral system, since voters cast preferences for candidates, not parties, and are required to evaluate the merits of candidates relative to one another by the transferable vote, which allows them to cast as many preferences as candidates run. In such contests where party is lessened in importance, and personalism and localism are to the fore, Independents can compete on a more even keel with party candidates, since their non-partisan status is less of a disadvantage than is the case under party-centred electoral systems.

Others have suggested that minority governments are more frequent occurrences under non-majoritarian electoral systems, especially the PR-STV variant (Moon 1995: 147–8). For example, in a study of Australian state governments, Moon found that Tasmania, the only state using STV to elect its assembly, had the longest period of rule by minority governments (34 years in total from 1910 to 1977; ibid.).

The influence of the electoral system does come with a slight caveat. Because Malta is the only other country using PR-STV to elect its lower house of parliament, it is difficult to test these premises on a comparative basis (especially because there have been no Independents elected in Malta since the country gained independence in 1964). Indeed, it is the relative uniqueness to Ireland of both the electoral system and the significant vote for Independents that has led many to draw the conclusion that there must be a positive relationship between the two variables. Gallagher rightly warns against the possible over-emphasising of the importance of PR-STV, asserting that while 'the distinctiveness of Ireland's electoral system makes it a fascinating object of study . . . at the same time, (it) opens up the danger of attributing far too much causal power to it' (2005: 529). Until the relationship is further explored – something which Weeks (2004) has tentatively done – the point must be stressed that it is not that PR-STV necessarily results in the election of Independents, but that it is easier for Independents to be elected under PR-STV than other electoral systems (Mitchell 2001: 197–198).

The cases

Given the frequent occurrence of minority governments in Ireland, as many as ten of the 27 governments in office from 1922–2006 have been dependent on the support of Independents (see Table 8.1). Across these ten examples, 37 Independent TDs supported the minority administrations, and these form the cases for analysis in the remaining sections of this chapter.

In seven of the ten instances of Independent support, there was no formal deal struck, with the Independents' participation predominantly limited to external parliamentary support.[11] However, in the three other examples, the parties looking to form a government negotiated an agreement with Independent TDs, in return for which the latter received compensation, predominantly in the form of particularistic benefits. As a precursor to an analysis of their time in governance, a brief section is required to describe the formation of these three governments and the role played by Independents.

Table 8.1 History of Independent support for governments, 1922–2006

Government dependent on Independents	Years in office	Deal formed?
Cumann na nGaedheal[a]	1927–30	No
Cumann na nGaedheal	1930–32	No
Fine Gael–Labour–National Labour– Clann na Poblachta–Clann na Talmhan	1948–51	Yes
Fianna Fáil	1951–54	No
Fianna Fáil	1961–65	No
Fine Gael–Labour	1981–82	No
Fianna Fáil	1982	Yes
Fianna Fáil	1987–89	No
Fianna Fáil–Progressive Democrats	1989–92	No
Fianna Fáil–Progressive Democrats	1997–2002	Yes

Note
a   Precursor to the Fine Gael party.

1948–1951 Fine Gael–Labour–National Labour–Clann na Poblachta–Clann na Talmhan

The first coalition government formed in the Irish state was a motley collection of five parties, ranging from the conservative Fine Gael to the radical Clann na Poblachta, and six Independents. The main stimulus impelling their coalescing was a shared desire to end 16 years of uninterrupted one-party rule by Fianna Fáil. Six of the 12 elected Independents, who had three years previously collaborated on the campaign of an Independent candidate during the 1945 presidential election, again came together to work as a single bargaining unit, nominating one of their representatives to negotiate on their behalf with the parties. The Independents were thus treated as an equal government partner, which was recognised by the securing of a ministerial portfolio for one of their group, who remains the only Independent to sit at cabinet in Irish political history.

1982 Fianna Fáil

The short-lived Fianna Fáil minority government of 1982, which lasted just nine months, was dependent on the support of two Independents, Tony Gregory and Neil Blaney. Both TDs had considerable organisations mobilised behind them that bore similarities to the movements that spawned new parties in other countries. For example, Gregory, known as a Community candidate, represented the many left-wing local community groups that sprang up around Dublin's inner city (his constituency) during the early 1980s. Blaney was a former Fianna Fáil minister who had left the party to form his own local organisation, known as Independent Fianna Fáil. Taking a large number of members and supporters from Fianna Fáil, it was a considerable political machine that had representatives elected at both local and national level.

Given Blaney's Fianna Fáil background, he did not place too many demands upon the Taoiseach, Charles Haughey, and a verbal agreement between the two was negotiated without a hitch. Gregory's support was far more difficult to secure, especially since he was being courted by the leaders of the two alternative governments, a situation that was described as akin to a tail wagging two dogs. Haughey was desperate to return to power to the extent that his response to Gregory's list of demands was 'you're pushing an open door' (Joyce and Murtagh 1983: 49). Not surprisingly then, Gregory decided to back Haughey's nomination as Taoiseach as the latter promised him a raft of particularistic benefits for his constituency in an arrangement known as the 'Gregory Deal'.

1997–2002 Fianna Fáil–Progressive Democrats

Falling four seats short of a majority, the Fianna Fáil–Progressive Democrats coalition initially formed separate deals with three Independents, and a year into the administration negotiated the support of an additional Independent. Each of the Independents presented a 'shopping list' of concerns to the government, most of which the latter agreed to, motivating one Independent to rue his not asking for more (O'Connor 2000a). The agreements reached were all of a verbal form, as the Independents were not in favour of a written document that could be released to the public under the Freedom of Information Act. Unlike previous Fianna Fáil-led minority administrations, the Independents were not ignored once they had voted the Taoiseach into office, and the government chief whip met them weekly to check their support for proposed legislation and to hear any concerns they had to air. This access made them the envy of many government backbenchers, resulting in the Independents being known as the 'Gang of Four'.

Consequences of participation in government

Policy benefits

The first area of consequence to be examined is the policy benefits received by Independents in return for their support. In the seven cases where Independents did not negotiate an agreement with the governing parties, there is not much evidence of their having received any clear policy concessions. However, the respective governments did sometimes dangle a carrot during times of instability. For example, it was believed that the 1989 Fianna Fáil–Progressive Democrats coalition looked favourably on the retention of a regional hospital that had been threatened with closure because an Independent TD who supported them in the Dáil was the representative of an interest group formed to lobby for its retention (Rafter 2000). Nevertheless, such 'favours' pale in significance to the extensive range of policy benefits received by Independents in the three cases where they struck a deal with the government, details of which are provided below.

The main concession achieved by Independents in the 1948–51 government was the securing of a cabinet post in the Department of Agriculture. Since the six Independents involved were all from rural constituencies where agriculture was the main industry, they shared a common interest in the government's plans for this sector of the economy. Achieving a ministerial appointee ensured their interests on such policies would be well represented at cabinet level. Given the backing of his former Fine Gael colleagues, the Independent minister managed to secure a number of policy concessions. These included the end of compulsory tillage, the negotiation of the Anglo-Irish Agreement (which improved the conditions for Irish farmers to export to the British market) and the introduction of the Land Project, the aim of which was to reclaim four million acres via a process of drainage and fertilisation, and the cost of which was between £40 million and £50 million (McCullagh 1998: 158–159).

An example of a non-agricultural policy on which Independents did exert an influence was the Social Welfare (Insurance) Bill, which sought to adopt the British model and extend the protection of workers via a redistributive insurance welfare scheme. Many of the Independents resented this perceived intrusion of the state into society, with one labelling it 'a slavish imitation of British Socialism' (McCullagh 1998: 194). They were also opposed to it practically, since the proposed scheme excluded casual workers and farmers, both of whom were a large source of support for Independents. In an attempt to secure their support, the Minister for Health amended the bill to include measures that would appease the Independents (notably pension increases and an easing of the means test for qualification to such a scheme), but they came at a cost of an extra £1.35 million, a sizeable amount when we take into account that total annual spending on the new social welfare scheme was estimated to be £10 million (McCullagh 1998: 195).

The 1982 Fianna Fáil minority government negotiated the infamous 'Gregory Deal', perhaps the closest such arrangements have come to a form of contract parliamentarism. While there was an explicit document written that was read out in parliament by the respective Independent, published in the newspapers, and signed by both the Taoiseach and Gregory, the government received no pledge of support from the latter beyond his promise to vote for their nominee as Taoiseach when parliament met. The contract that Gregory received was a lengthy (up to 30 pages) shopping list of pork-barrel benefits that the government pledged to provide, the total cost of which was estimated to be anything from £150 million to £300 million, a remarkable amount of money at a time when severe cutbacks were required to address the country's growing budget deficit problem. The particularistic concessions were primarily concerned with the inner city of Dublin, involving a major change of policy in relation to urban regeneration. For example, the 27-acre Dublin Port and Docks Board site, which was to have been used for offices, was now to be divided between houses, offices, and recreation space. £91 million was to be given to Dublin Corporation that year to construct 3,000 new houses. The maintenance budget for Dublin Corporation housing, which had been cut from £7.5 million to £2.7 million that year, was increased to £10 million. Free medical cards were to be provided for all pensioners, the supplementary welfare system was to be overhauled, the number of remedial teachers in Dublin inner city was to be increased, and £4 million was allocated to employ 500 extra men in the inner city, with 3,746 new jobs created in the same area within the following three years. There were also policy measures agreed on that were not detailed in the document, examples being a pledge by the Taoiseach to remove sales tax from books, and that rail fares would not be increased in the forthcoming year (see Joyce and Murtagh 1983: 59–66). Despite the wide range of largesse, no details were provided of where the funding for such projects was going to come from. The detrimental effect this threatened to have on the national economy was lifted when the government collapsed before the end of the year, leaving much of the Gregory Deal unimplemented.

The concessions achieved by Blaney were quite minuscule compared to Gregory's. While Haughey had agreed to his two demands of adopting a firm republican line on Northern Ireland, and of promoting employment via the development of the construction industry (Joyce and Murtagh 1983: 55), it is difficult to measure the extent to which these demands were met in the space of nine months. One clear concession was Haughey's appointment of a Blaney follower to the Seanad in return for Blaney's promise that his supporters would vote for Fianna Fáil candidates at the Seanad elections (Joyce and Murtagh 1983: 54–5).

The 1997–2002 'Gang of Four' Independents wielded a level of influence comparable to that of many other new parties in government. The Independents were all mainly concerned with securing largesse for their constituencies, to help ensure that they would not suffer the fate of many first-time Independent TDs (which three of them were, the other having been elected in a by-election the previous year) who fail to hold their seats. Because the government coffers were flush with monies from a booming economy, they were free to dole out large amounts of pork-barrel benefits to the Independents. At the succeeding election, one Independent listed in his campaign literature the cost of each piece of pork he had delivered, the total of which amounted to over £250 million. These included the securing of funding for hospitals, a new factory providing 300 jobs, and the general improvement of rural infrastructure. Such was the scale of his funding, it motivated political commentators to note that the Independent had 'redrawn the boundaries for the State's regionalisation programme' (Brennock 1998). This same TD was given an additional sweetener in the form of the chairmanship of the Dáil's Environment Committee. Another Independent extracted pledges of the provision of new hospital services, the upgrading of the road infrastructure, and the establishment of a district veterinary office for the constituency. The two other Independents received similar types of pork, one claiming to have secured £31 million of additional funding for his constituency (O'Connor 2000b). This latter Independent was the representative of a single-issue interest group, formed to prevent the closure of an illegal television deflector that provided British television stations free of charge in a constituency bordering with Northern Ireland. Despite intensive lobbying from multimedia companies that had invested hundreds of millions of pounds in purchasing rights to provide cable television, the government altered their communications policy and decided to legalise the status of such deflectors, which existed not just in the respective border constituency, but all over the country (O'Halloran 2002).

In terms of national policy, two Independents were concerned with the issue of abortion, which had been the subject of four controversial referendums between 1983 and 1992. In light of a Supreme Court ruling permitting abortion in certain circumstances, these Independents wanted the government to call another referendum on abortion to ensure a constitutional ban on its introduction. Despite his government partners, the Progressive Democrats, being against such a move, the Taoiseach kept a promise to the Independents and called a referendum in the last few months of the administration (ibid.). One of these Independents, hailing from a constituency bordering with Northern Ireland, and from a dynastic republican background, was also strongly committed to the achieving of a united Ireland. He wanted the government to adopt a republican line with respect to the Unionists in Northern Ireland (Mitchell 2001: 205), ensuring that there would be no changes to articles two and three of the constitution (which asserted a territorial claim over Northern Ireland) unless there was a settlement. While it is difficult to determine the overall influence this Independent wielded on Northern Ireland policy, the amendments to the aforementioned articles that did transpire were part of the settlement that was the 1998 Good Friday Agreement.

Two other national policies of note were also altered by the government in response to the demands of the Independents. The first concerned the allocation of funding from the European Union (EU). Due to a period of unprecedented economic growth that began in the mid-1990s, Ireland was no longer to retain Objective One status, and more importantly its accompanying massive levels of structural funding. However, since some of the country remained underdeveloped, the government drew up a regionalisation programme that split the country into a number of regions, the poorer of which (called the Border, Midlands and West region) would still retain Objective One status (and thereby the maximum level of structural funding). However, the constituency base of one of the Independents was excluded from the new BMW region, which provoked the outcry of his constituents. Such was his influence, he managed to persuade the government to redraw the programme to ensure his county would retain Objective One status (although this decision was later overruled by Brussels; anon. 1998).

The final policy area to be looked at is the government's intentions to introduce legislation banning the holding of multiple electoral mandates by politicians. For example, if an MEP wished to contest a general election, (s)he would have to resign either his/her European or Dáil seat if elected to the national parliament. Because the local constituency is the sole source of their votes, the Independent TDs like to also hold office in the local councils to ensure they are aware of all matters in their constituency, and also to protect their base of support. They were naturally opposed to this bill, and such was the vehemence of their protests, the Minister for the Environment was forced into a U-turn on a policy that had been favoured by both political commentators and the public alike (O'Halloran 2002).

Effect on organisation

Following a period of support for a government, an Independent has five options: (1) continue as an Independent; (2) form a new party from their own organisation or as a result of a merger with other Independents; (3) join another established party; (4) form an alliance of Independents; or (5) retire from political life.

Joining an established party would seem a logical move. Assuming that politicians strive for a long and successful career, party membership provides several obvious advantages for the continuous gain of office (Schlesinger 1966), ranging from an attractive 'brand name', to campaign resources, to a solution to the problem of collective action, whereby a politician can win more in parliament by being part of a team rather than on his own (Aldrich 1995: 35).

Regardless of whether or not one believes it is rational for an MP to join a parliamentary party, if an Independent already chose to neglect the party path both when running for political office, and on entering parliament, we should equally not expect them to join a party after supporting them in government. This should especially be the case for Independents who managed to secure recompense for their supporting a minority government. After all, if they had been a government party backbencher, they would have received no rewards for their support. The rationality of this situation was highlighted in 1997 when a Fianna Fáil activist, a party stalwart of over 30 years' standing failed to secure a nomination to run for the party. Running as an Independent, he won a seat and was a member of the pivotal 'Gang of Four' on whose support the 1997–2002 administration depended. If he had been elected as a Fianna Fáil backbench TD or joined the party in parliament, he would not have achieved a penny of funding. In such a situation, life as an Independent was clearly the rational choice.[12]

Of course, life on the Independent benches can be pretty lonely, and some politicians may prefer the collegiality and comradeship of being a member of a team, that is, a party. Having sampled a taste of such a life when supporting a government, they should therefore also have incentives to join the governing parties. Naturally, this strongly depends on how they get on with such parties. After all, if the latter resent the disproportional influence of the Independents, and party MPs openly express their dislike for their dependence on Independents, the latter may be less likely to join. In addition, we might expect that those who received little recompense for their support may be more likely to join a party. Of course, such a move all depends on whether the party is willing to invite them into their fold.

Looking at the various cases, these hypotheses seem to hold up. In the three cases where deals were done, all of the Independents involved retained their independent status at the next election. In three of the seven cases where Independents did not receive explicit benefits in return for their support, most of them changed their status shortly after. Of the 1932 crop, some of them helped to form a new party, the National Centre Party (NCP) in 1933. Four of the six Independents who supported Fianna Fáil in 1951 joined the party just two years later because they were frustrated at their inability to extract policy concessions from the government. Further, the group of Independents who had supported the 1948 government, and had expected to return to power in 1951 were dismayed at the declining influence of Independents in these years, and therefore also decided to join a party, with three of the original six signing up to Fine Gael in 1952. Finally, the socialist Independent who defeated the government's budget in 1982 founded the Democratic Socialist Party later that year.

It is not surprising that so few Independents choose to abandon their non-partisan status in favour of forming a new party. This is because it can be a lot easier to survive politically as an Independent than a new party. Established national parties tolerate the existence of localised Independents because they do not perceive them as a major electoral threat. However, a new party emergent on the national scene represents a challenge to all the parties, who usually then do their best to ensure the new party makes no inroads into their respective support bases. In addition, a new party can find it difficult to establish a clear identity in the minds of the voters, which explains why most of them tend to be flash parties, who disappear a few elections after an initially promising emergence. Of the four new parties (National Progressive Democrats, Socialist Labour Party, Democratic Socialist Party, NCP) formed by Independent TDs, none of them lasted for more than a decade. Besides their limited electoral prospects as a new party, forming such a party logistically is a major step for a local Independent to take, and many may be deterred at the effort this takes; for instance, they have to devise a constitution, write a manifesto, and face the might of the machines of the established national parties. Finally, Independents might find it harder to attract votes as a new party, since the electorate find it easier to switch to non-partisans than new parties, as it is less of a leap of volatility.[13]

The final option is to form an alliance of Independents, which represents somewhat of a halfway house between party and Independent status. Such a group can work together to achieve all the benefits accruing to parties (examples including the ability to negotiate as a single unit, as well as parliamentary benefits such as extra speaking rights and office facilities), without the negative repercussions from a betrayal of their independent status that forming a party would entail. All of the three groups of Independents who managed to extract pork from a dependent government had formed an alliance either before or after their agreeing to support the minority administration. The 1948 crop had previously worked together on the campaign of an Independent candidate at the presidential election three years previously, and in 1948 they nominated a representative to negotiate on their behalf with the party leaders. The 1954 group also worked together in a similar fashion. Although the 1997–2002 'Gang of Four' initially negotiated their own separate deals with the two governing parties, once in parliament they realised their interests could be furthered by working together; hence the 'gang' label. They agreed upon common policies, examples including their stance on regionalisation policy, abortion, and the state of the country's infrastructure, and met the government Chief Whip weekly to air their interests and discuss government legislation. Such was their success as a bargaining unit, there were several alliances of Independent candidates at the succeeding election in 2002, and 9 of the 13 TDs subsequently elected formed a parliamentary group to further their interests. They devised a common policy platform and appointed a whip to ensure the harmony of their representations. They formed a technical group that coalesced with the Green Party and Sinn Féin to secure more speaking time in the Dáil. In anticipation of the impending election in 2007, they proposed the formation of an alliance of Independents.

Electoral performance

Several theories can be expounded on the electoral impact for Independents of their supporting a minority government. Because Independent TDs forsake their independent status in favour of a partisan government, one might imagine that they would be punished by their respective electorates for a betrayal of their non-aligned status. However, since Irish voters' main priority at elections is to choose a candidate to look after the needs of the local constituency (Sinnott 1995: 169), the securing of pork for the district by an Independent would most likely offset any negative reaction from their decision to support a government. If, however, an Independent failed to secure such benefits, one would expect their participation to have a negative effect on their vote. The hypothesis is, therefore, where Independents attracted pork for their constituency, all other things being equal, their vote at the succeeding election should increase. If they failed to secure such pork, their vote should fall.

Of the 22 Independents who supported a minority government without any recompense, one did not stand again, while 14 saw a fall in their vote share at the next election, with an average decline of just under 2 per cent. Of the 15 Independents who did receive some benefits for their support, one did not stand again, while 6 of the remaining 14 gained votes at the next election. However, on average these Independents experienced a slight decline in support, at just over 1 per cent. These surprising results mean that the hypothesis concerning the influence of pork-barrel benefits must be rejected. Rather than being an indicator of the weakness of the hypothesis, it may be more a reflection of the difficulty in looking at the influence of a single variable on a candidate's vote, which is usually due to the interaction of a large number of complex factors.

Another theory is that some Independents fail to attract many votes because it is perceived that their winning a seat would be a waste as they can achieve little for the constituency. An Independent occupying a pivotal position in parliament and receiving policy concessions from a minority government can radically alter such a viewpoint. In theory, if voters can see the tangible benefits that Independents can accrue for a constituency, then at an election immediately after a period of rule by such a government, because Irish voters are constituency-oriented, one would therefore expect the overall vote for Independents to increase. While it is difficult to determine the validity of this theory with just three cases, in two of these examples the national vote for Independents increased by over 2 per cent. For instance, because the particularistic benefits achieved by the 'Gang of Four' Independents were well-publicised, the total Independent first preference vote jumped from just under 7 per cent in 1997 to almost 10 per cent in 2002, as many voters sought to elect a similar Independent in their respective constituencies. While it is difficult to form a theory from this, in five of the seven cases where they were supporting the government without any concessions, their vote declined.

Conclusion

Although appearing to be a deviant Irish phenomenon, Independents are, in many respects, not so different from new parties. They can be selected by an election committee, be subject to the wishes of an association, and have a large organisation mobilised to further certain policy interests. Further, the Independents who have come to prominence in Ireland could have registered their movements as parties, since they met the specific legal criteria that determine party status. Therefore, if we were studying these political actors in any other country in Europe, they would most likely be new parties, and would fit into a neat comparative framework. The aim of this chapter was to do just that, and it is to be hoped that the general reader is convinced of the validity of analysing Independents alongside new parties.

Although their role has been limited to support status in all cases bar one, Independents have had a significant role to play in the process of government formation. The decision to support minority governments is not as difficult for Independents to make as it is for new parties. The former are usually delighted to receive overtures from the major parties, and provided they can receive a tangible form of compensation for their support, they tend to be more than willing to support the formation of an administration. As a result, participation in government has generally had a positive effect for Independents when they managed to secure pork-barrel benefits for their constituencies. It has also affected their organisation on some occasions, when alliances formed in government led some Independents to form closer links with each other, and some to reject their non-partisan status by joining a party. To summarise, the role of Independents in supporting minority governments can be compared to that of a safety-valve. When the parties cannot form a majority coalition, which is frequently the case, Independents have provided the solution to a hung parliament, helping to prevent a period of stasis for parliamentary democracy.

In conclusion, a study of Independents can teach us a lot about why new parties emerge, since they are the next stage down from parties on the evolutionary chain of party formation. It can also work the other way, in that the success of Independents in supporting governments raises several questions concerning the rationality of (new) party status. Since new parties are in effect a grouping of previously 'independent' politicians, one can question whether they really are a rational path for aspirant individuals to follow. This, however, remains a question for another day and another study.

Notes

1 Pym Fortuyn was assassinated nine days before the legislative elections of 15 May 2002.
2 They are, however, not permitted to use this title on the official ballot paper to describe their candidacy. They can choose to refer to themselves as 'non-party', or simply leave their affiliation blank.
3 The Irish lower house of parliament.
4 They were sometimes recognised in parliament as such. For an example see William Davin, in Dáil Debates (1930) 34, col. 364.
5 An Irish MP. TD denotes 'Teachta Dála'.
6 As Pedersen says (1982: 5), this definition is not unusual and is typical of most definitions of parties. For example, see Downs 1957: 25; Sartori 1976: 64.
7 See the Electoral (Amendment) Act 2001, Section 11.
8 Although there were no formal deals per se, it was believed that government ministers were bound to look favourably on parliamentary questions concerning constituency matters submitted by the Independents helping to keep them in office (Anon. 2000).
9 A notable example occurred in January 1982 when the minority Fine Gael–Labour administration attempted to push through a fiscally stringent budget, without establishing whether its proposals had the backing of the Independents who had put them into power. The left-wing Independents voted against the budget, resulting in the fall of the government.
10 Also of relevance is the rejection by Labour of overtures from Fianna Fáil.
11 This does not necessarily mean that they did not occasionally receive some form of tangible reward from the government in return for their support. This could take the form of greater access to a minister to represent a case, or a particularistic benefit in the form of a pork-barrel project. While this ensured that they had a more privileged status than party backbenchers in terms of their ability to serve their constituents, there is no evidence that they had any influence on national policy (Farrell, 1987: 140).

12 Even if they decide not to support a party or parties, Independents' very presence can result in increased funding in a region, as the incumbent government attempts to woo back supporters with pork-barrel projects (Costar and Curtin 2004: 21). The irony of such a situation is that it supports Independents' argument that their presence does have an impact.
13 This is indicated by the proportionally higher levels of lower preferences Independents receive after voters have chosen their favoured party candidates (Weeks 2004).

Bibliography

Anon. (1998) 'Healy-Rae uses relationship to transform map', *The Irish Times*, 18 November.

Anon. (2000) 'Independent supporter of two Lemass-led Fianna Fáil governments during 1960s', *The Irish Times*, 7 October, p. 14.

Aldrich, J. (1995) *Why Parties?* Chicago: University of Chicago Press.

Aylott, N. and Bergman, T. (2004) 'Almost in government, but not quite: the Swedish Greens, bargaining constraints and the rise of contract parliamentarism', paper presented at Panel 6, ECPR Joint Sessions, Uppsala, Sweden, April 2004.

Bale, T. and Bergman, T. (2006). 'Captives no longer, but servants still? Contract parliamentarism and the new minority governance in Sweden and New Zealand', *Government and Opposition*, 41(3): 449–476.

Brennock, M. (1998) 'Keeping the Independent TDs happy', *The Irish Times*, 12 December, p. 8.

Browne, N. (1986) *Against the Tide*, Dublin: Gill and Macmillan.

Carty, R.K. (1981) *Party and Parish Pump: Electoral Politics in Ireland*, Ontario: Wilfried Laurier University Press.

Chubb, B. (1957) 'The independent member in Ireland', *Political Studies*, V: 131–41.

Chubb, B. (1992) *The Government and Politics of Ireland*, 3rd edn, New York: Longman.

Coakley, J. (1990) 'Minor parties in Irish political life, 1922–1989', *Economic and Social Review*, 21(3): 269–97.

Costar, B. and Curtin, J. (2004) *Rebels with a Cause: Independents in Australian Politics*, Sydney: UNSW Press.

Downs, A. (1957) *An Economic Theory of Democracy*, New York: Harper and Row.

Duverger, M. (1959) *Political Parties: Their Organization and Activity in the Modern State*, London: Methuen.

Farrell, B. (1987) 'Government formation and ministerial selection', in H.R. Penniman and B. Farrell (eds) *Ireland at the Polls, 1981, 1982 and 1987: A Study of Four General Elections*, Durham, NC: Duke University Press, pp. 131–55.

Gallagher, M. (1976) *Electoral Support for Irish Political Parties 1927–1973*, London: Sage.

Gallagher, M. (2005) 'Ireland: the discreet charm of PR-STV', in M. Gallagher and P. Mitchell (eds) *The Politics of Electoral Systems*, Oxford: Oxford University Press, pp. 511–535.

Gallagher, M. and Sinnott, R. (eds) (1990) *How Ireland Voted 1989*, Galway: PSAI Press.

Gallagher, M. and Laver, M. (eds) (1993) *How Ireland Voted 1992*, Dublin: PSAI Press.

Gallagher, M., Marsh, M. and Mitchell, P. (eds) (2003) *How Ireland Voted 2002*, London: Palgrave.

Harmel, R. and Robertson, J. (1985) 'Formation and success of new parties: a cross-national analysis', *International Political Science Review*, 6(4): 501–523.

Horgan, J. (2000) *Noel Browne: Passionate Outsider*, Dublin: Gill and Macmillan.

Joyce, J. and Murtagh, P. (1983) *The Boss: Charles J. Haughey in Government*, Dublin: Poolbeg Press.

Kelly, T. (2005) 'Cowley responds to Ring's view on Independents', *The Connaught Telegraph*, 1 June, p. 7.

Laver, M. and Schofield, N. (1990) *Multi-Party Government: the Politics of Coalition in Europe*, Oxford: Oxford University Press.

Lucardie, P. (2000) 'Prophets, purifiers and prolocutors: Towards a theory on the emergence of new parties', *Party Politics*, 6(2): 175–85.

Mair, P. (1987) *The Changing Irish Party System: Organisation, Ideology and Electoral Competition*, London: Frances Pinter.

Marsh, M. and Mitchell, P (eds) (1999) *How Ireland Voted 1997*, Boulder: Westview and PSAI Press.

McCullagh, D. (1998) *A Makeshift Majority: The First Inter-Party Government, 1948–51*, Dublin: Institute of Public Administration.

Mitchell, P. (2000) 'Ireland: from single-party to coalition rule', in W. Muller, and K. Strøm (eds) *Coalition Governments in Western Europe*, Oxford: Oxford University Press, pp. 126–158.

Mitchell, P. (2001) 'Divided government in Ireland', in R. Elgie (ed.) *Divided Government in Comparative Perspective*, Oxford: Oxford University Press, pp. 182–209.

Moon, J. (1995) 'Minority government in the Australian states: from ersatz majoritarianism to minoritarianism?', *Australian Journal of Political Science*, 30(Special Issue): 142–163.

O'Connor, A. (2000a) 'Blaney claims the government has agreed to pay £8m for Donegal bridge', *The Irish Times*, 7 August, p.14.

O'Connor, A. (2000b) 'Gildea getting benefits for Donegal constituency', *The Irish Times*, 8 August, p. 14.

O'Halloran, M. (2002) 'Building up a state of Independents', *The Irish Times*, 14 May, p. 7.

Pedersen, M. (1982) 'Towards a new typology of party lifespans and minor parties', *Scandinavian Political Studies*, 5(1): 1–16.

Penniman, H. and Farrell, B. (eds) (1987) *Ireland at the Polls 1981, 1982 and 1987: A Study of Four General Elections*, Durham: Duke University Press.

Rafter, K. (2000) 'Former TD Tom Foxe dies', *The Irish Times*, 9 February.

Rochon, T. (1985) 'Mobilizers and challengers: towards a theory of new party success', *International Political Science Review*, 6(4): 419–439.

Sartori, G. (1976) *Parties and Party Systems*, Cambridge: Cambridge University Press.

Schlesinger, J. (1966) *Ambition and Politics*, Chicago: Rand McNally.

Sinnott, R. (1995) *Irish Voters Decide: Voting Behaviour in Elections and Referendums since 1918*, Manchester: Manchester University Press.

Strøm, K. (1991) *Minority Government, Majority Rule*, Cambridge: Cambridge University Press.

Weeks, L. (2003) 'The Irish parliamentary election, 2002', *Representation*, 39(3): 215–26.

Weeks, L. (2004) 'Explaining voting for independents under STV Elections: the Irish Case', paper presented at the Annual Meeting of the American Political Science Association, Chicago, USA, September 2004.

9 The electoral fate of new parties in government

Jo Buelens and Airo Hino

Governing parties tend to lose at the polls (Rose and Mackie 1983; Müller and Strøm 2000). That raises the obvious and interesting question of whether parties that govern for the first time are more vulnerable than parties that have built up some experience as governing parties. At first sight the evidence is quite mixed. The German Greens entered a coalition with the Social Democrats (SPD) in 1998. In 2000 the Austrian Freedom Party (FPÖ) entered a coalition with the ÖVP. The fate of these two parties, however, differed remarkably in the subsequent general elections: in 2002 the German Greens won eight additional seats, while the Freedom Party lost 34 of its 52 seats. The two Belgian Green parties that joined the federal government in 1999, though, lost heavily four years later, with the Flemish Greens even losing all their seats in the federal parliament (see also Chapter 6). The contrast is striking: some new parties gain seats after participating in government, while others lose.

That leads us to a double question to be answered. First we need to analyse further the impact of governing on the electoral results of newly governing parties. And if there is indeed no clear picture of these effects, we should explore why some parties are able to win and others apparently lose. We assume that entering government is a move that affects parties, especially when they do it for the very first time. It means accepting both the opportunities and the risks of office. One of the major risks is not being able to convince the electorate that going for office was a good idea. Of course most parties do lose votes once in a while, but for parties new in government – especially if these are also new parties – the change to an office-seeking strategy might confront them for the very first time with (serious) electoral losses. That might be even more problematic if the party entered the coalition after winning at the polls. Governing then appears to put an end to a formerly successful vote-seeking strategy.

We will explore three factors that might influence the electoral effects of being new in government: party type (ideology), party size (significance) and electoral history. We first analyse 11 West European democracies in which we find both winning and losing (new) parties: Germany, Austria, Norway, Denmark, Italy, Spain, Sweden, Finland, The Netherlands, Ireland and Belgium.[1]

First, we examine the variations *between* established parties and newly governing parties. Next we look at the variation *amongst* the newly governing parties.

The electoral fate of newly governing parties

The effect of participation in government on parties was first examined by Rose and Mackie (1983). Their findings were straightforward: 66 per cent of the governing parties lost votes in the next elections and in only 5 per cent of the cases were all parties of a coalition government able to win. In other words: there was almost always at least one party of a government that lost votes after governing. More recently, Müller and Strøm (2000) looked at 277 coalitions and found that only 33 per cent of the governments were able to win at the subsequent elections. The basic pattern is obviously still there, but still needs to be explained.

We have constructed a dataset that should allow us to answer our question. Covering the period 1945–2004 we looked at all the parties and their electoral results at national elections. For parties participating in two consecutive elections, we looked at whether they won or lost. We used the performances of parties for the parliamentary elections in 11 different countries. We used the database of Caramani (1999) as a primary source and we completed it with the most recent information for each country from various sources. To identify the governing parties, we used the book on coalition formation in Western Europe by Müller and Strøm (2000).[2] The database has 1134 cases, with 432 cases of governmental parties. Among these governmental parties, we have 47 cases with parties for the first time in government. The number of governmental parties for each country is shown in Table 9.1.

Do newly governing parties lose after being in government? And do they lose more frequently than parties that have had previous experiences of government? Table 9.2 compares the electoral fate of newly and traditionally governing parties. We know that governing parties have more chance to lose than to win, and newly governing parties do indeed share that fate. Only 18 out of 68 new parties, or 26.5

Table 9.1 Number of governmental parties for each country (1945–2004)

	Traditional	First time	Second time	Total
Germany	35	1	1	37
Austria	27	3	-	30
Ireland	20	6	3	29
Norway	18	4	4	26
Sweden	22	4	3	29
Denmark	40	4	3	47
Finland	51	4	3	58
Belgium	60	6	1	67
Netherlands	53	4	1	58
Italy	31	9 (8)[a]	2	42
Spain	6	2	1	9
Total	363	47	22	432

Note
a In further analyses the party of PPI, SVP, PRI, UD, Prodi in Italy will not be included, as there was no electoral result after 1996 which could be calculated.

per cent, are capable of winning after participating in government, while 36.7 per cent of the traditional parties win. New parties in government thus seem to be even more vulnerable than the others, although the difference is not spectacular if we keep in mind that we are dealing with relatively small numbers.

Winning or losing might be a function of the party ideology. Some ideologies might be more flexible than others. Some more traditional ideologies might also be more flexible than newer ideologies. In order to check for variation between parties we have used a simple classification in party families, using the membership of the party groups in the European Parliament as the indicator.

Table 9.3 shows for each party family the proportion of parties winning or losing after spending time in opposition and in government. And that reveals quite some difference. For all party families we find more losing than winning parties after having been in government. But some families tend to lose or win more than others. Christian Democrats, liberals but also greens (only seven cases though) are able to win quite often – more than 40 per cent of the cases – after having been in government. Social democrats have a lower score (33.9 per cent) and are

Table 9.2 Electoral fate and parties' experiences in government

	Traditional	New (first and second time)	Total
Winning	36.7%	26.5%	35.1%
Losing	63.3%	73.5%	64.9%
N	357	68	425

Note
χ^2 value: 2,623 ($P = 0.105$).

Table 9.3 Winners and losers by party family and government participation (1945–2004)

	Opposition			Governing		
	Win	Lose	Total	Win	Lose	Total
Christian Democrats	53.2%	46.8%	77	41.6%	58.4%	113
Social Democrats	63.5%	36.5%	96	33.9%	66.1%	124
Liberals	47.4%	52.6%	95	42.3%	57.7%	78
Communists/Extreme left	44.2%	55.8%	113	0%	100.0%	9
Regionalists	41.2%	58.8%	51	24.1%	75.9%	29
Greens	60.6%	39.4%	33	42.9%	57.1%	7
Right-wing populists	46.9%	53.1%	31	16.7%	83.3%	6
Left libertarians	51.2%	48.8%	43	25.0%	75.0%	16
Agrarians	48.0%	52.0%	25	21.4%	78.6%	14
Conservatives	53.1%	46.9%	49	23.5%	76.5%	17
Single-issue	40.0%	60.0%	5			
Total	316	304	620	144	269	413
	51.0%	49.0%	100.0%	35.0%	65.0%	100.0%

followed by regionalists, left libertarians, agrarians and conservatives, all losing three times out of four. Two party families display very low scores. Of all the right-wing populist parties that entered a coalition only one (*Alleanza Nazionale* in 1994) was able to progress. And all communist parties ever joining a coalition paid a price for this at the polls.

For the extreme left and for the extreme right parties, the effect of governing is quite disastrous. This suggests that more radical ideologies have more problems adapting to the necessities of the compromising games of coalition life, or that voters of parties with radical ideologies cannot easily be convinced of the necessity to compromise. For supporters of Green parties the picture is not that clear though. There we will need explanations for the fact that some are able to increase their vote share after governing, while others are (sometimes severely) beaten.

Maybe size is the explanation. Smaller parties in a coalition are less able to put pressure on the partners, to put and to keep their items on the agenda. Smaller parties might then be less visible to the electorate at large and more vulnerable for their own core supporters. We calculated for each party its size in the coalition, i.e. the proportion of seats of the party in the total number of seats controlled by the coalition. Yet there is no correlation between the size of the parties in the coalition and the electoral performance afterwards (Pearson correlation: –0.048; significance, two-tailed: 0.328).

For new parties to become able to be a potential governing partner, they need to have won votes before. That goes without saying. Without having reached a reasonable size, their chances of being a potential and useful partner remain limited. Parties can, however, win enough votes and seats at their very first participation to make it straight into government. As a starting point, a vote-seeking strategy therefore seems quite obvious for most new parties. Dumont and Bäck (2006) have shown that, at least for Green parties, an experience of electoral loss – at least once – precedes accession to government. There is a plausible explanation for that: losing votes makes the party aware of the fact that the vote-seeking strategy might not pay for ever. This can lead to the beginning of a shift towards accepting the possibility of also pursuing an office-seeking strategy. A party is then possibly also better prepared to cope with the losses that often also come after the participation in government. For Green parties, the post-government fate is, however, more mixed than for others.

Why do some new parties survive while others fail?

The finding above leads us to investigate the second question of this chapter: Why do some new parties succeed in winning the subsequent election while others do not? Applying the common framework above, which runs the gamut of party type, party size, and electoral history, we examine here 20 new parties that have participated in government between 1950 and 2004 and compare their electoral fate. Note that we now shift our attention from the *between variation* of electoral fate between traditional and new parties to the *within variation* among new parties that have participated in government. The 20 new parties studied are listed in Table 9.4.

Table 9.4 List of 'new parties in government', 1945–2004

Party ID	Party name (English translation)	Country	First election after government participation
RW1	Rassemblement Wallon (Walloon Rally)	Belgium	17 April 1977
PPR1	Politieke Partij Radikalen (Radical Political Party)	Netherlands	25 May 1977
D66-1	Democraten '66 (Democrats '66)	Netherlands	25 May 1977
Volksunie1	Volksunie (Peoples' Union)	Belgium	17 December 1978
FDF1	Front Démocratique des Bruxellois Francophones (French Democratic Front)	Belgium	17 December 1978
FDF2	Front Démocratique des Bruxellois Francophones (French Democratic Front)	Belgium	8 November 1981
D66-2	Democraten' 66 (Democrats '66)	Netherlands	8 September 1982
LegaNord1	Lega Nord (Northern League)	Italy	21 April 1996
AN1	Alleanza Nazionale (National Alliance)	Italy	21 April 1996
D66-3	Democraten 66 (Democrats 66)	Netherlands	6 May 1998
VihreaLitto1	Vihrea Litto (Green Union)	Finland	21 March 1999
Verdi1	Federazione dei Verdi (Green Federation)	Italy	13 May 2001
D66-4	Democraten 66 (Democrats 66)	Netherlands	15 May 2002
Verts1	Les Verts (The Greens)	France	16 June 2002
Grüne1	Die Grüne (The Greens)	Germany	22 September 2002
FPÖ1	Freiheitliche Partei Österreichs (Austrian Freedom Party)	Austria	24 November 2002
LFP1	Lijst Pim Fortuyn (Pim Fortuyn's List)	Netherlands	15 January 2003
VihreaLitto2	Vihrea Litto (Green Union)	Finland	16 March 2003
Ecolo1	Ecolo (Ecologists)	Belgium	18 May 2003
Agalev1	Agalev (Live Differently)	Belgium	18 May 2003

Note
The table is compiled chronologically based on the first election after participating in government.

This sample is somewhat smaller and a bit more homogeneous than the one we analysed in the first part of this chapter. The cases are selected on the basis of two criteria. The first is 'participation in government', which denotes a party taking responsibility for an executive office. This precludes parties that have given 'external parliamentary support' to a government without being a cabinet member, such as the Danish People's Party (*Dansk Folkeparti*) since 2001 and the Swedish Greens since 1998.[3] In the second place we limit our cases to the new parties considered as belonging to the three main party families, i.e. the Greens, the new radical right parties and the regionalist parties.[4] We also leave out parties that were new in government in the period 1945–50.

The dependent variable in this analysis is 'Electoral Fate (ELECFATE)'. The 'Electoral Fate' variable represents the electoral outcome that new parties have at the subsequent election after their participation in government. It is operationalised by taking a ratio between the election T_1 (the election that led a new party to enter government) and the following election T_2 (the first election after its executive experience). Formally, the score is calculated as follows:

$$\text{ELECFATE (EF)} = \frac{Votes T_2}{Votes T_1} - 1$$

where $Votes T_2$ is the percentage of votes in T_2 (the subsequent election) and $Votes T_1$ is the percentage of votes in T_1 (the previous election).

To generate a variable with positive and negative values, 1 is deducted from the ratio of ELECFATE. If a party increases its share of votes in the next election (T_2), it gains a positive EF value; if a party loses votes in the subsequent election (T_2), it obtains a negative EF value. For example, the Greens of Germany scores a positive EF value (8.6 per cent in 2002 and 6.7 per cent in 1998, a ratio of +0.28), while Pim Fortuyn List in the Netherlands results in a negative EF value (5.7 per cent in 2003 and 17 per cent in 2002, generating a ratio of – 0.66). In a nutshell, the EF score captures the change over the elections before and after taking part in government.

Figure 9.1 shows the continuum on the Index of EF, illustrating the ways in which the new parties in government are distributed along the spectrum. The highest EF score is +0.31 for D66-1, and the lowest EF score is attained by LPF1 with –0.66. Between these two extremes, the 20 parties are scattered around the mean of –0.26, demonstrating that the electoral fate of new parties that have participated in government varies to a large extent. Consequently, the question arises: What accounts for such a variation? Does party family matter for their electoral fortunes at the following election? Or does party size or the party's role in coalition government matter at all? Or, alternatively, does their electoral record prior to joining the government pave a way to their survival or electoral defeat? In short, our aim here is to apply the same themes investigated above for the *between variation* and to elucidate the mechanisms by which some new parties survive while others fail at the next election.

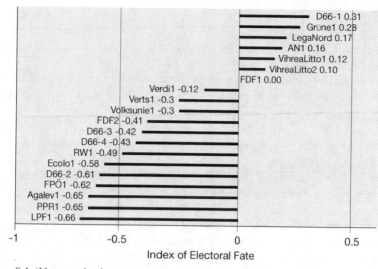
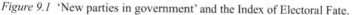

Figure 9.1 'New parties in government' and the Index of Electoral Fate.

Does party type matter?

As described in the above analyses, we test if the type of new parties (the Greens, the extreme-rights or the regionalists) has anything to do with the electoral fate of new parties, the extent to which a new party thrives or falters in the election after participating in government. As we have seen in the example of the Austrian Freedom Party, we expect that extreme right parties could have a harder time in reconciling their anti-establishment stance and executive experiences than other new parties.

Contrary to our expectation, the results show that there is no clear link between the party type and its electoral fate. Two out of three extreme-right parties face an electoral loss, while 12 out of 17 non-extreme-right parties which participated in government lost the subsequent elections (the χ^2 test suggests that there is no significant relationship). The only extreme-right party which managed to increase its votes after participating in government is once again the *Alleanza Nazionale* in Italy. Likewise, 8 out of 12 Greens lost in the following elections, while six out of eight other new parties in government faced an electoral defeat (χ^2 test suggests no significance). The story with the ethnoregionalist parties is similar to the above two types and no significant relationship is found. Given the small number of cases, it is difficult to infer a definitive pattern. New parties such as extreme-right parties, Green parties, and regionalist parties, tend to be ideological by default and the effects of ideology seem to be less pronounced among the new parties than the comparative analyses with traditional parties.

If the party family does not matter, how about the status of incumbency at the time of election? A party could be either blamed or praised; being part of government at the time of election as an incumbent party could reasonably affect their electoral performance (Kramer 1971; Fiorina 1981). When their performance in coalitions is negatively judged, in particular, it may result in an electoral punishment (Key 1966). There are three patterns of governmental participation between two consecutive elections: (1) a party enters government after an election but leaves before the next election; (2) a party enters government after an election and remains in government until the next election; (3) a party enters government through cabinet changes or reshuffles and remains until the next election.[5] Based on these three variables, a binary variable is created to reflect the status of new parties at the time of election.

Among the 20 new parties that have participated in government, 15 of them were still part of their government at the election, and five of them left their government before the election. A cross-tabulation (Table 9.5) reveals that 12 of the 15 incumbent new parties lost in the following elections (80.0 per cent) while only two of the five non-incumbent new parties (40 per cent) faced an electoral defeat (the difference is significant at $P < 0.10$ level). These two cases are both Belgian parties: the defeat of the French Democratic Front in 1981 and of Ecolo in 2003; and the three non-incumbent new parties that survived were the National Alliance and the Northern League in the 1996 Italian election, and the Finnish Green Union in 2003. Given the distribution of countries, the ways in which the parties are punished may be different across the countries as well.

Does party size matter?

Now we examine whether party size has anything to do with their electoral fate. Here we mean party size by the significance of new parties within the coalition government. We measure this first by the portfolio ratio, the percentage of ministers that a new party possesses within its coalition, and second by the type of coalition governments that new parties take part in (e.g. minimum winning coalitions, surplus coalitions).

Table 9.5 Cross-tabulation between electoral fate and incumbent status

			Incumbency at the time of elections		Total
			0: No	1: Yes	
Electoral fate	0: Down	*Frequencies*	2	12	14
		% incumbency	40.0%	80.0%	70.0%
	1: Up	*Frequencies*	3	3	6
		% incumbency	60.0%	20.0%	30.0%
Total		*Frequencies*	5	15	20
		% incumbency	100.0%	100.0%	100.0%

Note
χ^2 value: 2.857 ($P = 0.091$).

We could expect that taking many ministerial responsibilities may harm new parties' vote winning potentials (in particular, the post that they hold could undermine their anti-establishment appeals). Given that the total number of ministerial posts varies across countries and governments, the absolute number of ministerial posts does not fully reflect the extent to which new parties play a significant role in coalition formation. We thus employ a 'portfolio ratio' which can be calculated simply by dividing the number of ministerial posts that a new party holds by the total number of ministerial posts in the government. For instance, the portfolio ratio of D66 in the purple government of the Netherlands since 1994 is computed as 0.25 (i.e. four ministers out of 16 ministers in total). The simple correlation with the Index of Electoral Fate produces an insignificant result of -0.227 ($P = 0.167$).

We now examine if the type of government has anything to do with the variation of 'electoral fate' of new parties. Theoretically, to be an essential and important member in coalition government could either favour or harm an electoral outcome in the next election. To put it simply, if the government performs well, coalition members benefit from their good performance; conversely, if the government performs poorly, they suffer from the popular punishment accordingly. Hence, we hypothesise that being an essential member in a minimum number coalition government could have an amplifying effect on their electoral fate together with other relevant variables, that is to say, the extent to which new parties gain or lose in the next election.

In terms of the dataset, the governments up to 1998 derive from the compilation by Woldendorp, Keman and Budge (2000) while those up to date are supplemented by the annual 'Political Data' volumes of *European Journal of Political Research* (Katz and Koole 1999, 2000, 2001, 2002, Katz 2003). The type of government varies from single-party government, through minimum winning coalition, surplus coalition, single-party minority government, multiparty minority government, to caretaker government in the dataset. We examine how the type of government relates to the electoral performance of new parties and how it interacts with other relevant variables.

The results suggest that there is no direct link between the type of government that new parties take part in and their electoral fate at the bivariate level. Table 9.6 reports the cross-tabulation between the electoral fate of new parties and whether or not they were part of a minimum winning coalition. There seems to be virtually no direct link between the two variables. The same applies for other types of government. This does not come as a surprise, since we expect that this variable would only have an amplifying effect when other variables are taken into consideration.

For example, the electoral fate of new parties could also be affected by how well coalition partners do in the same election. As the previous research has shown, only 5 per cent of all government parties have won the following election all together (Rose and Mackie 1983). This suggests that there is a 'zero-sum' game going on among coalition partners, where new parties in government have to win not only against the opposition parties but also against their own coalition

Table 9.6 Cross-tabulation between electoral fate and minimum winning coalition (MWC)

			Minimum winning coalition		Total
			0: No	1: Yes	
Electoral fate	0: Down	Frequencies	8	6	14
		% of MWC	72.7%	66.7%	70.0%
	1: Up	Frequencies	3	3	6
		% of MWC	27.3%	33.3%	30.0%
Total		Frequencies	11	9	20
		% of MWC	100.0%	100.0%	100.0%

Note
χ^2 value: 0.087 ($P = 0.769$).

partners. Hence, it is reasonable to test whether the size of coalition partners, i.e. the electoral performance of coalition partners, matters for the electoral fate of new parties. As the later multivariate analyses will show, the electoral perform-ance of coalition partners does indeed have a significant effect on the electoral fate of new parties, especially when the competition among coalition partners is severe, as in the case of a minimum winning coalition.

Does electoral history matter?

If a new party makes a huge gain in the election immediately prior to entering office, it is more difficult to maintain that boost over more than two elections. The electoral performance at the last election (LASTELEC) is calculated with the equivalent formula to 'electoral fate' (ELECFATE):

$$LASTELEC = \frac{Votes T_1}{Votes T_0} - 1$$

where $Votes T_1$ is the percentage of votes in T_1 (the previous election) and $Votes T_0$ is the percentage of votes in T_0 (the election before the last).

The result shows that new parties do indeed have difficulty in maintaining their electoral success in the previous elections (Pearson's correlation = −0.345, $P = 0.074$). The better the electoral record is before entering in government, the harder it is for new parties to win more votes in the following election. This cor-responds to the above finding that new parties tend to enter into government after experiencing electoral losses in the past.

The multivariate analyses

Based on the explorative findings above, we apply the Qualitative Comparative Analysis (QCA) method here to examine more complex relations among these variables.[6] The QCA is powerful in extracting the essence of the interactions among variables (conditions) and minimise a causal link to the outcome (Ragin 1987; De Meur and Rihoux 2002). The dependent variable (*outcome*) and the independent variables (*conditions*) to be considered are as follows:

- Outcome
  - FATE (1: electoral gains/0: electoral losses at the second election)
- Conditions
  - INCUMBENCY (1: part of coalition/0: out of coalition at the time of election)
  - COALFATE (1: electoral gains/0: electoral losses by coalition partners)
  - LASTELEC (1: substantial gains/0: losses or status quo at the first election)[7]
  - MWC (1: part of minimum winning coalition /0: not part of minimum winning coalition)

The 'truth table' for all 20 cases is presented in the Appendix (Table 9.1A). The Venn diagram shown in Figure 9.2 visualises the results of QCA and illustrates how the combination of the four conditions is linked to their outcome.

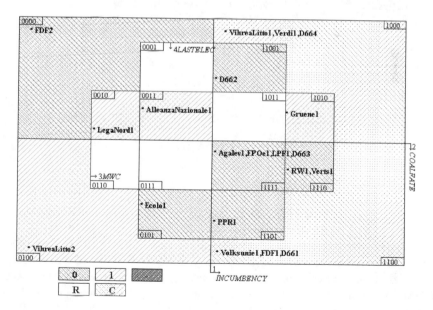

Note 1: R denotes 'Remainders' (logical cases) and C denotes 'Contradictions'.

Note 2: The diagram is created by using TOSMANA Ver 1.254 (Cronqvist 2006).

Figure 9.2 The Venn diagram for 'new parties in government'.

We will now discuss the results of Boolean minimisation. First, the Boolean equation for explaining '1' (FATE: all the cases with an 'upwards' electoral fate) is calculated. This results in the following formula (Note that CAPITAL letters indicate the value '1' and lower-case letters indicate the value '0').[8]

$$FATE = coalfate*MWC*lastelec +$$
$$incumbency*coalfate*MWC +$$
$$incumbency*COALFATE*mwc*lastelec \qquad (1)$$

To decipher the Boolean formula, FATE (the '1' zone in Figure 9.2) is conditioned by the combination of coalfate*MWC*lastelec (cells '0010' and '1010'), incumbency*coalfate*MWC (cells '0010' and '0011'), and incumbency*COALFATE *mwc*lastelec (cell '0100').

Next, the formula is further reduced by minimising the 'remainders' (the white 'R' zones in Figure 9.2), often known as 'logical' cases where no empirical cases are found. This operation results in the following Boolean formula.

$$FATE \text{ (including R)} = \quad coalfate*MWC +$$
$$incumbency*COALFATE*lastelec \qquad (2)$$

Second, the Boolean formula for explaining '0' (fate: all the cases with a 'downwards' electoral fate) is calculated. The following formula accounts for the new parties that lost electoral ground after participating in government.

$$fate = \qquad INCUMBENCY*COALFATE*MWC +$$
$$COALFATE*mwc*LASTELEC +$$
$$INCUMBENCY*mwc*LASTELEC +$$
$$incumbency*coalfate*mwc*lastelec \qquad (3)$$

Again, the formula is further minimised by including the remainders.

$$fate \text{ (including R)} = \quad COALFATE*MWC +$$
$$mwc*LASTELEC +$$
$$incumbency*coalfate*mwc \qquad (4)$$

Now, what do we make of these formulae? First, the results of this Boolean minimisation suggest that being a member of a minimum winning coalition (MWC) in conjunction with the electoral fate of coalition partners (COALFATE) is important in determining the electoral fate of new parties. Both minimal formulae for the cases of electoral gains and losses produce an intersection between MWC and COALFATE. That is to say, for electoral gains (i.e. formula 2), coalfate*MWC is obtained. As shown in Figure 9.2, this combination (covering cells '1010', '0011', and '0010') includes the German Greens (Grüne1), the Italian National Alliance (AlleanzaNazionale1), and Northern League (LegaNord1). All three parties made electoral gains after participating in a minimum winning coalition by having a coalition partner defeated at the same election.

Similarly for electoral losses (i.e. formula 4), COALFATE*MWC is obtained. These cases apply to the Flemish Greens (Agalev1), Austrian Freedom Party (FPÖ1), List Pim Fortuyn (LPF1), the third coalition participation of Democrats '66 (D66–3), Walloon Rally (RW1), and French Greens (Verts1). All six parties shared the same conditions and outcome: being in a minimum winning coalition government and having a partner who made electoral gains at the subsequent election (covering cells '1110', '1111', '0111', and '0110' in Figure 9.2).

Together with the interaction of coalfate*MWC (formula 2), the result from the interaction of COALFATE*MWC (formula 4) suggests that MWC is an important variable once mediated through the electoral performance of coalition partners (COALFATE). This was not found in the earlier cross-tabulation, in which the possibility of interaction effects with other variables was not explored. The Boolean analysis brought out this interaction effect between MWC and COALFATE, and recast the relevance of the minimum winning coalition. This finding sheds light on the oft-neglected aspects of coalition politics. The 'zero-sum' game takes place between the partners of the minimum winning coalition and coalition partners have to win the 'within competition' on top of the competition against opposition parties. 'New parties in government' must win the battle against the coalition partner at the subsequent election especially if they are part of a tight coalition government such as a minimum winning coalition.

Second, the interaction of mwc*LASTELEC resulted in electoral losses of new parties in formula 4 (covering cells '1001', '0001', '1101', and '0101' in Figure 9.2). This interaction effect suggests that all those that made substantial gains in the election prior to entering a surplus coalition government were destined to lose votes in the subsequent election. The examples are the Dutch Radical Political Party (PPR1), the second participation of Democrats '66 (D66-2), and the Walloon Greens (Ecolo1).

Other than the above two findings, a patchy picture emerges for parties in a surplus coalition government or multi-party minority government[9] (those outside the MWC zone in Figure 9.2). There are two 'Contradiction' zones (identified as 'C'): INCUMBENCY*COALFATE*mwc*lastelec (cell '1100') and INCUMBENCY*coalfate*mwc*lastelec (cell '1000'). In the former cell, Democrats '66 (D66–1) gains but the People's Union (Volksunie1) and the French Democratic Front (FDF1) lose; in the latter cell, the Finnish Greens (VihreaLitto1) gain but the Italian Greens (Verdi1) and the fourth participation of Democrats '66 (D66–4) lose votes at the subsequent election. To sort out these contradictions, a further operation, such as the introduction of additional conditions, may be necessary.

For the remaining two zones, a definite outcome is obtained but with a single case. For the combination of incumbency*COALFATE*mwc*lastelec in formula 1 (cell '0100' in Figure 9.2), the second participation in government by Finnish Greens (VihreaLitto2) increases their seats in the next election. For the combination of incumbency*coalfate*mwc*lastelec in formula 3 (cell '0000'), the second participation by the Francophone Democratic Front in Belgium loses in the next election. Given that each zone only accommodates a single case, interpretations of these results should be reserved.

To further investigate the multiplicative relationships, we ran a multiple regression analysis. We include in the model the variables initially found relevant in the above section such as 'electoral performance in the previous election', 'incumbent status', and 'electoral fate of coalition partners'. We also include the interaction effect between the electoral fate of coalition partners and Minimum Winning Coalition, the co-occurrence of conditions found important in the Boolean analysis.

The regression model is specified based upon the above findings as follows:

$$Y = \alpha + \beta_1 X_1 + \beta_2 X_2 + \beta_3 X_3 + \beta_4 X_4 + \beta_5 X_3 * X_4 + \varepsilon$$

where

$Y =$ Index of EF (Electoral Fate)
$\alpha =$ Intercept
$X_1 =$ INCUMBENCY (1: party is incumbent/0: party is not incumbent)
$X_2 =$ LASTELEC (1: substantial gain of votes <20 per cent>/0: no substantial gains)
$X_3 =$ coalfate (1: electoral losses/0: electoral gains of coalition partners)[10]
$X_4 =$ MWC (1: in Minimum Winning Coalition/0: not in Minimum Winning Coalition)
$\varepsilon =$ Error term

The dependent variable is the variation of electoral fate of new parties as measured by the Index of Electoral Fate. The estimates of the respective β coefficients and α intercept are reported in Table 9.7.[11]

As shown in the table, the interaction term 'coalfate*MWC' and the independent variables LASTELEC and MWC appear significant with expected signs. The high positive magnitude for 'coalfate*MWC' demonstrates that being part of MWC government and having coalition partners whose share of the vote de-

Table 9.7 Multiple regression analysis on the Index of Electoral Fate

Variables	Index of Electoral Fate (EF)				
	Un-standardised coefficient			Standardised coefficient	
	b	Standard error		β	Significance
Intercept (α)	−0.279	0.179		–	0.142
INCUMBENCY (β₁)	0.043	0.160		0.055	0.793
LASTELEC (β₂)	−0.236	0.132		−0.347	0.095
Coalfate (β₃)	0.220	0.169		0.318	0.213
MWC (β₄)	−0.351	0.159		−0.514	0.045
Coalfate*MWC (β₅)	0.899	0.273		0.946	0.005

Notes
$N = 20$; $R^2 = 0.59$ (adjusted $R^2 = 0.44$).

clines or stagnates in the second election significantly increases the chances of new parties surviving the next election. Contrarily, the negative coefficient for LASTELEC implies that a large gain at the last election tends to lead to a 'reversal of fortunes' at the election after being in government.

These results from the multiple regression analysis coincide with the findings obtained from the QCA. The high significance of the interaction term 'coalfate*MWC' is reasonable given that all nine cases of this interaction [i.e. Walloon Rally (RW1), Northern League (LegaNord1), National Alliance (AlleanzaNazionale1), the third participation of Democrats '66 (D66-3), and French Greens (Verts1), German Greens (Grüne1), Austrian Freedom Party (FPÖ1), List Pim Fortuyn (LPF1), Flemish Greens (Agalev1)] fit perfectly without any contradiction (Figure 9.2). Likewise, the moderate significance of LASTELEC seems valid as only one out of eight cases [i.e. National Alliance (AlleanzaNazionale1)] makes an electoral gain at the second election; all the other seven cases [Radical Political Party (PPR1), the second participation of Democrats '66 (D66–2), the third participation of Democrats '66 (D66-3), Austrian Freedom Party (FPÖ1), List Pim Fortuyn (LPF1), Walloon Greens (Ecolo1), and Flemish Greens (Agalev1)] gained substantially in the election that led up to their participation in government but experience electoral losses in the subsequent election.

Concluding remarks

The aim of this chapter was to describe and explain the electoral fate of new parties in government. The analyses confirmed the existing knowledge that parties tend to lose more as governmental parties than as opposition parties. This was the same for both traditional parties and new parties. We have examined whether new parties tend to lose more than traditional parties after participating in government. The analyses suggested that they are rather similar, and new parties are no more unfortunate than traditional parties. The difference between new parties and traditional parties was marginal and not statistically significant. The comparison of the electoral fate between new parties and traditional parties indeed revealed that both of them tend to lose after participating in government.

To explain why some parties survive after government participation while others fail to do so, we have examined party type (party ideology), party size, electoral history, and coalition partnership thematically. Party ideology seemed to matter in accounting for which party family is more susceptible to an electoral defeat after participating in government. The electoral fate of the extreme-left and extreme-right parties in government point in the direction that strong ideology has a negative influence on the electoral result at the next election. *Aleanza Nationale* in Italy was the only exception but this case also revealed the difficulty in measuring ideology as it might shift over time. From our analyses, we could speculate that the stronger the ideology is, the harder it is for parties to reconcile its own extreme-left or extreme-right programme with governmental responsibilities. Nonetheless, party ideology did not appear a crucial factor in explaining the variation of the electoral fate among new parties. Given that new parties tend to be ideologically driven by default, this finding was not surprising.

Next, party size did not appear to be a crucial factor in explaining the variation of electoral performance. However, the electoral history of governmental parties seemed to account for the electoral path of governing parties afterwards. First of all, losing in the past seemed to be a great incentive for new parties to join a coalition. It became clear that new parties that decided to take up the executive role tended to have experienced an electoral loss in the past before entering government. Also, a large gain at the election which led a new party to enter into government tended to end in an electoral loss at the following election. It became evident that it is difficult for new parties to continue their winning streak if they have a large electoral boost before entering a coalition government. These findings suggest that it is important to keep the time-series perspective in analysing the electoral fate of new parties in government, and we believe that future research should also integrate the cross-temporal dimension into the analysis.

Our analyses also added a new finding: winning at elections seems to be a zero-sum game within governmental parties. To predict the electoral fate of a new party in government, the result of the coalition partner is useful, certainly if this new party enters in a tight coalition such as a minimum winning coalition. All new parties that survived after participating in government had their coalition partners lose in the following election (especially if in a minimum winning coalition). This finding corresponds to the earlier observation of Rose and Mackie (1983) that only in 5 per cent of the cases all governmental parties were able to win. This finding sheds light on the zero-sum aspects of coalition politics. Coalition partners are, so to speak, 'enemies within'. On one hand, coalition partners have to fight against opposition parties in election campaign together as a team, but on the other hand, they have to fight against each other for a common pie and gain votes at the expenses of partners' loss. The analyses here uncovered the competitive aspects of coalition politics and could have a further implication in future research. The law of the jungle lives in coalition politics.

Appendix

Table 9.1A Truth table for Boolean analysis

Case	FATE	INCUMBENCY	COALFATE	MWC	LASTELEC
Volksunie1	0	1	1	0	0
RW1	0	1	1	1	0
FDF1	0	1	1	0	0
FDF2	0	0	0	0	0
LegaNord1	1	0	0	1	0
VihreaLitto1	1	1	0	0	0
VihreaLitto2	1	0	1	0	0
Verdi1	0	1	0	0	0
Verts1	0	1	1	1	0

Grüne1	1	1	0	1	0
Ecolo1	0	0	1	0	1
Agalev1	0	1	1	1	1
AlleanzaNazionale1	1	0	0	1	1
FPÖ1	0	1	1	1	1
LFP1	0	1	1	1	1
PPR1	0	1	1	0	1
D66–1	1	1	1	0	0
D66–2	0	1	0	0	1
D66–3	0	1	1	1	1
D66–4	1	1	0	0	0

Notes

1 France was omitted due to the frequent use of cartels by the parties, which made it difficult to create a comparable dataset.

2 By comparing the two sources, we corrected the figure on a couple of instances. For the Netherlands, DS70 loses 1.2 per cent in 1971 instead of gaining 1.8 per cent, and D66 gains 1.3 per cent in 1977 instead of losing 1.2 per cent. For Belgium, the FDF loses 0.5 per cent in 1978 instead of gaining 2 per cent.

3 In Denmark, the Danish People's Party supports the coalition government of the Liberal Party and the Conservative People's Party, but formally remains outside of the Rasmussen cabinet. In Sweden, the Greens have supported the Social Democratic Party minority government after the 1998 and 2002 elections (see Chapter 5 for more details).

4 We include the new parties that participated in government for the third and fourth time. For example, D66 in the Netherlands in the 90s is considered as a viable case.

5 Theoretically, two more patterns are possible: (1) a party may participate in government between the two elections and leave before the next election arrives; (2) a party may enter in government after the first election and leave in the middle, and re-enter government to remain until the next election. Despite the theoretical possibilities, neither pattern is empirically observed in the 20 cases examined here.

6 We have also investigated the coalition role of new parties, the number of coalition partners, reasons for government termination, the duration of government, and cabinet reshuffles, but they did not appear to be related to the electoral fate of new parties.

7 LASTELEC derives from the index of electoral performance at the last election calculated above. The index is dichotomised based upon the threshold of '0.2' (i.e. electoral gains above 20 percentage points are considered as 'substantial gain').

8 The Boolean reduction was performed by TOSMANA Ver 1.254 (Cronqvist 2006).

9 Verdi1 is the only party that qualifies as a multiparty minority government across the 20 cases.

10 The variable is recoded to facilitate more intuitive interpretations by switching the value of 0 to 1 and the value of 1 to 0.

11 For the independent variables, all four *conditions* investigated in the QCA are included. The electoral performance prior to participating in government is dichotomised at 20 percent to distinguish substantial gains from others. Note that coalfate*MWC is an interaction term, reflecting the effects revealed in the QCA (i.e. the configurations 'coalfate*MWC' and 'COALFATE*MWC').

Bibliography

Caramani, D. (1999) *Elections in Western Europe since 1815: Electoral results by Constituencies*, London: Macmillan.

Cronqvist, L. (2006) *Tosmana – Tool for Small-N Analysis [SE – Version 1.254]*. Marburg. Available at: http://www.tosmana.net (accessed 23 May 2006).

De Meur, G. and Rihoux, B. (2002) *L'Analyse Quali-Quantitative Comparée: Approache, techniques et applications en sciences humaines*, Louvain-la-Neuve: Bruylant-Academia.

Dumont, P. and Bäck, H. (2006) 'Why so few, and why so late? Green parties and the question of governmental participation, *European Journal of Political Research*, 45: 35–67.

Fiorina, M.P. (1981) *Retrospective Voting in American National Elections*, New Haven: Yale University Press.

Katz, R. (2003) 'Political Data in 2002', *European Journal of Political Research*, 42: 873–9.

Katz, R. and Koole, R. (1999) 'Political Data in 1998', *European Journal of Political Research*, 36: 307–15.

Katz, R. and Koole, R. (2000) 'Political Data in 1999', *European Journal of Political Research*, 38: 303–12.

Katz, R. and Koole, R. (2001) 'Political Data in 2000', *European Journal of Political Research*, 40: 223–32.

Katz, R. and Koole, R. (2002) 'Political Data in 2001', *European Journal of Political Research*, 41: 885–96.

Key, V.O. (1966) *The Responsible Electorate, Rationality in Presidential Voting, 1936–1960*, Cambridge: Belknap Press of Harvard University Press.

Kramer, G. H. (1971) 'Short-term fluctuations in U.S. Voting Behavior, 1896–1964', *American Political Science Review*, 65: 131–43.

Müller, W.C. and K. Strøm (eds) (2000) *Coalition Governments in Western Europe*, Oxford: Oxford University Press.

Ragin, C. (1987) *The Comparative Method: Moving beyond Qualitative and Quantitative Strategies*, Berkeley: University of California Press.

Rose, R. and Mackie, T. (1983) 'Incumbency in government: asset or liability?', in H. Daalder and P. Mair (eds) *Western European Party Systems: Continuity and Change*, London: Sage, pp. 115–37.

Woldendorp, J., Keman, H. and Budge, I. (2000) *Party Government in 48 Democracies (1945–1998): Composition – Duration – Personnel*, Dordrecht: Kluwer Academic Publishers.

10 Populists in power

Attitudes toward immigrants after the Austrian Freedom Party entered government

Elisabeth Ivarsflaten[1]

Introduction

As three Western European democracies – Austria, the Netherlands, and Italy – have survived the inclusion of a populist right party in government and these parties all experienced severe electoral losses immediately thereafter, government responsibility seems to be the best cure available for ridding Western European voters of their taste for radical right-wing populism. However, many scholars, politicians, and commentators worried about such inclusions not primarily because they feared improved electoral performance by populist right parties. Instead, elites were worried about the signal that such inclusion would send to voters concerning the acceptability of anti-immigrant sentiment. After all, populist right parties across several Western European countries had risen from insignificance to substantial political influence since the mid-1980s mainly because of the attention that their provocative exclusionist statements on asylum and immigration policy had granted them and the way in which these statements resonated with parts of the public (Carter 2005; Ivarsflaten 2005; Norris 2005). Contrasting the recent Austrian experience with that of Denmark and Flanders, this chapter examines the extent to which including a populist right party as a legitimate government partner fuels anti-immigrant sentiment.

This chapter argues and shows that, in the Austrian case, including the populist right Freedom Party (FPÖ) in government did not fuel anti-immigrant sentiment, but rather that it most likely somewhat dampened the expression of such sentiments in the short term. I argue and show some supportive evidence to suggest that this unexpected dampening effect has two causes. First, I argue that populist right parties in government are structurally constrained in their communication with voters in a way that populist right parties in opposition are not, and that these constraints limit the extent to which populists in government can incite anti-immigrant sentiment. Second, I argue that the particular way in which the government inclusion of the Freedom Party was handled in Austria sent a strong signal to the Austrian public that suggested, on the one hand, that the mainstream right party, ÖVP, did not agree with the radical anti-immigrant proposals of the FPÖ, and on the other, that parts of the FPÖ's legacy and personnel were still unacceptable. Comparing the Austrian case to Denmark and Flanders, where populist right parties were not included in government, this chapter concludes that including populist right parties in government is not more likely to fuel anti-immigrant sentiment than the two main alternatives. However, the extent to which more tolerance will be the result depends on the particular way in which such inclusion is handled.

Theories of how parties interact with public opinion

Since the 1950s political science has fostered two powerful, yet contradictory, schools for understanding how political parties interact with public opinion – spatial theory and opinion leadership models. The main claims of these two schools and how they apply to our question of interest will be discussed in this section. In the following sections, arguments will be put forward to fill gaps in existing opinion leadership models that result from their narrow application to the two-party context of the US.

Spatial theory of party competition holds that for most intents and purposes the public's policy preferences are influenced by events and prior convictions and are therefore unaffected by the argumentation of political parties. Political parties, in this account, compete for votes by strategically altering their policy positions and/ or the choice situations for voters to their advantage. They do so, for example, by adopting winning policy positions on issues and/or promoting the importance of their winning issue over others. They do not, by contrast, significantly alter the distribution of voter preferences, so opinion towards immigrants do not depend on parties' opinion leadership (Downs 1957; Riker 1982; Laver and Hunt 1992; Kitschelt 1994; Kitschelt and McGann 1995; Meguid 2005).

Opinion leadership models, by contrast, hold that the public does not form solid opinions on a range of issues. Bombarded by information and with only limited interest in politics, most people trust elites to do the work of how to respond to complex and changing social, political and economic phenomena for them. The extreme version of this idea is captured in V.O. Key's much cited phrase, "the voice of the people is but an echo" (1966). When elites disagree, voters, according to the dominant contemporary account in this school of thought, follow the cues of the party or elite to which they have a prior affinity (Zaller 1992). Political parties thus perform an important function in shaping the public's response to political events. They not only compete by jostling to be on the right side of public opinion, they also do so by trying to bring as much of the public as possible to their side.

For the purposes of this analysis, the spatial theory perspective functions mostly as a null hypothesis. Spatial theory would lead us to expect that the public's response to the immigration crisis of the 1980s and 1990s in Western Europe[2] was mainly influenced by the experience of receiving a large number of refugees or immigrants, on the one hand, and their prior convictions about the desirability of and obligation to accepting such individuals, on the other. These prior convictions could concern, for instance, beliefs about the obligation to help people in need and about the costs and benefits of accepting immigrants. However, parties' positions on immigration policy should not have any direct impact on voters' attitudes towards immigrants, according to the most commonly used assumptions of spatial theory.

The hypotheses emerging from opinion leadership models are more complex, and being more complex the burden of evidence lays on their shoulders. From this perspective, if the major parties take a firm stance against the populist right – for example forming a *cordon sanitaire* as was done in Belgium in the late 1980s and onwards – they will clearly signal that the populist right is illegitimate and that its views on immigration are unacceptable. Following these strong elite cues, voters with a prior affinity towards the major parties will, according to this perspective, express less anti-immigrant sentiment. In fact, the opinion leadership model predicts that mainstream parties will be able to convince a substantial number of their key voters that a moderate or liberal policy response to the immigration crisis is appropriate.

By contrast, if the mainstream right makes a high-profile effort to propose more restrictive immigration policies, as was done in Denmark in the 2001 election campaign, the expected outcome according to the opinion leadership model is that voters with a prior affinity to the mainstream right will express more anti-immigrant sentiment and call for restrictive immigration policies. The change in public perception will come about because the mainstream right will send cues to the effect that more restrictive immigration policies are in their voters' interest and that the claim for such policies is legitimate within liberal democracies.

Government inclusion as a new dimension

Including new parties into a governing coalition, as was done in Austria in 1999, is a behavioral dimension that is not usually considered by these opinion leadership models of how parties interact with public opinion. Simply extending the theory as stated above, it could be argued that a mainstream right party that includes a populist right party into government sends a signal to voters that all policy differences between the two parties are small or irrelevant. Thus, the effects of government inclusion could be analogous to the policy co-option model described above, where the mainstream right adopts more restrictive immigration policies.

However, while government inclusion of populist right parties doubtless signals that such parties are largely acceptable to the mainstream right, it is not clear a priori that, if assuming opinion leadership, the effects on people's attitudes towards immigrants should be the same as when the mainstream right itself campaigns for much more restrictive immigration policies. The two responses can be thought of as different because a mainstream right party that includes a populist right party in a coalition after an election can position itself on the moderate side in the immigration and multiculturalism debates, while a mainstream right party that itself wants to become the proponent of restrictive immigration policies cannot do so.

In the case of policy co-option, the mainstream right party will seek to emphasize, explain and justify its change of position as much as possible and, if opinion leadership is strong, the mainstream right party is likely to persuade voters that it is in their interest to restrict immigration. The case for restrictions on immigration and the costs of multiculturalism was indeed adamantly argued by the Danish mainstream right, *Venstre*, in the campaign leading up to the 2001 general elections. If major mainstream parties exercise opinion leadership on sentiment towards immigrants, we should as a consequence see more anti-immigrant sentiment among *Venstre*-partisans after the 2001 election.

By contrast, even if we expect a high degree of opinion leadership by the major mainstream parties, the inclusion of the populist right into government may not lead to much of a shift in public opinion towards immigrants. Mainstream parties may state before the election that a coalition with the populists is undesirable because of the party's incitement of racism, and they may campaign on a ticket of moderate or status-quo immigration policies. If, after the election, it turns out that the populist right party gained a very substantial amount of votes, the mainstream right may reluctantly enter into a coalition with the populist right party arguing that they are responding to the voice of the people although they dislike the populist right parties' policies.

Moreover, they may seek symbolic and substantive concessions from the populist right party. As will be discussed further below, this account resembles what the mainstream right in Austria, ÖVP, did when it entered into a governing coalition with the Freedom Party after the 1999 general elections. If government inclusion is an important and overlooked dimension in existing opinion leadership models, we should therefore expect less anti-immigrant sentiment expressed by Austrian ÖVP-partisans, following the government inclusion of the Freedom Party in 1999, than by Danish *Venstre*-partisans following the 2001 election campaign.

Opinion leadership of the populist right parties themselves as a new variable

The traditional theory of opinion leadership was formulated for the US context where it makes sense to assume that opinion leadership will be exercised only by the two main parties (Zaller 1992). In the context of European multiparty systems, it is however possible that parties other than the major mainstream left and right parties exercise considerable opinion leadership. In the three contexts considered here, the populist right parties are large parties that have existed for a long time (especially in Austria and Denmark, where they were established in the 1950s and 1970s respectively). It is therefore possible that these parties exercise a considerable amount of opinion leadership, especially in the area of immigration and asylum, where they have sought the role as populist "truth-tellers" (Rydgren 2005).

If the populist right themselves exercise opinion leadership, then it is possible that the effectiveness of this leadership varies when the populist right is included in government, as in Austria, and when it is excluded, as in Denmark and Flanders. When excluded from government responsibility, populist right parties can use all their resources to campaign on persuading the public at large, and their key electorate more specifically, about the negative consequences of immigration and the problems associated with the integration of new minorities. When included in government, many of their resources will by practical necessity be diverted to other policy areas. Moreover, they will be in a position where they cannot just criticize immigration policy, but will have to defend the status quo. It is therefore possible that populist right parties in a governing position will be a less persistent, single-minded and effective advocate of anti-immigrant views and sentiments than populist right parties out of government.

Summary of hypotheses

In spite of the one-dimensional focus of opinion leadership models, the discussion above revealed that mainstream parties' responses to the asylum crisis can in fact be thought of as two-dimensional. As Figure 10.1 illustrates, the first dimension consist of policy positions and changes in them. In the three cases studied here, moderate policies predominated on this dimension.[3] The exception is the Danish mainstream right, which changed its policies and started proposing restrictive immigration policies before and during the 2001 election campaign. Because of the debate above about whether or not inclusion of the populist right in the government coalition changed the immigration policy signal sent by the Austrian ÖVP as much as that of the Danish *Venstre*, the Austria 1999 case appears in between the moderate and restrictive categories. By contrast, their coalition policy was evidently inclusionary at that point. The two other cases considered (and all mainstream right parties in the three cases earlier on, in the 1990s) pursued exclusionary coalition policies towards the populist right.

The empirically testable proposition that derives from the above discussion can be summarized as follows:

- P0 (following spatial theory assumptions): Neither immigration policy changes by major parties nor government inclusion of populist right parties influences the level or composition of anti-immigrant sentiment.
- P1 (following traditional opinion leadership accounts): If a mainstream party adopts more restrictive immigration policies, the partisans of this party will express more anti-immigrant sentiment.

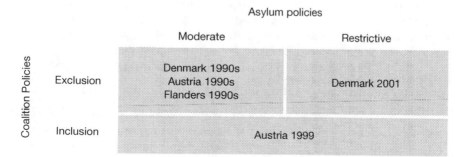

Figure 10.1 Mainstream parties' immigration and coalition policies in Austria, Denmark and Flanders. Source: Lubbers (2001); own research.

- P2 (new opinion leadership hypothesis): A mainstream right party that reluctantly includes an anti-immigrant party in government will not lead its partisans towards expressing more anti-immigrant sentiment.
- P3 (new opinion leadership hypothesis): A well-established populist right party in government will be less effective at inciting anti-immigrant sentiment among its partisans than a well-established populist right party in opposition.

Empirical evaluation of the hypotheses

Ideally, we would have an all European multiwave panel study conducted at regular intervals between the early 1980s and today to evaluate the hypotheses above. This study should have asked respondents about their absolute and relative asylum and immigration policy preferences, indirectly tapped their prejudice against minorities, and also asked about their vote and party affinities. Such survey data would have allowed fine-tuned and precise tests of the hypotheses above. Unfortunately, no such data exist, and we therefore have to answer what I consider to be a crucial question in Western European politics – about the extent of parties' opinion leadership on immigration attitudes – by creatively using and interpreting the data that were gathered in this period.

Unfortunately, good time series data on immigration attitudes in Austria is lacking.[4] The best studies that chart attitudes towards immigrants over time in the relevant period were found to be Eurobarometer surveys (1997, 2000, 2003). Unfortunately, these surveys do not ask about party affinity or party membership and the questions that are asked in all three years tap policy preferences more than prejudice or anti-immigrant preferences. The Eurobarometer data can therefore be used only to get a sense of the movement of attitudes towards immigration policies over the relevant time period.

To analyse how anti-immigrant sentiment relates to partisanship, it was therefore necessary to rely on a cross-sectional study. The first wave of the European Social Survey (Jowell *et al.* 2003) includes all three countries, measures of party affinity and membership, and measures of anti-immigrant sentiment and can therefore be used to compare the role of party affinity in the formation of these attitudes across countries. Since the propositions discussed above primarily concern how partisanship influence anti-immigrant sentiment, and not the overall movement of immigration policy attitudes over time, the most crucial evidence will be found in the European Social Survey data.

Attitudes toward immigration and asylum policy over time

As pointed out above, our propositions mostly concern the relationship between partisanship and anti-immigrant sentiment on the individual level. However, if party cues strongly affect public opinion towards immigration, we would expect to see aggregate traces of such effects. Only being able to examine aggregate public opinion towards immigrants and immigration policy at three points in time, however, we will not be able to distinguish the effects of opinion leadership from other possible exogenous influences. The evidence about over time changes in aggregate public opinion in Austria discussed in this section is therefore only suggestive.

Changes over time in attitudes towards immigration and asylum policy in Austria are depicted in Figure 10.2. The figure shows the percentage of Austrian voting-age respondents who expressed that they wished to see more restrictions on asylum (Asylum), that legal immigrants should not have the right to family reunification (Family), that legal immigrants who had committed serious criminal offences should be expelled (Crime), or that legal immigrants who were long-term unemployed should be expelled (Employment). While one of these measures (Asylum) asks about preferences relative to the present, the other three ask about absolute preferences. The pattern seen across all measures is largely the same. Opposition to immigration was more widespread in 1997 than immediately after the inclusion of FPÖ in government in 2000. Between 2000 and 2003, however, opposition to immigration increased.

As pointed out above, aggregate evidence gives us a general sense of the move-ment of attitudes in this area, but we cannot say if this movement was caused by the actions of political elites or by other events or both. The data are not suited for time-series modeling and we do not have the indicators of party affinity neces-sary for evaluating the opinion leadership hypothesis. However, Figure 10.2 is informative in that it shows that public opinion of immigration restrictions in Austria was not at an all-time high after the inclusion of the Freedom Party in

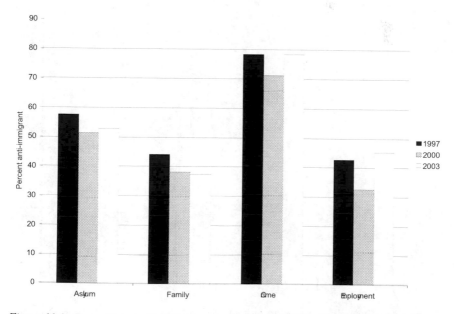

Figure 10.2 Opposition to immigration in Austria in 1997, 2000 and 2003 (Source: Eurobarometer 47.1, Eurobarometer 53, and Eurobarometer 59.2).

government. On the contrary, right after the government inclusion of the populist right in 2000, opposition to immigration was lower than in 1997 and 2003.[5]

Figure 10.3 compares changes in immigration attitudes between 1997 and 2000 in Flanders, Austria and Denmark.[6] It shows, first, that the movement towards less opposition observed in the Austrian case in Figure 10.1 was not unique. Second, it shows that the decline in Austria was more pronounced than in the two other cases. In Denmark and Austria, the decline was of a similar magnitude. In Austria, the difference between the averages is in excess of 7 percentage points (in 1997 on average 56 percent expressed opposition to immigration whereas in 2000 on average 48 percent did so). In Denmark the difference is around 5 percentage points (in 1997 on average 59 percent expressed opposition to immigration whereas in 2000 on average 54 percent did so). Unlike in Denmark and Austria, the decline was very small and not statistically significant in the Flemish case.

In the absence of panel data or more extensive time series we will not be able to establish for certain what explains the patterns seen below, but we will be better able to evaluate our hypotheses when we in the next section turn to using cross-sectional data on party affinity and party membership. Here we simply conclude that after the Freedom Party was included in government we did not observe an increase in the level of opposition to immigration; on the contrary, we observed a decrease of between five and ten percentage points depending on the question asked. Compared to Austria, this decline in opposition to immigration was equally or somewhat less pronounced in Denmark and clearly less pronounced in Flanders.

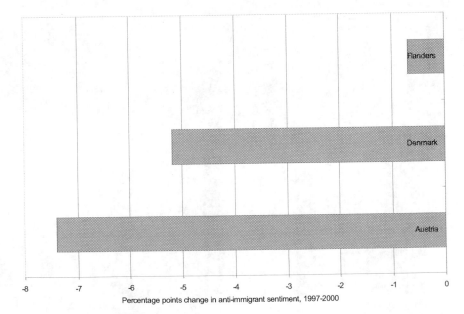

Figure 10.3 Comparing changes in attitudes towards immigrants in Austria, Denmark, and Flanders between 1997 and 2000 (Source: Eurobarometer 47.1, Eurobarometer 53, and Eurobarometer 59.2).

Partisanship and anti-immigrant sentiment

Turning to examine the cross-sectional data collected in 2002–03, both after *Venstre's* immigration policy change in Denmark and after the inclusion of FPÖ in government in Austria, we will be better able to address the propositions above, albeit still only in a suggestive way. If, contrary to P0 and P1 but in line with P2, opinion leadership by *Venstre* in Denmark spurred an increase in anti-immigrant sentiment among *Venstre*-partisans and no similar leadership was exercised by the ÖVP, we would expect that more of those who felt close to *Venstre* expressed anti-immigrant sentiment than those who felt close to the ÖVP in Austria. This would happen because *Venstre* had spent more time and effort campaigning to convince their voters that immigrants posed a problem, while the ÖVP had not done so. On the contrary, the ÖVP had sought to distinguish itself from the immigration stances of the Freedom Party by insisting that Haider not be a part of the government and that the Freedom party sign a declaration of abidance to democratic norms.

Figure 10.4 shows that in all three countries more of those who had affinities with parties of the right expressed anti-immigrant sentiment than the average in the respective publics in 2002–03.[7] However, in addition to this uniform trend, Figure 10.3 also shows, in line with P2, that the pull towards anti-immigrant sentiment for *Venstre* partisans in Denmark is significantly stronger than the pull on mainstream right partisans in Flanders and Austria. Among *Venstre* partisans, the number of people who expressed anti-immigrant sentiment exceeded the national average by 9 percent. The comparable figures for Austrian and Flemish mainstream right partisans were 4 and 5 percent respectively.

These results, which support the refined opinion leadership proposition P2,

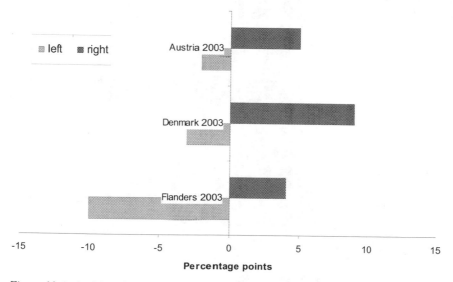

Figure 10.4 Anti-immigrant sentiment by party affinity: difference from national averages, 2002–03 (Source: European Social Survey 2003).

would be severely undermined if they were caused only by switches of party affinities, meaning that in Denmark a significant number of those who had anti-immigrant views had started feeling close to *Venstre* while a significant number of those who did not hold such views had stopped feeling such affinity. However, both the mainstream right and the populist right increased their number of votes in the 2001 election, so it is unlikely that the high number of *Venstre* partisans who expressed anti-immigrant sentiment were caused by a massive shift in affinities from the populist to the mainstream right or by a massive desertion of *Venstre* by its traditional electorate.

Moreover, as shown in Figure 10.5, the correspondence between the opinion leadership thesis and the levels of anti-immigrant sentiment among *members* of mainstream right parties in Denmark, Austria, and Flanders is strong. The figure shows that the proportion of *Venstre* members who expressed anti-immigrant sentiment exceeded the national average by 27 percentage points. The comparable numbers for Austria and Flanders are 6 and 3 percentage points respectively.

Party memberships are less easily changeable than party affinities, and it is therefore less likely that switching will have caused the results in Figure 10.4. Some voters may have given up their membership in the Danish *Venstre* in disagreement with the party's change in asylum policy, but it is unlikely that such protests happened only in Denmark and not in Austria where the mainstream right entered into government with the FPÖ. While not proving proposition 2, therefore, the results in Figures 10.4 and 10.5 do support it.

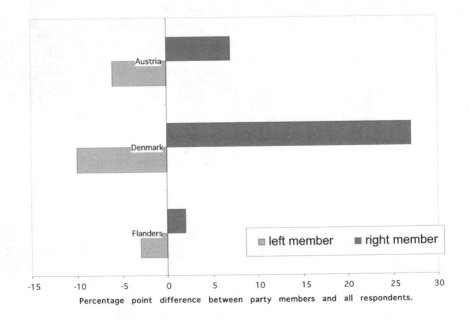

Figure 10.5 Anti-immigrant sentiment by mainstream party membership in Austria, Denmark and Flanders, 2003 (Source: European Social Survey 2003).

Government inclusion

In this final section we investigate the extent to which populist right parties themselves also exercise opinion leadership. We do so by seeking to determine whether or not the data are consistent with proposition 3, which suggested that government participation by populist right parties hampers their ability to incite anti-immigrant sentiment.

By assuming government responsibility, the populist right in Austria all of a sudden found itself in a position where it had to defend the government's practices in the area of immigration. Moreover, and these are the issues that predictably tore the FPÖ apart, the party had to focus on other policy areas than immigration. Thereby it lost some of its capacity earlier spent on persuading the public that radical restrictions on immigration were in their best interest.

By contrast, the populist right parties in both Flanders and Denmark were excluded from government responsibility and were, because of their positions as government outsiders, uniquely placed to continue their campaign to sway public opinion towards opposing immigration. These structurally different positions of the populist right parties in Denmark and Flanders, on the one hand, and in Austria, on the other, inspired proposition 3, which suggested that the FPÖ would be less able to lead its partisans towards expressing anti-immigrant sentiment than would the Danish People's Party or Vlaams Blok.

The data in Figure 10.6 support this proposition. They show that, in 2002–03,

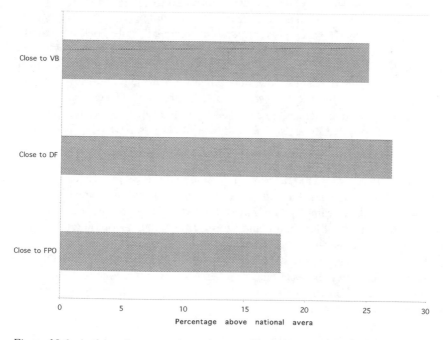

Figure 10.6 Anti-immigrant sentiment by populist right-wing party affinity in Austria, Denmark and Flanders, 2003 (Source: European Social Survey 2003).

the FPÖ exercised a significantly weaker pull towards anti-immigrant sentiment on those who felt close to this party than did the DF and the VB. Among those who felt a close affinity to the DF and the VB, the number of people who expressed prejudice exceeded the national averages by 27 and 25 percent respectively. By contrast, the comparative figure for those who felt an affinity for FPÖ in 2002–03, after the government inclusion and fiasco, was only 18 percent.

Conclusion

This chapter finds evidence, yet not conclusive evidence, to suggest that whether or not populist right parties are included in government, and how this inclusion is handled, matters for opinion towards immigrants. However, a simplistic notion of opinion leadership does not explain the patterns of change across time and countries found in the public opinion data. First, it does not seem to be the case that only mainstream parties influence the public's views in this area. The data are consistent with the hypothesis that populist right parties exercise opinion leadership in the area of immigration, and that they are particularly effective at doing so as government outsiders. Second, the data presented here suggest, contrary to the implicit assumptions of the opinion leadership literature, that drawing a distinction between government inclusion and policy co-option is crucial for understanding how parties and public opinion towards immigrants interact.

Western Europe's arguably boldest mainstream party effort at collectively opposing the populist right, in Flanders, was more effective in preventing partisans from opposing immigrants than the Danish strategy of approaching the populist right on policy terms. It was however not more effective than the Austrian version of approaching the populist right by including the FPÖ in government. Whereas the Danish case cautions against disregarding opinion leadership, the Flemish case, where we saw opposition towards immigration at the highest level among the three cases studied in all three years (1997, 2000, and 2003) cautions against overestimating it. In particular, the evidence presented here suggests that populist right parties themselves exercise a fair amount of opinion leadership in the area of immigration policy.

Finally, the Austrian case suggests very strongly that the cues that are sent to the public with regards to tolerance towards immigrants are significantly different when the populist right is reluctantly included in government than when the mainstream right seeks to campaign on a more restrictive immigration policy agenda itself. The argument for how this could happen from within an opinion leadership perspective has both a structural and an agency component. In terms of structure, in contrast to *Venstre* the ÖVP did not have to significantly change its immigration policy position before the election campaign. Moreover, the Freedom Party was hampered in its effort to emphasize the negative aspects of immigration by its position as a governing party.

The agency component relates to how the ÖVP included the FPÖ in government. The ÖVP leadership clearly demarcated itself from the unacceptable parts of the FPÖ's personnel and legacy. In practical terms, this meant that Haider was not part of the government and that a declaration of abidance to democratic norms had to be signed. Popular demonstrations as well as the international response also sent clear signals to the Austrian people and may have contributed to the overall decline in observed opposition towards immigration in Austria right after the dramatic events of 1999.

The trends in this chapter thus caution us against adopting a simple spatial model to understand party competition over immigration policy in Western Europe. The data are not good enough and a sufficiently sophisticated set of empirical tests were therefore not possible, but through careful examination of the best evidence available, I found strong enough support for the claims that parties lead public opinion that this possibility needs to be studied further rather than assumed not to exist. It looks likely that parties do not simply respond to voters when they change their immigration policies, but that they also affect the very public opinion environment within which they operate. This chapter suggests that they do so in somewhat more complex ways than predicted by the opinion leadership literature, but that this added complexity easily can be modeled theoretically and with better data can also be rigorously analysed empirically.

Notes

1 I would like to thank participants in the New Parties in Government workshop at the ECPR conference in Uppsala, April 13–25, 2004, for their helpful comments on an earlier version of this chapter, and the Norwegian Research Council for funding.
2 It has been called a crisis because Western European countries received a large number of asylum applications and/or illegal immigrants in spite of often strict bans on immigration. In addition, governments in Western Europe were not well prepared for the increased demands on the immigration and asylum fronts (UNHCR 1995).
3 See Lubbers (2001) for expert survey data confirming this statement about these major mainstream parties' immigration policy positions.
4 Pooling national surveys was not possible, because the questions asked about immigration and attitudes towards new minorities were not comparable over time and/or across countries.
5 It is hard to interpret the change between 2000 and 2003. Possibly the increase in anti-immigrant sentiment is due to the events following 11 September 2001.
6 The measure shown is the difference between the average percentage point score on the four measures presented in Figure 10.1 in 2000 and in 1997.
7 The means were 48 percent for Flanders, 37 percent for Denmark and 34 percent for Austria. The question used taps anti-immigrant sentiment by asking how many people from different races, religions, and cultures should live in the respondent's ideal neighborhood. The percentage quoted refers to those who answered 'almost none'.

Bibliography

Carter, E. (2005) *The Extreme Right in Western Europe: Success of Failure?*, Manchester: Manchester University Press.
Downs, A. (1957) *An Economic Theory of Democracy*, New York: Harper & Row.
Eurobarometer (1997) 47.1 (principal investigator Anna Melich) [Computer file]. Conducted by INRA (Europe), Brussels on request of the European Commission, 1st edition, Cologne, Germany: Zentralarchiv fur Empirische Sozialforschung.

Eurobarometer 53 (2000) [Computer file]. Conducted by INRA (Europe), Brussels on request of the European Commission.

Eurobarometer 59.2 (2003) [Computer file]. Conducted by INRA (Europe), Brussels on request of the European Commission.

European Social Survey (2003) Conducted by Jowell, R. and Central Co-ordinating Team, London: Centre for Comparative Social Surveys, City University. The datafile and more information about it is distributed and made available by the Norwegian Social Science Data Services (NSD).

Ivarsflaten, E. (2005) *Immigration Policy and Party Organization: Explaining the Rise of the Populist Right in Western Europe*, D.Phil. Thesis, Oxford: University of Oxford.

Key, V.O., Jr. with M. Cummings (1966) *The Responsible Electorate*, Cambridge, MA: Harvard University Press.

Kitschelt, H. (1994) *The Transformation of European Social Democracy*, Cambridge: Cambridge University Press.

Kitschelt, H. in collaboration with A.J. McGann (1995) *The Radical Right in Western Europe*, Ann Arbor: University of Michigan Press.

Laver, M. and Hunt, W.B. (1992) *Policy and Party Competition*, New York: Routledge.

Lubbers, M. (2001) *Exclusionistic Electorates: Extreme Right-Wing Voting in Western Europe*. PhD dissertation, Nijmegen: Interuniversity Center for Social Science Theory and Methodology, Nijmegen University.

Meguid, B. (2005) 'Competition between unequals: the role of mainstream party strategy in niche party success', *American Political Science Review*, 99(3): 347–59.

Mendelberg, T. (2001) *The Race Card: Campaign Strategy, Implicit Messages, and the Norm of Equality*, Princeton: Princeton University Press.

Norris, P. (2005) *Radical Right: Voters and Parties in the Electoral Market*, Cambridge: Cambridge University Press.

Riker, W.H. (1982) *Liberalism Against Populism: A Confrontation Between the Theory of Democracy and the Theory of Social Choice*, San Francisco: W.H. Freeman.

Rydgren, J. (2005) 'Is extreme right-wing populism contagious? Explaining the emergence of a new party family', *European Journal of Political Research,* 44(3): 413–38.

UNHCR (1995) 'Asylum under threat', *Refugee Magazine: Asylum in Europe*, Issue 101, Geneva: UNHCR.

Zaller, J.R. (1992) *The Nature and Origins of Mass Opinion*, Cambridge University Press.

Index

Abedi, A. 25
Accornero, A. *et al.* 48
actors: executive actors 36; new parties as
    organizational actors 21–3, 30, 31, 32,
    38; party actors 10–11; political actors
    17, 23, 153; strategic actors 17
Adamu, Semira 107
adaptation 2, 9–14, 26–7, 102; anticipatory
    adaptation 14; and change, common
    patterns of 8, 9–14; identification
    of processes for 33; ideological
    adaptations 6; to leadership change 80;
    organizational adaptations 6, 26–7; to
    parliamentary life 102; survival through
    38
Agalev (Flemish Greens) 26, 161, 169,
    171, 173
Aimer, P. 93
Aldrich, J. 150
Alliance for Free Finland 124
Alliance Party of New Zealand 8, 86, 87,
    88, 95–6, 102
AN (Italian National Alliance) xviii, 11,
    47, 56, 58–9, 61n3, 161, 163, 164, 168,
    171, 173
Anderton, Jim 85, 86, 88, 95
Andeweg, R.B. and Irwin, G.A. 66
anti-participationists in Belgium 107–8
AOV (Dutch General Association of Old
    Aged People) 69, 80
ARP (Dutch Anti Revolutionary Party) 65,
    66, 68, 72, 77, 80
Assemblé Générale (AG) in Belgium 108
Austria 9, 11, 65, 175–87; asylum policy
    and immigration, attitudes over time
    to 180–2, 187; FPÖ (Freedom Party)
    xix, 9, 10, 11, 40n14, 157, 161,

169, 171, 173, 175–87; government
    inclusion as new dimension 177–8;
    immigrants, attitudes towards after
    FPÖ in government 175–87; opinion
    leadership, agency component
    186–7; opinion leadership, empirical
    evaluation of hypotheses 180, 186;
    opinion leadership, government
    inclusion, party co-option and
    186; opinion leadership, structural
    component 186–7; opinion leadership,
    summary of hypotheses 179–80;
    ÖVP (People's Party) 157, 175, 178,
    179, 183, 186; partisanship and anti-
    immigrant sentiment 183–4; populist
    right, government inclusion 185–6,
    186–7; populist right, new variable of
    opinion leadership for 178–9; public
    opinion, parties' interactions with
    176–7
authorization stage in new party life 3, 8
Aylott, N. and Bergman, T. 141

Baccetti, C. 50
Bäck, M. and Möller, T. 90
Bale, T. and Bergman, T. 8, 40n10, 88,
    100, 142
Bale, T. and Dunphy, R. 2
Bale, T. and Wilson, J. 96
Bale, T. *et al.* 87
Bale, Tim xv, 7–8, 85–103
Bardie, L. 46
Bardie, L. and Ignazi, P. 46
Bardie, L. and Morlino, L. 46
bargaining power 25, 28–30, 100
Bartolini, S. 1
Bartolini, S. and Mair, P. 12, 45

Printed in the United States
by Baker & Taylor Publisher Services